Curren
Experimental Philosophy

Experimental philosophy is one of the most active and exciting areas in philosophy today. In *Current Controversies in Experimental Philosophy*, Edouard Machery and Elizabeth O'Neill have brought together twelve leading philosophers to debate four topics central to recent research in experimental philosophy. The result is an important and enticing contribution to contemporary philosophy which thoroughly reframes traditional philosophical questions in light of experimental philosophers' use of empirical research methods, and brings to light the lively debates within experimental philosophers' intellectual community. Eight chapters are dedicated to the following four topics:

- Language (Edouard Machery & Genoveva Martí)
- Consciousness (Brian Fiala, Adam Arico, and Shaun Nichols & Justin Sytsma)
- Free Will and Responsibility (Joshua Knobe & Eddy Nahmias and Morgan Thompson)
- Epistemology and the Reliability of Intuitions (Kenneth Boyd and Jennifer Nagel & Joshua Alexander and Jonathan Weinberg).

Preliminary descriptions of each chapter, annotated bibliographies for each controversy, and a supplemental guide to further controversies in experimental philosophy (with bibliographies) help provide clearer and richer views of these live controversies for all readers.

Edouard Machery is Professor of History and Philosophy of Science at the University of Pittsburgh.

Elizabeth O'Neill is a graduate student in the Department of History and Philosophy of Science at the University of Pittsburgh.

Current Controversies in Philosophy

In venerable Socratic fashion, philosophy proceeds best through reasoned conversation. **Current Controversies in Philosophy** provides short, accessible volumes that cast a spotlight on ongoing central philosophical conversations. In each book, pairs of experts debate four or five key issues of contemporary concern, setting the stage for students, teachers and researchers to join the discussion. Short chapter descriptions precede each chapter, and an annotated bibliography and study questions conclude each debate. In addition, each volume includes both a general introduction and a supplemental guide to further controversies. Combining timely debates with useful pedagogical aids allows the volumes to serve as clear and detailed snapshots, for all levels of readers, of some the most exciting work happening in philosophy today.

Series Editor:

John Turri
University of Waterloo

Volumes in the Series

Current Controversies in Philosophy of Mind
Edited by Uriah Kriegel

Current Controversies in Epistemology
Edited by Ram Neta

Current Controversies in Experimental Philosophy
Edited by Edouard Machery and Elizabeth O'Neill

Current Controversies in Metaphysics
Edited by Elizabeth Barnes

Current Controversies in Political Philosophy
Edited by Thom Brooks

Current Controversies in Virtue Ethics
Edited by Mark Alfano

Current Controversies in
Experimental Philosophy

Edited by
Edouard Machery and Elizabeth O'Neill

Routledge
Taylor & Francis Group

NEW YORK AND LONDON

First published 2014
by Routledge
711 Third Avenue, New York, NY 10017

and by Routledge
2 Park Square, Milton Park, Abingdon, Oxon, OX14 4RN

Routledge is an imprint of the Taylor & Francis Group, an informa business

© 2014 Taylor & Francis

The right of the editors to be identified as the author of the editorial material, and of the authors for their individual chapters, has been asserted in accordance with sections 77 and 78 of the Copyright, Designs and Patents Act 1988.

All rights reserved. No part of this book may be reprinted or reproduced or utilized in any form or by any electronic, mechanical, or other means, now known or hereafter invented, including photocopying and recording, or in any information storage or retrieval system, without permission in writing from the publishers.

Trademark notice: Product or corporate names may be trademarks or registered trademarks, and are used only for identification and explanation without intent to infringe.

Library of Congress Cataloging-in-Publication Data

CIP data has been applied for

ISBN: 978-0-415-51966-3 (hbk)
ISBN: 978-0-415-51967-0 (pbk)
ISBN: 978-0-203-12288-4 (ebk)

Typeset in Minion
by Apex CoVantage, LLC

Printed and bound in the United States of America
by Edwards Brothers Malloy

Contents

Introduction: Experimental Philosophy: What Is It Good For?   vii
Elizabeth O'Neill and Edouard Machery

Part I
Language   1

1 What Is the Significance of the Demographic Variation
   in Semantic Intuitions?   3
   Edouard Machery

2 Reference and Experimental Semantics   17
   Genoveva Martí

Part I Suggested Readings   27

Part II
Consciousness   29

3 You, Robot   31
   Brian Fiala, Adam Arico, and Shaun Nichols

4 The Robots of the Dawn of Experimental Philosophy of Mind   48
   Justin Sytsma

Part II Suggested Readings   65

Part III
Free Will and Responsibility   67

  5 Free Will and the Scientific Vision   69
     Joshua Knobe

  6 A Naturalistic Vision of Free Will   86
     Eddy Nahmias and Morgan Thompson

Part III Suggested Readings   104

Part IV
Epistemology and the Reliability of Intuitions   107

  7 The Reliability of Epistemic Intuitions   109
     Kenneth Boyd and Jennifer Nagel

  8 The "Unreliability" of Epistemic Intuitions   128
     Joshua Alexander and Jonathan M. Weinberg

Part IV Suggested Readings   146

Supplemental Guide to Further Controversies   149

Contributors   151

Index   155

Experimental Philosophy
What Is It Good For?

ELIZABETH O'NEILL AND EDOUARD MACHERY

[E]ven if experimental philosophy is interesting, this doesn't necessarily mean that it is important. Those who insist that it marks a revolution in philosophy owe us some explanation of its significance.

—Papineau (2011, p. 83)

This volume covers four of the most intensely debated topics in experimental philosophy—semantic intuitions (Part I of the book), the folk concept of consciousness (Part II of the book), free will and responsibility (Part III of the book), and the reliability of epistemological intuitions (Part IV)—and it touches on issues that are important in the central areas of philosophy in general: language, mind, action and ethics, and epistemology. Each part presents two chapters that disagree with one another about these central topics.

The goal of this introduction is to describe several philosophical projects whose completion requires experimentation and, more generally, empirical methods, and to position the chapters of this volume in relation to those projects. The importance of empirical methods to some of these projects has already been extensively discussed, but the relevance of empirical methods for others is less widely recognized. By describing these projects in relation to experimental philosophy, we hope to make clear how important empirical methods are for philosophers and to show that such methods should be viewed as part and parcel of philosophers' toolkit. We also hope to broaden the scope of experimental philosophy and encourage it in new directions.

Here is how this introduction proceeds: In Section 1 of the introduction, we describe what experimental and other empirical methods offer to what we will call "traditional" philosophical projects. In Section 2, we review the contribution of experimental philosophy to metaphilosophical debates. In Section 3, we highlight the importance of experimentation and other empirical methods for naturalist philosophers.

1. Experimental Philosophy for Traditionalists

We start by discussing four ways experimental philosophy should be incorporated into "traditional philosophical projects"—that is, the kind of arguments, debates, views, issues, topics, and so on that contemporary philosophers in general recognize as being obviously part of philosophy (so, on this view, debates about free will and permissibility are in and debates about the causal nature of natural selection are out). First, experimental philosophy should often inform projects involving conceptual analysis. Second, some traditional philosophical arguments have empirical premises, which call for experimental and other empirical methods. Third, findings from experimental philosophy can be employed in traditional debunking arguments. Fourth, experimental philosophy provides us with information about biases that may affect the practice of philosophy, including biases influencing judgments about philosophical cases. These uses of experimental philosophy for traditional purposes are of course interrelated, and no doubt there are other uses as well. We offer these as just a few key ways experimental and other empirical methods should be employed in traditional philosophical projects.

1.1 Analysis, Explication, and Experimental Philosophy

Some philosophers think of the business of philosophy as conceptual analysis (e.g., Goldman, 2007). Conceptual analysis can be understood in various ways, and we embrace an inclusive conception of this task here: Analyzing a concept consists in identifying other concepts that must be possessed by anybody who possesses the analyzed concept. We call "components of concepts" the concepts that are mentioned in the analysis of a concept. Component concepts can provide separately necessary and jointly sufficient conditions for the application of a concept, or just necessary conditions, or conditions that make it likely the analyzed concept applies. Philosophers may be able to analyze some concepts well enough on their own (for instance, the concepts of a limit or a bachelor), perhaps because in some such cases, their own concepts are of interest. However, when philosophers' aim is to analyze a concept as it is employed by some population, such as the folk or a set of experts (e.g., scientists in some discipline), using empirical methods to get at the concept has important advantages. Philosophers' concepts may differ from the concepts possessed by lay people or by some population (e.g., biologists or psychologists), and the former may lead philosophers astray when the latter are of interest (Livengood & Machery, 2007; Sytsma & Machery, 2010). Concepts may vary from one population to the other, and this conceptual variation, which may be of philosophical interest, would be overlooked if philosophers analyze only their own concepts. Bracketing these two issues, a fine-grained analysis of a concept often requires experimental methods. Even if philosophers can correctly identify the components of a particular concept, they are unlikely to be in a position to correctly assess the weight or importance of those components. By contrast, statistical methods like regression and analysis of variance applied to large data sets can do this successfully (e.g., Griffiths, Machery, & Linquist, 2009). Finally, philosophers often identify the components of a concept by examining how judgments vary across different cases. Philosophers often underestimate how difficult it is to understand which features of these cases result in different judgments, particularly when two potentially critical features are highly correlated across cases or when some features are more salient than others. Sophisticated statistical methods like structural equation modeling and causal search algorithms applied to large data sets can be usefully applied to this issue (Rose, Livengood, Sytsma, & Machery, 2012). Many important disputes in traditional philosophy could benefit from this treatment, such as the debate about Gettier cases, because it is still unclear which of their features lead most philosophers to conclude that knowledge is not present.

Some experimental philosophers have provided relevant evidence for conceptual analysis, studying folk concepts of free will and responsibility (e.g., Nahmias, Morris, Nadelhoffer, & Turner, 2006; Nichols & Knobe, 2007; Woolfolk, Doris, & Darley, 2006; Part III of this book), causation (e.g., Alicke, Rose, & Bloom, 2011; Danks, Rose, & Machery, forthcoming; Hitchcock & Knobe, 2009; Sytsma, Livengood, & Rose, 2012; see the Supplementary Guide), and a variety of other topics (see the Supplementary Guide), as well as experts' concepts of innateness (Knobe & Samuels, 2013), and gene (Stotz, Griffiths, & Knight, 2004), among others.

One might object that experimental philosophy, as currently practiced, is not the right way to analyze concepts because survey studies collect quick, unreflective judgments, which are not an appropriate source of evidence about concepts. However, the methods of experimental philosophy are not limited to surveys about whether a concept applies in particular cases. Other empirical methods are relevant as well, including studies of usage, interviews, and cross-cultural linguistic studies, among others. For instance, Reuter (2011) examined the occurrences of "feeling pain" and "having pain" on the Web in order to determine whether laypeople distinguish the appearance and the reality of pain, whereas Knobe and Prinz (2008) have examined how often mental states are ascribed to collective entities on the Web.

One might also object that analyzing folk concepts (or perhaps even the concepts possessed by experts) does not reveal anything about their referent. Thus, analyzing the concept of knowledge may not be useful to understand what knowledge is (Kornblith, 2002, 2013). This is a complex issue that cannot be addressed in sufficient depth here, and we will only make three brief points. First, this objection does not bear on those philosophical projects that are only concerned with the concepts themselves (e.g., Griffiths et al., 2009). Second, on some views of concepts (e.g., Jackson, 1998; Thomasson, 2012), for all concepts, or perhaps for some of the concepts that interest philosophers, such as the concepts of knowledge or culture, one's concept of *x* determines what *x* could and could not be. Thus, analyzing a concept provides some information about its referent. Finally, even if one does not embrace this view of concepts, in some domains, people's concepts are likely to be accurate. For instance, Boyd and Nagel (this volume) argue that it is plausible that the folk are good at picking out cases of knowledge because it would have been adaptive for our ancestors to have the capacity to distinguish conspecifics that know certain propositions from those that do not. So, their concept of knowledge is likely to be accurate.

In addition to fitting naturally with conceptual analysis, Schupbach (2013) has recently argued that experimental methods make an important contribution to explication. In contrast to analysis, explication *modifies* a given concept in light of various goals (for instance, in Carnap's conception of explication, to provide a useful tool for some science). When the goal is to clarify and precisify a folk concept, philosophers involved in explication need to show that the proposed explication (the "explicans") does not stray too far from the concept to be explicated (the "explicandum"). Experimental methods can be used to establish this point. Furthermore, explicantia can be compared with respect to their closeness to the explicandum. Schupbach (2011) does exactly this for the concept of explanatory power, experimentally comparing various formal measures of explanatory power with laypeople's assessment of how good an explanation is.

1.2 Empirical Premises

Many traditional philosophical arguments involve empirical premises, even though they reach nonempirical conclusions. These premises should be evaluated: If some philosophical conclusion hangs on the solution of some still controversial empirical question, intellectual probity requires philosophers to contribute to its solution instead of just assuming that the facts are one way or the other.

Several such cases come from meta-ethics. For instance, Mackie's argument from disagreement for an error theory about ethics relies on an empirical premise: "The argument from relativity has as its premise the well-known variation in moral codes from one society to another and from one period to another, and also the differences in moral beliefs between different groups and classes within a complex community" (1977, p. 36). This diversity of moral beliefs, Mackie (1977, p. 37) argues, is better explained as the expression of cultural values than by variation in people's perception of objective values. Whether there is in fact widespread cross-cultural disagreement about moral questions is an issue that experimental philosophers investigated early on, and further work is called for (Brandt, 1954; see also Machery, Kelly, & Stich, 2005). Similarly, moral philosophers interested in the moral consequences of the evolution of morality (e.g., Joyce, 2006) should not just assume that morality evolved; rather, they should closely examine the empirical literature and, if necessary, they should contribute to this literature (Machery, 2012b; Machery & Mallon, 2010).

Empirical premises in traditional arguments are sometimes implicit; in other cases, the empirical nature of the relevant premises goes unacknowledged. But one need not look long before finding many relevant examples. Many arguments in ethics depend on claims about moral psychology that are best investigated empirically (Doris & the Moral Psychology Research Group, 2010; Doris & Stich, 2005), such as what sorts of behavior human beings are capable of, whether human beings are ultimately concerned with the welfare of others (Stich, Doris, & Roedder, 2010), and whether moral character exists (Doris, 2002). The same is true of arguments in applied ethics and political philosophy. Singer's (1972) argument that we should give foreign aid hinges on the claim that various types of foreign aid are likely to reduce suffering. Indeed, any questions about the means for achieving an end are likely to involve empirical issues that can be investigated empirically. For instance, some have investigated whether a veil of ignorance is a good mechanism for achieving impartiality (Aguiar, Becker, & Miller, 2013). Examples are not limited to practical philosophy. To focus only on the philosophy of science, Laudan et al. (1986) make a strong case that theories about scientific change (including whether it is rational) should be tested against systematic studies in history of science. As they put it,

> [N]ot one of these "post-positivist" theories [of scientific change] has itself been tested in more than the most perfunctory and superficial manner. Nothing resembling the standards of testing that these very authors insist upon within science has ever been met by any of their theories about science. . . . In our view, it is time to put this situation right. (Laudan et al., 1986, p. 142)

In an important series of papers, Meehl (1992, 2002, 2004) has similarly argued that epistemological theories about confirmation, induction, and so on can and should be tested against systematic studies of the history of science, and he has described various tools and methods to bring this research program to fruition.

It would be natural to respond that experimental philosophers, with their paper-and-pencil studies examining people's responses to vignettes, are poorly equipped to tackle the empirical questions mentioned in this section. But we are not so much concerned with defending experimental philosophy as it is currently practiced than in making a case for the inclusion of experimentation and other empirical methods as an important tool for the philosopher.

It would also be erroneous to object that philosophers should just be concerned with the validity of arguments, leaving it to science to determine the truth of their premises. Waiting for science to evaluate the empirical premises our arguments rely on will just means slower progress in philosophy because scientists are not always interested in the premises of interest to us. If we are seriously committed to the conclusions of our arguments, it behooves us to broaden our conception of philosophy, and to investigate, alone or in collaboration with scientists, the truth of our empirical premises.

1.3 Debunking Arguments

An important form of argument in traditional philosophy consists in debunking a belief. This may be done by showing that the belief is the product of a causal process that is not connected in the right way to the fact of the matter. Experimental philosophy can provide evidence that supports these debunking arguments. Debunking might be thought of a subcategory of traditional arguments for nonempirical conclusions that involve an empirical premise, where the empirical premise here has to do with the causal origins of the belief.

For instance, Griffiths et al. (2009) use information about the nature of folk judgments about innateness to undermine philosophical analyses of the concept of innateness (mutatis mutandis, philosophical theories about innateness). They argue that philosophers' analyses are only attractive because such analyses pick out one of the three components of the folk concept of innateness and identify innateness with this component. They conclude that the attractiveness of these analyses can be explained away as the product of a folk notion. To give only another example, Singer (2005) has used Joshua Greene's empirical work on the causal sources of moral judgment to debunk intuitions against consequentialism.

1.4 Warrant and Psychological Processes

There are other, less dramatic ways of using information about the causal sources of beliefs and judgments (including judgments about cases; see Section 2 of this introduction on the role of these judgments in philosophy).

In particular, one can use such information to identify potential biases and to take these into account in philosophizing. Knobe and Nichols (2008) describe what they view as "the first major goal of experimental philosophy" as follows:

> The goal is to determine what leads us to have the intuitions we do about free will, moral responsibility, the afterlife. The ultimate hope is that we can use this information to help determine whether the psychological sources of the beliefs undercut the warrant for the beliefs. (p. 7)

Experimental philosophy has already produced results about possible biases, including framing effects and the influence of various demographics factors. This research is discussed further in the next section. It should now be the business of traditional philosophers to pay heed to empirical data about the possible biases influencing philosophizing and, indeed, to engage in empirical work themselves to assess the reliability of the cognitive processes involved in doing philosophy.

2. Experimental Philosophy for Metaphilosophers

2.1 The Method of Cases

An important feature of contemporary analytic philosophy is the role played by cases, or thought experiments, in philosophical argumentation. Philosophers consider an actual or, more often, a counterfactual, situation and judge that a particular fact holds in this situation. For instance, as part of the argument against descriptivism,[1] Kripke (1972) describes a case in which a speaker associates a proper name, "Gödel," with a description that is not true of the original bearer of the name but that is true of someone else, called "Schmidt" in the story (for discussion of this case, see Part I of this book). Descriptivist theories of reference typically entail that in this situation "Gödel" refers to the man originally called "Schmidt." But, Kripke maintains, this is just wrong:

> On the [descriptivist] view . . . when our ordinary man uses the name "Gödel," he really means to refer to Schmidt, because Schmidt is the unique person satisfying the description "the man who discovered the incompleteness of arithmetic." . . . But it seems we are not. We simply are not. (1972, p. 84)

So, in this situation, Kripke assumes that, in the counterfactual situation just described, "Gödel" would refer to Gödel rather than to Schmidt.

Turning from the philosophy of language to ethics, we find Thomson and Foot debating trolley cases. Thomson (1985) describes Foot's so-called switch case as follows:

> Some years ago, Philippa Foot drew attention to an extraordinarily interesting problem. Suppose you are the driver of a trolley. The trolley rounds a bend, and there come into view ahead five track workmen who have been repairing the track. The track goes through a bit of valley at that point, and the sides are steep, so you must stop the trolley if you are to avoid running the five men down. You step on the brakes, but alas they don't work. Now you suddenly see a spur of track leading off to the right. You can turn the trolley onto it, and thus save the five men on the straight track ahead. Unfortunately, Mrs. Foot has arranged that there is one workman on that spur of track. He can no more get off the track in time than the five can, so you will kill him if you turn the trolley onto him. Is it morally permissible for you to turn the trolley? Everyone to whom I have put this hypothetical case says, Yes, it is. (p. 1395)

So, just like Foot, Thomson assumes that in this case it would be morally permissible to save five people by causing the death of one individual.

Cases are put to many different uses in contemporary analytic philosophy. Sometimes they are simply put forward for illustrative purpose: They are meant to show how the characterization of a concept (be it an analysis, an explication, or a stipulative proposal) or a particular philosophical theory (e.g., about knowledge or permissibility) applies to a particular situation. In other circumstances (e.g., Goldman, 2007), cases are put forward because the judgments they elicit are taken to constitute evidence about the philosophically relevant concepts or beliefs people possess (e.g., the concept of knowledge or of permissibility). The assumption here is that people judge one way rather than another when they are confronted with a particular case because they possess one concept rather than another. Finally, other cases are put forward because, by considering them, philosophers come to know, or come to be justified in believing, that some particular facts hold in the situations described by these cases and can thus be assumed, at least defeasibly, in a philosophical debate. The implications or philosophical significance of these facts are then a matter of philosophical argumentation. The claim that a fact holds in a particular situation can naturally be defeated by arguments or other examples. In what follows, we are only concerned with this third use of the method of cases.

It is difficult to overestimate the importance of the method of cases in contemporary philosophy. While it is not the only method available to philosophers, it plays a very large role in areas such as epistemology (see Part

IV of this volume), metaphysics, ethics, philosophy of language (see Part I of this volume), philosophy of mind, and action theory (see Part III of this volume).

The method of cases has been understood and described in many different ways, and it is beyond the scope of this introduction to discuss them all. However, two issues are important for our present purpose. First, what kind of mental state is elicited when one considers a case of philosophical interest? Philosophers have been prone to describe philosophical cases as eliciting intuitions, and experimental philosophers have often followed suit (e.g., Machery, Mallon, Nichols, & Stich, 2004; Weinberg, Nichols, & Stich, 2001). There is, however, little consensus on what intuitions are. Some compare intuitions to perceptual experiences, and identify them with intellectual seemings (e.g., Bealer, 1996). Others identify them with specific kinds of judgment or specific kinds of inclination to judge. In particular, many identify them with non-inferred, unreflective, immediate judgments (Gopnik & Schwitzgebel, 1998) or inclinations to judge. Others identify them with judgments or inclinations to judge that have a particular modal content (about what is necessarily or possibly the case) and that hold a particular relation to what is essentially involved in possessing a concept—what they call "conceptual competence" (Sosa, 2007). Others view them as simply judgments, and doubt that they form a distinctive type of judgment (Machery, 2011; Williamson, 2007). Finally, yet others shy away from any psychological description of the mental states elicited by philosophical cases, preferring to describe the relevant assumed facts as being part of "the common ground" among philosophers (Cappelen, 2012).

The second issue concerns the nature and source of the warrant for philosophers' assumption that a particular fact holds in a philosophically relevant case. Some, such as Ludwig (2007) or Sosa (2007), propose that we know a priori that a particular fact holds in a given case. For example, we know a priori that in a Gettier case (e.g., the clock case) the agent does not know the relevant proposition. Others focus on other types and sources of justification. Chudnoff (2011) argues that intuiting that p gives the intuiter a prima facie defeasible justification for judging that p. Yet others (Machery, 2011; Williamson, 2007) propose that, if they are justified, judgments about philosophical cases are justified on exactly the same grounds as everyday judgments. If I am justified in judging that the agent does not know the relevant proposition in a Gettier case, it is on the same grounds that I am justified in ascribing and refusing to ascribe knowledge in every day circumstances—probably because I have reliable skills for distinguishing knowledge from lack-of-knowledge cases. For all the philosophical positions just described, something about one's judgment provides some sort of justification to the assumption that a particular fact holds in a situation of philosophical relevance. By contrast, some philosophers have little to say about the nature and source of philosophers' warrant for taking for granted (at least defeasibly) particular facts about philosophical cases (Cappelen, 2012).

2.2 Skepticism About the Method of Cases

An influential tradition within experimental philosophy has challenged the role the method of cases plays in contemporary philosophy (Alexander & Weinberg, this volume; Feltz & Cokely, 2012; Machery, 2011; Machery et al., 2004; Swain, Alexander, & Weinberg, 2008; Weinberg, 2007; Weinberg et al., 2001). There are several distinct views about the details of experimental philosophers' challenge to the method of cases, which focus on different epistemological properties (compare Weinberg, 2007, and Machery, 2011), such as reliability or hopefulness (a source of evidence is hopeful if one has the capacity to detect its errors).[2] Here we will focus on reliability. One way of putting the objection against the method of cases goes as follows:

The Argument From Unreliability Against the Method of Cases

1. The judgments elicited by philosophical thought experiments are significantly influenced by factors that do not track the fact of the matter.
2. If a judgment is significantly influenced by factors that do not track the fact of the matter, that judgment is not reliable.
3. If a judgment is not reliable, it cannot provide warrant for assuming its content.
4. Hence, the judgments elicited by thought experiments do not provide warrant for assuming their content.

If the judgments elicited by thought experiments do not provide warrant for taking their content for granted, then philosophers are not warranted to assume on the basis of such judgments that some facts hold in the situations described by these thought experiments. As a result, the method of cases cannot play the role it is meant to play in contemporary philosophy.

The empirical evidence collected for about a decade by experimental philosophers can be used to support Premise 1 of this argument (Parts I and IV of this book). Two main kinds of factors have been examined. First and foremost, experimental philosophers have examined whether demographic variables (culture, age, gender, language, personality variables, etc.) influence the judgments elicited by some thought experiments. For instance, Part I of this book discusses at length the evidence that judgments about the reference of proper names in situations like Kripke's Gödel case vary across cultures. Colaço, Buckwalter, Stich, and Machery (in press) provide evidence that age influences some epistemological judgments: Older people are less likely to ascribe knowledge in fake-barn cases. Second, some evidence suggests that the way vignettes are presented (including their order) influences these judgments (Liao, Wiegmann, Alexander, & Vong, 2012; Swain et al., 2008; Wright, 2010). Assuming, plausibly enough, that the matters of fact do not vary as a function of the relevant demographic variables or the ways in which cases are presented, experimental philosophers conclude that the judgments elicited by some thought experiments are influenced by non-truth-tracking factors. They then conclude inductively that in general the judgments elicited by thought experiments are influenced by such factors.[3] Premises 2 and 3 deserve some discussion and defense, but for the sake of space, we bracket this task here.[4]

2.3 Objections and Responses

A critic could first criticize Premise 1 of the argument from unreliability against the method of cases by questioning whether the existing studies show that philosophical judgments about cases are significantly influenced by non-truth-tracking factors. These studies may be poorly designed (see, e.g., Ludwig, 2007, vs. Machery, Sytsma, & Deutsch, in press); they may not reveal people's judgments clearly (Turri, 2013); they may not reveal the judgments of the right people;[5] or they may target judgments that are of no philosophical relevance (see, e.g., Martí, 2009, this volume, vs. Machery, Olivola, & de Blanc, 2009, and Machery, this volume; see also Devitt, 2011, vs. Machery, Mallon, Nichols, & Stich, 2013). Alternatively, while conceding that some judgments elicited by thought experiments are significantly influenced by non-truth-tracking factors, one may reject the inductive conclusion that these judgments are in general significantly influenced by such factors as well as the weaker conclusion that they may be so influenced (see Note 3 of this chapter). Jennifer Nagel has been pressing this point by arguing theoretically (Nagel, 2012, 2013; but see Stich, 2013) and empirically (Nagel, San Juan, & Marr, 2013) that judgments about cases that are of key importance in epistemology are not significantly influenced by non-truth-tracking demographic variables.

So, are we in a position to claim that the judgments elicited by thought experiments are significantly influenced by non-truth-tracking factors? That would be premature. We have good evidence that *some* judgments are so influenced (see Machery, this volume, for a defense of this claim), but the extent to which demographic variables and ways of presentation influence the judgments elicited by thought experiments remains unclear. A recent large-scale research project led by Edouard Machery and Steve Stich ("Intellectual Diversity and Intellectual Humility in Philosophy") will hopefully cast some light on the extent and nature of these influences.[6]

Second, one could challenge the way the method of cases is described by experimental philosophers, and argue that, because it has been misdescribed, experimental philosophers' empirical results are irrelevant. In particular, according to Cappelen (2012), judgments about cases play no essential role in the method of cases (see also Deutsch, 2009; Machery, this volume); rather, facts about the situations described by the philosophical cases are simply part of the common ground in philosophy. As he puts it, "a central goal of experimental philosophy is to criticize the philosophical practice of appealing to intuitions about cases" and "[t]he entire project of experimental philosophy only gets off the ground by assuming Centrality" (Cappelen, 2012, p. 219; viz., the assumption that intuitions play a central role in philosophy).

However, Cappelen (2012) says nothing about what warrants viewing some assumed facts as belonging to the common ground. Why are we warranted in assuming, for example, that it is permissible to cause someone's death in the switch version of the trolley case? Further, and more important, an argument closely related to the argument from unreliability can be deployed against the method of cases as Cappelen understands it. Studies probing the role of demographic variables on judgments about philosophical cases reveal that there is a fair amount of disagreement about whether the assumed fact (e.g., that the agent does not know the relevant proposition in a Gettier case) really holds. Now, although the epistemology of disagreement is intricate (Christensen, 2009), and although we do not argue for any specific view here, we hold that, except if there are reasons to discount the judgments of dissenters (perhaps because we are experts and they are not), it is unwarranted to accept some alleged fact into the common ground of philosophical debate when millions of people would doubt this fact. So, by providing evidence for massive disagreement, experimental philosophers cast doubt on whether some facts about the situations described by thought experiments can be justifiably considered in the common ground. Thus, the relevance of experimental philosophers' findings for the method of cases is not removed by simply denying the role of intuitions or judgments in this philosophical method.

Finally, one may object that the argument from unreliability against the method of cases shows too much. In particular, supposing that the judgments elicited by thought experiments are not a particular type of judgment or are not grounded in intellectual seemings, doubting their reliability should lead us to question the reliability of similar judgments in everyday life. For instance, if judgments about what causes what or about whether someone knows something are unreliable when elicited by thought experiments, why would they be reliable when they occur in everyday life—for example, when we judge that smoking causes cancer, when a professor judges that a student does not know her lesson, and so on. And if the latter skepticism is implausible (after all, e.g., our judgments about people's proper names are generally reliable), then the former kind of skepticism should be implausible too (Williamson, 2007).

There are two distinct lines of response to this argument, which we describe only briefly in this introduction. First, one could attempt to identify properties that distinguish the judgments elicited by thought experiments from everyday judgments, before arguing that experimental philosophers' empirical results only cast doubt on the reliability of judgments with these properties (Machery, 2011; for a criticism of this strategy, see Cappelen, 2012, Chapter 11). This strategy may lead a critic of the method of cases to acknowledge the reliability of the judgments elicited by some thought experiments, provided that these do not possess the properties in question, as well as lead her to extend her skepticism to some everyday judgments that possess these properties. Alternatively, one can reformulate the argument from unreliability against the method of cases to turn it into a piecemeal argument. Rather than questioning in general the reliability of the judgments elicited by thought experiments or the reliability of the judgments about proper names elicited by thought experiments, experimental philosophers would merely claim, for example, that the judgment about who "Gödel" refers to in the Gödel case is unreliable or that judgments elicited by fake-barn cases are unreliable. Because these judgments differ from most everyday judgments, experimental philosophers' skepticism about them does not generalize, implausibly, to everyday judgments. Because these cases are philosophically important, the piecemeal skepticism about the method of cases would be philosophically significant.

So, experimental philosophy continues to serve important purposes for metaphilosophers. It provides evidence about the influences on and diversity in judgments about cases that can be employed to argue against the method of cases, or, as in Nagel's arguments, to defend the method of cases in particular domains.

3. Experimental Philosophy for Naturalists

In this section, we examine the use naturalistic philosophers can make of experimental philosophy. It is common to distinguish between methodological and metaphysical naturalism, and we will follow this tradition. Metaphysical naturalists, a family resemblance kind rather than a homogenous group of philosophers, hold various views about the nature of reality, typically endorsing reductive or non-reductive materialism and the causal completeness of physics. By contrast, methodological naturalism has less to do with the nature of reality than with the nature of philosophizing, with methodological naturalists often embracing the (vague) slogan that "philosophy is continuous with the sciences." Roughly, they hold, first, that, just like scientific theories, philosophical theories (or at least many of them) are about things in the world (mind, cognition, knowledge, etc.)—we call the questions about these things "first-order questions." This contrasts with the view that philosophical theories are about the concepts of these things (the concepts of mind, knowledge, etc.) or the meaning of the words referring to these things (e.g., the meanings of "mind," "knowledge," etc.)—we call questions about concepts or meaning "second-order questions." Second, they hold that there is no distinctive philosophical method (i.e., no philosophical method that is not also found in other disciplines), and third, they hold that, to meet their theoretical goals, philosophers should rely on any method and data found in the sciences. Here we are concerned with the promises of experimental philosophy to methodological naturalists.

3.1 Naturalists' Reservations

Naturalists have often expressed reservations about experimental philosophy. In a nutshell, on their view, experimental-philosophy studies proceed by eliciting judgments about particular cases, which are typically, although not always, drawn from or inspired by the philosophical literature. Their results can, at best, provide evidence about how experimental participants—typically laypeople—conceptualize various things, such as reference (see Part I of this volume), consciousness (see Part II of this volume), intentional action (see the Supplemental Guide), or causation (see the Supplemental Guide), but not about the nature of these things. As a result, findings in experimental philosophy have little to bring to the naturalists. Papineau (2011) expresses this concern, although he ends up finding two minor roles for experimental philosophy: assessing the trustworthiness of the judgments elicited by thought experiments (Sections 1.4 and 2 of this introduction and Parts I and IV of this volume) and describing people's philosophically relevant judgments and the psychological mechanisms behind them (Parts II and III of this book).

As a result, experimental-philosophy studies often appear to naturalists to be a return to a foregone area of philosophy, one concerned with concepts or meaning (Papineau, 2013, pp. 188–189). In a recent essay, Kornblith (2013) puts his views about experimental philosophy as follows:

> [M]uch (though not all) of the work that experimental philosophers have done and wish to do is misdirected, indeed, . . . it is misdirected in much the same way, I believe, that a good deal of armchair theorizing in philosophy is. So I will be arguing in defense of a thoroughly empirically informed approach to epistemology, but one which is fundamentally different from that pursued by the experimental philosophers. (p. 197)

In the remainder of this section, our goal will be to alleviate naturalist philosophers' reservations toward experimental philosophy and bridge the rift between the two. In a nutshell, we advise experimental philosophers to expand the reach of experimental philosophy, and we advise naturalist philosophers to more fully embrace their naturalism by engaging in empirical work.

3.2 Broadening Experimental Philosophy

Naturalists' reservations toward experimental philosophy are grounded in their characterization of what experimental philosophers do—examine the judgments elicited by philosophically relevant thought-experiments—and of what can be learned from examining these judgments—at most the trustworthiness or untrustworthiness of these judgments and the nature of the concepts these judgments are derived from. Because this characterization is partly correct—for instance, Nadelhoffer and Nahmias (2007, p. 123) state that existing experimental philosophy "shares a commitment to using controlled and systematic experiments to explore people's intuitions and conceptual usage and to examine how the results of such experiments bear on traditional philosophical debates"—naturalists' reservations about experimental philosophy should be viewed as an invitation to broaden the kind of research currently done in experimental philosophy.[7]

What does a broadening of experimental philosophy amount to? At least two things: a broadening of subject matter and a broadening of methods. First and foremost, it consists in expanding what experimental philosophers hope to learn from their experimental research. In its current state, experimental philosophy already extends beyond the narrow notion some naturalists may have of it as just collecting intuitions about cases out of an interest in the content and trustworthiness of those intuitions. As illustrated in this book, although much of experimental philosophy today has to do with identifying patterns of judgments about cases and the causes of such judgments for the purpose of assessing the trustworthiness of such judgments (e.g., judgments about cases from epistemology—see Part IV of this volume; judgments about the reference of proper names—see Part I of this volume), experimental philosophers are also engaged in projects to develop accounts of the psychological mechanisms underlying certain domains of judgments (e.g., folk theories about free will and responsibility—see Part III of this volume). Many studies eliciting judgments from vignettes are less interested in the exact content of these judgments than in characterizing the psychological mechanisms underlying them. Danks, Rose, and Machery (forthcoming) have recently examined whether causal learning is influenced by the moral valence of the causal relations to be learned. Causal judgments about cases were elicited, but Danks and colleagues were not interested in the content of these judgments. Rather, the pattern of judgments they observed was used to infer that, in contrast to explicit and verbalized causal judgments, causal learning is not influenced by morality. In his recent work on the role of emotions in moral judgment, Jesse Prinz examined whether consuming a bitter liquid (assumed to elicit a disgust reaction) or hearing unpleasant noises influence people's moral judgments, which were elicited by various vignettes (Eskine, Kacinik, & Prinz, 2011; Seidel & Prinz, 2013). As was the case for Danks and colleagues, the content of these judgments is of no particular interest to Prinz. Thus, part of what experimental philosophers are doing is investigating some of the first-order questions that naturalistic philosophers deplore experimental philosophers ignore.

An even broader experimental philosophy of mind or psychology (for instance) would bear on understanding what beliefs are, whether the mind is computational, whether perceptual experiences are penetrated by propositional attitudes, what role attention plays in action, and so on. Naturally, there is no reason to limit the broadening of experimental philosophy to the field of psychology: Issues in biology, chemistry, or physics that are of interest to naturalist philosophers would fall within the purview of experimental philosophy as well.

In fact, to a large extent, this more extensive broadening of experimental philosophy is already occurring. Many studies are explicitly about issues other than describing the content of people's judgments or identifying factors that influence those judgments out of interest in the content and trustworthiness of those judgments. Schwitzgebel has examined whether studying moral philosophy resulted in more moral behavior, a claim often found in classical philosophy. Instead, he found that moral philosophers are more likely to steal books from library and to leave trash in conference rooms than other philosophers (Schwitzgebel, 2009; Schwitzgebel, Rust, Huang, Moore, & Coates, 2012). Livengood, Sytsma, Feltz, Scheines, and Machery (2010) have examined whether philosophers possess some distinctive epistemic virtues, and they have found that, at every level of education, philosophers are more likely to distrust their spontaneous judgments (their gut reactions) than equally educated people.

Expanding the kind of questions addressed within experimental philosophy requires expanding the range of experimental methods to which experimental philosophers appeal. They should avail themselves of the complete range of experimental methods used in the sciences. Nonexperimental empirical methods such as interviews and qualitative studies could also be fruitfully used by experimental philosophers. Some experimental philosophers are leading by example. Adam Arico and colleagues (Arico, Fiala, Goldberg, & Nichols, 2011; see Part II of this volume) measured people's reaction times to identify the cues people use to decide whether an entity can have conscious experiences, whereas Young, Nichols, and Saxe (2010) used functional magnetic resonance imaging (fMRI) to study judgments about moral luck. Machery and Cohen (2012) use quantitative citation analysis to study evolutionary psychologists' acquaintance with evolutionary biology.

In addition, some philosophers not usually categorized as experimental philosophers have long incorporated certain empirical methods into their work. Philosophers of science are likely to engage in scientific work themselves, both to investigate the operations of the sciences and to investigate scientific questions that bear on topics that interest them. For instance, philosophers of biology have employed simulations for the purpose of learning about phenomena such as generative entrenchment and the emergence of social norms (Muldoon, Lisciandra, Bicchieri, Hartmann, & Sprenger, in press; Wimsatt & Schank, 1988). Philosophers of science frequently employ case studies, ethnographic methods, and other social-scientific tools to investigate the operation of the sciences, including questions about conceptual change and the nature of things such as models (e.g., Giere, 1988; Hull, 1988; Nersessian, 2012). Those philosophers who now employ these various empirical methods might think of themselves as within the fold of experimental philosophy, broadly understood, and are encouraged to employ the range of empirical methods that might bear on the philosophical questions that interest them.

That said, pencil-and-paper studies examining people's judgments about cases (a.k.a. vignettes) can be brought to bear on a larger range of questions than critics of experimental philosophy realize (which is not to say that pencil-and-paper studies do not raise specific methodological problems). Variation in judgments across cases as a function of carefully controlled variables provides evidence about the cues that influence judgments, and thus about the cognitive mechanisms outputting these judgments. Psychologists have fruitfully used this methodology. To give a single example among many, Kahneman, Tversky, and the researchers working in the heuristics-and-biases tradition have extensively used vignettes to provide evidence about the heuristics underlying decision and judgment (see, e.g., the yellow and blue cab case or the mammography vignette).

One may perhaps feel that, although interesting, the issues examined in this broadened experimental philosophy fall entirely beyond the scope of philosophy (Papineau, 2011). In their influential manifesto, Knobe and Nichols (2008) responded to a similar concern by arguing that, because past philosophers (e.g., Aristotle, Hume, Descartes) were concerned with these very first-order questions or with similar ones, these issues clearly fall within philosophy. They write that

> [T]the only legitimate controversy here is about whether this sort of inquiry can legitimately be considered philosophy. That is, someone might think that it is all well and good to launch an inquiry into basic questions about human nature but that such an inquiry should not take place in a philosophy department . . . Now, it is true that some philosophers have thought that questions about how the mind works lie outside the proper domain of philosophy, but this is a relatively recent development. Throughout almost all of the history of philosophy, questions

about the workings of the mind were regarded as absolutely central. Philosophers wanted to know whether the mind was composed of distinct parts (reason, the passions, etc.) and how these parts might interact with each other. (. . .) There simply wasn't anything wrong with the traditional conception of philosophy. The traditional questions of philosophy—the questions that animated Plato, Aristotle, Spinoza, Hume, Nietzsche, and so many others—are just as profound and important today as they were when they were first posed. If experimental philosophy helps to bring our discipline back to these issues, we think that is cause for celebration. (Knobe & Nichols, 2008, pp. 13–14)

We are unconvinced by this argument: If it were correct, issues in theoretical physics, systematics, meteorology, developmental biology, and so on, would fall within philosophy too. Come to think of it, very few topics would not fall within philosophy! Perhaps Knobe and Nichols (2008) would respond that issues about meteorology have never been central to philosophy, whereas issues about the mind have. Although this is perhaps true about meteorology, many issues in physics (e.g., space, the structure of matter, the nature of motion, etc.) and in biology have been as central to the history of philosophy as the issues they mention.

A better response just denies that there is anything more to being a philosophical topic than being a topic of scholarly interest among philosophers. On this view, whether judgments about the intentional nature of actions are influenced by moral considerations (see the Supplemental Guide) is a philosophical topic these days, whereas meteorological issues are not part of philosophy anymore. We do not intend to defend this view about the nature of philosophical topics in this introduction; we simply note that any substantial characterization of what a philosophical topic is will have a hard time covering issues as diverse as whether natural selection is a force, whether emotions or concepts form a natural kind, whether ascriptions of knowledge is sensitive to stakes, whether there is only one thing, and so on. Ultimately, what matters is that there are many questions bearing on topics that currently interest philosophers that are susceptible to empirical investigation.

3.3 Toward a Mature Methodological Naturalism

Methodological naturalists typically take empirical facts to be relevant to some or all of their philosophical theorizing. We find it puzzling that many of them have not embraced enthusiastically the use of experimental, or more generally empirical, tools to further their philosophical interests. It is doubtful that all the empirical questions that are relevant for philosophical theorizing in this tradition have already been collected. If relevant first-order empirical questions have not yet been settled, naturalistic philosophers should engage in the relevant scientific work, alone or in collaboration with scientists. Furthermore, the philosophical theories that are developed on the basis of existing evidence undoubtedly have empirical consequences that have not yet been assessed. To avoid the charge that they are merely developing post hoc theories that fit existing data, philosophers should test these philosophical consequences.

There are many fine examples of this experimental broadening of methodological naturalism (in addition to Prinz's, 2008, work on emotions and moral judgments cited earlier, see, e.g., Nichols, 2002, on the evolution of etiquette norms). For instance, Lloyd (2005) criticized the existing evolutionary theories about female orgasm and the findings alleged to support them, and proposed that female orgasm was simply a by-product of male orgasm. Recently, moving beyond relying on existing findings, she has been providing some new empirical evidence (by reanalyzing existing data sets) in favor of her hypothesis (Wallen & Lloyd, 2008, 2011). Similarly, Griffiths (Griffiths et al., 2009; Linquist, Machery, Griffiths & Stotz, 2011) has recently examined experimentally whether the lay concept of innateness conflates three dimensions—the universality of a trait, the robustness of its development, and its functional nature—as he proposed in 2002 on the basis of existing data and psychological theories.

Prinz (2008) distinguishes between empirical and experimental philosophy. Empirical philosophy really amounts to what we have been calling methodological naturalism: It is simply the practice of using empirical facts in one's philosophical theorizing. What we propose, in effect, is that, to fulfill their goals, empirical philosophers should often turn themselves into experimental philosophers.

Notes

1. We bracket the debate about the exact role of the Gödel case in Kripke's argument against descriptivism (Devitt, 2011; Ichikawa, Maitra, & Weatherson, 2012).
2. See also Alexander and Weinberg (this volume) on reliability.
3. In a weaker formulation of the argument, instead of concluding inductively that the judgments elicited by thought experiments are in general influenced by non-truth-tracking factors, experimental philosophers conclude that these judgments may be influenced by such factors and hold that they cannot provide warrant if this possibility is not defeated.
4. In particular, when truth-tracking factors can compensate for non-truth-tracking factors (e.g., in perceptual judgments), Premise 2 is dubious. One may also wonder whether Premise 3 should appeal to the knowledge of unreliability rather to unreliability itself.
5. In particular, the Expertise Defense holds that, because experimental-philosophy studies focus on lay people's judgments, they do not show anything about philosophers' judgments (Devitt, 2011). For discussion, see Machery (2011, 2012a); Schulz, Cokely, and Feltz (2011); Tobia, Buckwalter, and Stich (2013); Schwitzgebel and Cushman (2012); Weinberg, Gonnerman, Buckner, and Alexander (2010); and Williamson (2011).
6. Supported by the Fuller Theological Seminary/Thrive Center in concert with the John Templeton Foundation.
7. For another argument in support of a broad view of experimental philosophy, see Rose and Danks (2013).

References

Aguiar, F., Becker, A., & Miller, L. (2013). Whose impartiality? An experimental study of veiled stakeholders, involved spectators and detached observers. *Economics and Philosophy, 29*, 155–174.

Alicke, M.D., Rose, D., & Bloom, D. (2011). Causation, norm violation, and culpable control. *Journal of Philosophy, 108*, 670–696.

Arico, A., Fiala, B., Goldberg, R.F., & Nichols, S. (2011). The folk psychology of consciousness. *Mind & Language, 26*, 327–352.

Bealer, G. (1996). A priori knowledge and the scope of philosophy. *Philosophical Studies, 81*, 121–142.

Brandt, R.B. (1954). *Hopi ethics: A theoretical analysis*. Chicago, IL: The University of Chicago Press.

Cappelen, H. (2012). *Philosophy without intuitions*. Oxford, England: Oxford University Press.

Christensen, D. (2009). Disagreement as evidence: The epistemology of controversy. *Philosophy Compass, 4*, 756–767.

Chudnoff, E. (2011). The nature of intuitive justification. *Philosophical Studies, 153*, 313–333.

Colaço, D., Buckwalter, W., Stich, S.P., & Machery, E. (in press). Epistemic intuitions in fake-barn thought experiments. *Episteme*.

Danks, D., Rose, D., & Machery, E. (forthcoming). Demoralizing causation. *Philosophical Studies*.

Deutsch, M. (2009). Experimental philosophy and the theory of reference. *Mind & Language, 24*, 445–466.

Devitt, M. (2011). Experimental semantics. *Philosophy and Phenomenological Research, 82*, 418–435.

Doris, J.M. (2002). *Lack of character*. New York, NY: Cambridge University Press.

Doris, J., & Stich, S.P. (2005). Moral psychology: Empirical approaches. In E.N. Zalta (Ed.), *The Stanford encyclopedia of philosophy*. Retrieved from http://plato.stanford.edu/archives/win2012/entries/moral-psych-emp/

Doris, J.M., & the Moral Psychology Research Group. (Eds.). (2010). *The moral psychology handbook*. Oxford, England: Oxford University Press.

Eskine, K.J., Kacinik, N.A., & Prinz, J.J. (2011). A bad taste in the mouth: Gustatory disgust influences moral judgment. *Psychological Science, 22*, 295–299.

Feltz, A., & Cokely, E.T. (2012). The philosophical personality argument. *Philosophical Studies, 161*, 227–246.

Giere, R.N. (2010). *Explaining science: A cognitive approach*. Chicago, IL: University of Chicago Press.

Goldman, A.I. (2007). Philosophical intuitions: Their target, their source, and their epistemic status. *Grazer Philosophische Studien, 74*, 1–26.

Gopnik, A., & Schwitzgebel, E. (1998). Whose concepts are they, anyway? The role of philosophical intuition in empirical psychology. In M.R. dePaul (Ed.), *Rethinking intuition* (pp. 75–91). Lahman, MD: Rowman and Littlefield.

Griffiths, P.E. (2002). What is innateness? *The Monist, 85*, 70–85.

Griffiths, P.E., Machery, E., & Linquist, S. (2009). The vernacular concept of innateness. *Mind & Language, 24*, 605–630.

Hitchcock, C., & Knobe, J. (2009). Cause and norm. *Journal of Philosophy, 11*, 587–612.

Hull, D.L. (1988). *Science as a process: An evolutionary account of the social and conceptual development of science*. Chicago, IL: University of Chicago Press.

Ichikawa, J., Maitra, I., & Weatherson, B. (2012). In defense of a Kripkean dogma. *Philosophy and Phenomenological Research, 85*, 56–68.

Jackson, F. (1998). *From metaphysics to ethics: A defence of conceptual analysis*. Oxford, England: Oxford University Press.

Joyce, R. (2006). *The evolution of morality*. Cambridge, MA: MIT Press.

Knobe, J., & Nichols, S. (2008). An experimental philosophy manifesto. In J. Knobe & S. Nichols (Eds.), *Experimental philosophy* (pp. 3–14). Oxford, England: Oxford University Press.

Knobe, J., & Prinz, J. (2008). Intuitions about consciousness: Experimental studies. *Phenomenology and the Cognitive Sciences, 7*, 67–83.

Knobe, J., & Samuels, R. (2013). Thinking like a scientist: Innateness as a case study. *Cognition, 128*, 72–86.

Kornblith, H. (2002). *Knowledge and its place in nature.* New York, NY: Oxford University Press.

Kornblith, H. (2013). Is there room for armchair theorizing in epistemology? In M.C. Haug (Ed.), *Philosophical methodology: The armchair or the laboratory?* (pp. 195–216). New York, NY: Routledge.

Kripke, S. (1972). *Naming and necessity.* Cambridge, MA: Harvard University Press.

Laudan, L., Donovan, A., Laudan, R., Barker, P., Brown, H., Leplin, J., . . . Wykstra, S. (1986). Scientific change: Philosophical models and historical research. *Synthese, 69*, 141–223.

Liao, S.M., Wiegmann, A., Alexander, J., & Vong, G. (2012). Putting the trolley in order: Experimental philosophy and the loop case. *Philosophical Psychology, 25*, 661–671.

Linquist, S., Machery, E., Griffiths, P.E., & Stotz, K. (2011). Exploring the folk biological conception of human nature. *Philosophical Transactions of the Royal Society B, 366*, 444–453.

Livengood, J., & Machery, E. (2007). The folk probably don't think what you think they think: Experiments on causation by absence. *Midwest Studies in Philosophy, 31*, 107–127.

Livengood, J., Sytsma, J., Feltz, A., Scheines, R., & Machery, E. (2010). Philosophical temperament. *Philosophical Psychology, 33*, 313–330.

Lloyd, E.A. (2005). *The case of the female orgasm: Bias in the science of evolution.* Cambridge, MA: Harvard University Press.

Ludwig, K. (2007). The epistemology of thought experiments: First person versus third person approaches. *Midwest Studies in Philosophy, 31*, 128–159.

Machery, E. (2011). Thought experiments and philosophical knowledge. *Metaphilosophy, 42*, 191–214.

Machery, E. (2012a). Expertise and intuitions about reference. *Theoria, 72*, 37–54.

Machery, E. (2012b). Delineating the moral domain. *The Baltic International Yearbook of Cognition, Logic and Communication, 7.* doi:http://dx.doi.org/10.4148/biyclc.v7i0.1777

Machery, E., & Cohen, K. (2012). An evidence-based study of the evolutionary behavioral sciences. *The British Journal for the Philosophy of Science, 63*, 177–226.

Machery, E., Kelly, D., & Stich, S.P. (2005). Moral realism and cross-cultural normative diversity. *Behavioral and Brain Sciences, 28*, 830.

Machery, E., & Mallon, R. (2010). Evolution of morality. In J.M. Doris & the Moral Psychology Research Group (Eds.), *The moral psychology handbook* (pp. 3–46). Oxford, England: Oxford University Press.

Machery, E., Mallon, R., Nichols, S., & Stich, S.P. (2004). Semantics, cross-cultural style. *Cognition, 92*, B1–B12.

Machery, E., Mallon, R., Nichols, S., & Stich, S.P. (2013). If intuitions vary, then what? *Philosophy and Phenomenological Research, 86*, 618–635.

Machery, E., Olivola, C., & de Blanc, M. (2009). Linguistic and metalinguistic intuitions in the philosophy of language. *Analysis, 69*, 689–694.

Machery, E., Sytsma, J., & Deutsch, M. (in press). Speaker's reference and cross-cultural semantics. In A. Bianchi (Ed.), *On reference.* Oxford, England: Oxford University Press.

Mackie, J. (1977). *Ethics: Inventing right and wrong.* New York, NY: Penguin Books.

Martí, G. (2009). Against semantic multi-culturalism. *Analysis, 69*, 42–48.

Meehl, P.E. (1992). Cliometric metatheory: The actuarial approach to empirical, history-based philosophy of science. *Psychological Reports, 71*, 339–467.

Meehl, P.E. (2002). Cliometric metatheory: II. Criteria scientists use in theory appraisal and why it is rational to do so. *Psychological Reports, 91*, 339–404.

Meehl, P.E. (2004). Cliometric metatheory III: Peircean consensus, verisimilitude and asymptotic method. *The British Journal for the Philosophy of Science, 55*, 615–643.

Muldoon, R., Lisciandra, C., Bicchieri, C., Hartmann, S., & Sprenger, J. (in press). On the emergence of descriptive norms. *Politics, Philosophy & Economics.*

Nadelhoffer, T., & Nahmias, E. (2007). The past and future of experimental philosophy. *Philosophical Explorations, 10,* 123–149.

Nagel, J. (2012). Intuitions and experiments: A defense of the case method in epistemology. *Philosophy and Phenomenological Research, 85,* 495–527.

Nagel, J. (2013). Defending the evidential value of epistemic intuitions: A reply to Stich. *Philosophy and Phenomenological Research, 87,* 177–189.

Nagel, J., San Juan, V.S., & Mar, R.A. (2013). Lay denial of knowledge for justified true beliefs. *Cognition, 129,* 652–661.

Nahmias, E., Morris, S.G., Nadelhoffer, T., & Turner, J. (2006). Is incompatibilism intuitive? *Philosophy and Phenomenological Research, 73,* 28–53.

Nersessian, N.J. (2012). Modeling practices in conceptual innovation: An ethnographic study of a neural engineering research laboratory. In U. Feest & F. Steinle (Eds.), *Scientific concepts and investigative practice* (pp. 245–269). Berlin, Germany: DeGruyter.

Nichols, S. (2002). On the genealogy of norms: A case for the role of emotion in cultural evolution. *Philosophy of Science, 69,* 234–255.

Nichols, S., & Knobe, J. (2007). Moral responsibility and determinism: The cognitive science of folk intuitions. *Nous, 41,* 663–685.

Papineau, D. (2011). What is x-phi good for? *The Philosophers' Magazine, 52,* 83–88.

Papineau, D. (2013). The poverty of conceptual analysis. In M.C. Haug (Ed.), *Philosophical methodology: The armchair or the laboratory?* (pp. 166–194). New York, NY: Routledge.

Prinz, J. (2008). Empirical philosophy and experimental philosophy. In J. Knobe & S. Nichols (Eds.), *Experimental philosophy* (pp. 189–208). Oxford, England: Oxford University Press.

Reuter, K. (2011). Distinguishing the appearance from the reality of pain. *Journal of Consciousness Studies, 18,* 9–10.

Rose, D., & Danks, D. (2013). In defense of a broad conception of experimental philosophy. *Metaphilosophy, 44,* 512–532.

Rose, D., Livengood, J., Sytsma, J., & Machery, E. (2012). Deep troubles for the deep self. *Philosophical Psychology, 25,* 629–646.

Schulz, E., Cokely, E.T., & Feltz, A. (2011). Persistent bias in expert judgments about free will and moral responsibility: A test of the expertise defense. *Consciousness and Cognition, 20,* 1722–1731.

Schupbach, J.N. (2011). Comparing probabilistic measures of explanatory power. *Philosophy of Science, 78,* 813–829.

Schupbach, J.N. (2013). *Experimental explication.* Manuscript in preparation.

Schwitzgebel, E. (2009). Do ethicists steal more books? *Philosophical Psychology, 22,* 711–725.

Schwitzgebel, E., & Cushman, F. (2012). Expertise in moral reasoning? Order effects on moral judgment in professional philosophers and non-philosophers. *Mind & Language, 27,* 135–153.

Schwitzgebel, E., Rust, J., Huang, L.T.L., Moore, A.T., & Coates, J. (2012). Ethicists' courtesy at philosophy conferences. *Philosophical Psychology, 25,* 331–340.

Seidel, A., & Prinz, J. (2013). Sound morality: Irritating and icky noises amplify judgments in divergent moral domains. *Cognition, 127,* 1–5.

Singer, P. (1972). Famine, affluence, and morality. *Philosophy & Public Affairs, 1,* 229–243.

Singer, P. (2005). Ethics and intuitions. *The Journal of Ethics, 9,* 331–352.

Sosa, E. (2007). Experimental philosophy and philosophical intuition. *Philosophical Studies, 132,* 99–107.

Stich, S.P. (2013). Do different groups have different epistemic intuitions? A reply to Jennifer Nagel. *Philosophy and Phenomenological Research, 87,* 151–178.

Stich, S.P., Doris, J., & Roedder, E. (2010). Altruism. In J.M. Doris and the Moral Psychology Research Group (Eds.), *The moral psychology handbook* (pp. 147–205). Oxford, England: Oxford University Press.

Stotz, K., Griffiths, P. E., & Knight, R. (2004). How biologists conceptualize genes: An empirical study. *Studies in History and Philosophy of Science Part C: Studies in History and Philosophy of Biological and Biomedical Sciences, 35*, 647–673.

Swain, S., Alexander, J., & Weinberg, J. M. (2008). The instability of philosophical intuitions: Running hot and cold on Truetemp. *Philosophy and Phenomenological Research, 76*, 138–155.

Sytsma, J., Livengood, J., & Rose, D. (2012). Two types of typicality: Rethinking the role of statistical typicality in ordinary causal attributions. *Studies in History and Philosophy of Science Part C: Studies in History and Philosophy of Biological and Biomedical Sciences, 43*, 814–820.

Sytsma, J., & Machery, E. (2010). Two conceptions of subjective experience. *Philosophical Studies, 151*, 299–327.

Thomasson, A. L. (2012). Experimental philosophy and the methods of ontology. *The Monist, 95*, 175–199.

Thomson, J. J. (1985). The trolley problem. *Yale Law Journal, 94*, 1395–1415.

Tobia, K., Buckwalter, W., & Stich, S. (2013). Moral intuitions: Are philosophers experts? *Philosophical Psychology, 26*, 629–638.

Turri, J. (2013). A conspicuous art: Putting Gettier to the test. *Philosophers' Imprint, 13*, 1–16.

Wallen, K., & Lloyd, E. A. (2008). Clitoral variability compared with penile variability supports nonadaptation of female orgasm. *Evolution & Development, 10*, 1–2.

Wallen, K., & Lloyd, E. A. (2011). Female sexual arousal: Genital anatomy and orgasm in intercourse. *Hormones and Behavior, 59*, 780–792.

Weinberg, J. M. (2007). How to challenge intuitions empirically without risking skepticism. *Midwest Studies in Philosophy, 31*, 318–343.

Weinberg, J. M., Gonnerman, C., Buckner, C., & Alexander, J. (2010). Are philosophers expert intuiters? *Philosophical Psychology, 23*, 331–355.

Weinberg, J. M., Nichols, S., & Stich, S. (2001). Normativity and epistemic intuitions. *Philosophical Topics, 29*, 429–460.

Williamson, T. (2007). *The philosophy of philosophy*. Malden, MA: Blackwell.

Williamson, T. (2011). Philosophical expertise and the burden of proof. *Metaphilosophy, 42*, 215–229.

Wimsatt, W. C., & Schank, J. C. (1988). Two constraints on the evolution of complex adaptations and the means for their avoidance. In M. Nitecki (Ed.), *Progress in evolution* (pp. 213–273). Chicago, IL: University of Chicago Press.

Woolfolk, R. L., Doris, J. M., & Darley, J. M. (2006). Identification, situational constraint, and social cognition: Studies in the attribution of moral responsibility. *Cognition, 100*, 283–301.

Wright, J. C. (2010). On intuitional stability: The clear, the strong, and the paradigmatic. *Cognition, 115*, 491–503.

Young, L., Nichols, S., & Saxe, R. (2010). Investigating the neural and cognitive basis of moral luck: It's not what you do but what you know. *Review of Philosophy and Psychology, 1*, 333–349.

PART **I**

Language

CHAPTER 1

What Is the Significance of the Demographic Variation in Semantic Intuitions?

EDOUARD MACHERY

Abstract

In this article, I review the empirical evidence for the claim that judgments about the reference of proper names in actual and possible cases vary across cultures. I then respond to two objections by Max Deutsch and by Genoveva Martí, who have both argued that this variation has no significant implications for theorizing about reference.

How do proper names refer to their bearers? What makes it the case that "Barack H. Obama" refers to the 44th president of the United States of America? Philosophers of language have offered two fundamentally different kinds of answer to such questions. According to descriptivist theories of reference (Jackson, 1998; McGinn, 2012; Searle, 1958), a proper name refers to whatever satisfies the description associated with this proper name. So, "Paris" refers to the capital of France because the capital of France is the only city that satisfies the description associated with the proper name "Paris." This basic insight of descriptivist theories of reference can naturally be declined in various ways, depending on what one takes the descriptions associated with proper names to be, on whose descriptions count for securing reference, and so on. But all descriptivist theories of reference stand in sharp contrast to the causal-historical theories of reference (Devitt, 1981; Kripke, 1972/1980). According to these latter theories, a proper name refers to its bearer because of a particular causal chain linking the proper name to its bearer. So, "Paris" refers to the capital of

France because the capital of France is causally connected (in the right way) to current uses of "Paris."

Which of these two approaches of reference is right? Before being in a position to answer this question, however, another issue must be addressed: How does one know which of these approaches to the reference of proper names is correct? That is, what kind of evidence or what type of consideration would favor one approach over the other? Surprisingly, for a long time, philosophers have ignored, or perhaps not addressed explicitly, this question in semantic epistemology. Recently, however, an intense debate, fuelled by findings in experimental philosophy (Beebe & Undercoffer, 2013a, 2013b; Genone & Lombrozo, 2012; Grau & Pury, in press; Lam, 2010; Machery, 2012a; Machery et al., 2010; Machery, Mallon, Nichols, & Stich, 2004; Machery, Olivola, & de Blanc, 2009; Sytsma & Livengood, 2011; Sytsma, Livengood, Sato, & Oguchi, 2012) has been raging about the methods used to identify the correct theory of reference (Andow, in press; Cohnitz & Haukioja, 2013; Deutsch, 2009, 2010; Devitt, 2011, 2012a, 2012b; Ichikawa, Maitra, & Weatherson, 2012; Jackman, 2009; Ludwig, 2007; Machery, 2012b; Machery, Mallon, Nichols, & Stich, 2013; Machery & Stich, 2012; Mallon, Machery, Nichols, & Stich, 2009; Martí, 2009, 2012, this volume; Maynes, in press; Maynes & Gross, 2013; Ostertag, 2013; Reimer, 2009; for review, see Genone, 2012). In previous work, I have argued that when theorizing about the reference of proper names, philosophers of language typically appeal to their judgments about what proper names refer to in actual and possible situations (a method called "the method of cases") and that evidence about various forms of demographic variation in this type of judgment (which are often, but somewhat misleadingly, called "intuitions") raise a challenge for this method. The goal of this chapter is to defend this argument against two criticisms: First, the claim that, appearances notwithstanding, philosophers of language do not rely on judgments about reference (Deutsch, 2009, 2010); second, the claim that to determine the referential properties of proper names (and probably other kinds of word), speakers' use of these words, not their judgments about reference, should be examined (Devitt, 2012a; Martí, 2009, 2012, this volume).

Here is how this chapter proceeds: In Section 1, I review the argument put forward in my previous work. In Section 2, I address the objection that philosophers of language do not appeal to judgments about reference when they theorize about reference and that, as a consequence, demographic variation in judgments about the reference of proper names is irrelevant. In Section 3, I address the objection that use, but not judgments about reference, should be examined to determine the referential properties of proper names.

1. Against the Method of Cases

1.1 The Method of Cases

The method of cases is straightforward. Theories of reference entail that some proper names (e.g., "Barack H. Obama") refer to particular individuals in actual or merely possible situations (or "cases"). These theories are supported if we judge that these names do refer to these individuals, and they are undermined if we judge that they do not refer to them. Our judgments about the reference of proper names in actual and possible situations play this evidential role because they are taken to be true. So, if we judge that a proper name does not refer to an individual in a merely possible situation, then in this situation, this proper name does not refer to this individual. Naturally, judgments about reference only provide defeasible support or evidence against theories of reference.

The method of cases is well illustrated by Kripke's (1972/1980) original defense of the causal-historical theory. In *Naming and Necessity*, Kripke considers a counterfactual case in which a proper name, "Gödel," is associated with a description, "the man who proved the incompleteness of arithmetic," that is false of the original bearer of the name but true of someone else, originally called "Schmidt." Because descriptivist theories of reference hold that a name refers to the individual that best satisfies the description competent speakers associate with it, descriptivist theories entail that "Gödel" refers to the man originally called "Schmidt." In contrast, causal-historical theories of reference hold that "Gödel" continues to refer to its original bearer because he is the person causally-historically linked with contemporary uses of the name. To provide evidence discriminating these two competing kinds of theory, Kripke asks who an ordinary man would be referring to in this situation:

> Suppose that Gödel was not in fact the author of [Gödel's] theorem. A man called "Schmidt," whose body was found in Vienna under mysterious circumstances many years ago, actually did the work in question. His friend Gödel somehow got hold of the manuscript and it was thereafter attributed to Gödel. On the [descriptivist] view . . . when our ordinary man uses the name "Gödel," he really means to refer to Schmidt, because Schmidt is the unique person satisfying the description "the man who discovered the incompleteness of arithmetic." So, since the man who discovered the incompleteness of arithmetic is in fact Schmidt, we, when we talk about "Gödel," are in fact always referring to Schmidt. But it seems we are not. We simply are not. (1972/1980, pp. 83–84)

Taken at face value, this passage provides a striking illustration of the use of the method of cases in debates about reference: Implications of theories of reference for particular cases are examined; judgments about these cases are made; these judgments are taken to bear on the truth of the theories because they are taken to be true.

1.2 Demographic Variation in Intuitions

A decade ago, Ron Mallon, Shaun Nichols, Steve Stich, and I decided to examine whether judgments about the reference of proper names vary across cultures. Influenced by psychologist Richard Nisbett's (2003) then ground-breaking cross-cultural research in psychology, according to which East Asians (primarily Chinese, Japanese, and Koreans) and Westerners (primarily Americans) tend to have different cognitive styles, we hypothesized that judgments about reference may vary across cultures (Machery et al., 2004). Specifically, we hypothesized that East Asians may be more likely to make descriptivist judgments (i.e., judgments consistent with descriptivist theories of reference) than Westerners.

To test this hypothesis, we presented participants in Hong Kong and in the United States with cases closely inspired by Kripke's (1972/1980) Gödel case (quoted earlier), such as the following case (for further detail, see Machery et al., 2004):

> Suppose that John has learned in college that Gödel is the man who proved an important mathematical theorem, called the incompleteness of arithmetic. John is quite good at mathematics and he can give an accurate statement of the incompleteness theorem, which he attributes to Gödel as the discoverer. But this is the only thing that he has heard about Gödel. Now suppose that Gödel was not the author of this theorem. A man called "Schmidt," whose body was found in Vienna under mysterious circumstances many years ago, actually did the work in question. His friend Gödel somehow got hold of the manuscript and claimed credit for the work, which was thereafter attributed to Gödel. Thus, he has been known as the man who proved the incompleteness of arithmetic. Most people who have heard the name "Gödel" are like John; the claim that Gödel discovered the incompleteness theorem is the only thing they have ever heard about Gödel. When John uses the name "Gödel," is he talking about:
>
> (A) the person who really discovered the incompleteness of arithmetic? or
> (B) the person who got hold of the manuscript and claimed credit for the work?

Another case, the Tsu Ch'ung Chih case, had the same structure, but used names of Chinese individuals. (I collectively call these cases "Gödel-style cases.")

As we had predicted, we found that East Asians were more likely to make descriptivist judgments about the Gödel and the Tsu Ch'ung Chih cases than were Americans. In fact, most Americans made causal-historical judgments, whereas most East Asians made descriptivist judgments. We also found a substantial amount of within-culture variation.

Follow-up studies have provided further empirical support for the hypothesis that judgments about the reference of proper names vary across cultures. Beebe and Undercoffer (2013a) have independently replicated our original finding and have shown that it is robust: It is still found when the formulation of the vignettes and of the questions about reference is varied. They have also provided some suggestive evidence that East Asians are more likely to make descriptivist judgments about reference in Jonah cases (i.e., cases in which a proper name is associated with an entirely false description and in which people are asked whether the proper name refers to anything or fails to refer). Sytsma and colleagues (2012) have shown that, just like Chinese, Japanese tend to make descriptivist judgments about the reference of proper names in Gödel-style cases, suggesting that the cultural hypothesis put forward in Machery et al. (2004) may well be correct. Machery and colleagues (2009) have shown that in Gödel-style cases judgments about the reference of proper names and judgments about the truth-value of sentences involving these names are in sync with one another: In a given culture, when people tend to report, say, descriptivist judgments about the reference of "Gödel" in the Gödel case, they tend to judge that a sentence such as "Gödel was a great mathematician" uttered in this case would be true. Machery et al. (2010) have shown that Chinese participants make similar judgments when Gödel-style cases are presented in English (as was originally done in Machery et al., 2004) and in Chinese. Machery, Sytsma, and Deutsch (in press) have shown that people are genuinely reporting their judgments about the semantic reference of proper names in Gödel-style cases (roughly, what a proper name refers to according to the language to which it belongs) and not about the speaker's reference of these names (roughly, what the speaker intends to refer to with a proper name in a given occasion). Finally, Machery (2012a) has provided some tentative evidence that, among experts, judgments about the reference of proper names is influenced by experts' disciplinary background.

1.3 Philosophical Implications

This expanding body of empirical evidence has various philosophical implications (for discussion, Machery, 2011; Machery et al., 2013; Mallon et al., 2009), but in this chapter, I only focus on their implications for the methodology of semantic theorizing about reference.

If judgments about reference really vary, philosophers of language interested in the reference of proper names need to accommodate such variation.

One option would be to maintain that names refer in the same way in all languages and thus infer that variable judgments are not reliable guides to the semantic properties of names. Philosophers of language who adopt this view would reject the method of cases, and they in turn owe an account of how the correct theory of reference is to be determined.

Alternatively, philosophers of language interested in reference could maintain that judgments about reference are reliable guides to the semantic properties of names and go on to infer that names refer differently in different cultures. If they endorse this second option, philosophers of language would need to examine the judgments of ordinary competent speakers empirically, which would lead to a sea change in their methods and might compel them to devise new theories of reference (Machery & Stich, 2012).

A third option would be to insist that some sources of judgments, but not others, are reliable guides to the semantic properties of names. For example, they could suggest that academic philosophers, or linguistic experts, or Westerners, or members of some other special cultural group, make reliable judgments about reference while others do not. The burden for this line of argument is justifying the claim that the favored group of people or of judgments is privileged. Again, arguably, this option would require empirical validation of the reliability of these judgments, and it would require a sharp departure from the blind reliance on philosophers' judgments (see Machery, 2012a, for some concerns with this option).

It is not clear at all which option philosophers of language should embrace, but, fortunately, this is not *my* problem!

2. Doing Away With Intuitions?

Some philosophers of language may well object that the three options described at the end of Section 1 do not exhaust the range of possible responses. In particular, they may deny that judgments play any role in semantic epistemology: According to this view, judgments about the reference of proper names in actual and possible situations play no role in deciding which theory of reference is correct. If this is true, the variation in semantic judgments across and within cultures is irrelevant to semantic epistemology. In the remainder of this chapter, I flesh out this argument in more detail and respond to it.

Max Deutsch (2009, 2010) has forcefully argued that judgments about reference are not used to identify the correct theory of reference. He writes that

> Mallon et al. misunderstand the way in which Kripke, for example, argues for and against the claims about reference of interest to him. . . . [N]othing in Kripke's famous argument against the descriptivist theory

of reference for proper names hinges on assuming anything about people's intuitions. (Deutsch 2009, p. 445)

His argument seems straightforward:

> Like any other theory, a theory of reference is true only if it makes true predictions. But the predictions of a theory of reference concern terms and their referents, not competent speakers and their intuitions. For example, *D* [i.e., descriptivism] predicts that, in Kripke's fiction, the relevant speaker's uses of "Gödel" refer to Schmidt, not Gödel. If the prediction is false, so is the theory, but the theory makes no predictions at all concerning who will intuit what. Hence, in presenting the Gödel case, Kripke does not, and need not, make any claims about competent speakers' intuitions. (Deutsch, 2009, p. 448)

So, according to Deutsch, judgments about reference are not used in the philosophy of language because theories of reference such as descriptivist theories make predictions about what proper names refer to in particular situations, and not about what speakers judge that proper names refer to in these situations.

This objection is clearly a nonstarter. Deutsch is obviously right that the implications of theories of reference bear on what proper names refer to in actual and possible situations, and not on people's semantic judgments. Causal-historical theories of reference entail that the proper name "Gödel" refers to Gödel in the Gödel case, and they do not entail anything about people's judgments. But this noncontroversial observation raises the question, How do we know that "Gödel" refers to Gödel, and not to Schmidt, in the Gödel case? This is when judgments about reference play a role: The judgment that "Gödel" refers to Gödel in the Gödel case is taken to be evidence that "Gödel" refers to Gödel in the Gödel case, plausibly because this type of judgment is taken to be reliable.

Not only is this objection a nonstarter; Deutsch also knows it is because he quickly acknowledges that Mallon, Nichols, Stich, and I "would likely" make that response. Indeed, not only would we; in fact, this is also exactly the role that, in our view, judgments about reference play in the philosophy of language.

Before examining what Deutsch has to say in response, let me note that some of Deutsch's remarks are strangely self-defeating. He rightly remarks that philosophers of language do not always take their theory to be undermined when it conflicts with some judgments. Rather, they sometimes try to explain these judgments away, appealing for instance to pragmatic principles. As Deutsch (2009) puts it, "they argue instead that the intuitions of competent speakers are not the final arbiter of correctness for a semantic theory and attempt to 'explain away' the contrary intuitions in a way that leaves their semantic view unscathed" (p. 449). But, surely, if judgments were really irrelevant, as Deutsch claims, philosophers of language would not need to explain *any* judgment away: They could just ignore them. Rather, the fact that they feel the need to explain some judgments away only makes sense if on their view these judgments somehow bear on the truth of their claims.

In his response to the claim that judgments about reference provide evidence about what proper names refer to in actual and possible situations, Deutsch grants that some philosophers treat judgments about reference as evidence and that these judgments may well be evidence, but he insists that "Kripke's argument against descriptivism, and Evans' argument against the causal-historical theory, [do] not depend on treating intuitions as a source of evidence. Even if intuitions are evidence, they need not be treated as such in the case of these two arguments" (pp. 450–451). His main argument is that three *other* considerations besides the Gödel case undermine descriptivist theories of reference (Deutsch, 2009, pp. 451–452): First, the counterfactual Gödel case has actual counterparts (e.g., many people associate the proper name "Peano" with a single definite description, namely, "the man who discovered the axioms of arithmetic," whereas these axioms were actually discovered by Dedekind); second, if descriptivism were true, one could never be mistaken when asserting that "*a* is the *F*" where "*F*" is the definite description associated with the proper name "*a*" (e.g., "Gödel is the discoverer of the incompleteness of arithmetic"); and, third, Kripke defends an alternative to descriptivism. However, this response fails on at least two grounds.

First, if the considerations Deutsch alludes to were sufficient to undermine descriptivist theories of reference, one wonders why Kripke bothered putting forward the Gödel case at all. And, if this case plays any role in Kripke's argument, as seems likely, one wonders how one could know what "Gödel" refers to in the counterfactual situation described by Kripke. Deutsch seems to be evading the question.

Deutsch would be wrong to respond that our knowledge of the reference of proper names in actual counterparts to the Gödel case—for instance, our knowledge that "Peano" refers to Peano and not Dedekind—shows that "Gödel" refers to Gödel in the counterfactual Gödel case. The Dedekind/Peano case differs from the Gödel case in important respects: In particular, in the Dedekind/Peano case, but not in the Gödel case, experts know that the original bearer of the proper name do not fulfill the description nonexperts associate with the name (i.e., they know that Peano was not the first one to formulate the axioms of arithmetic), and as a consequence, they associate another description with "Peano."

Second, the three considerations Deutsch alludes to fail to undermine descriptivism decisively. As just noted, the Peano and other cases are not counterparts of the Gödel case. Deutsch's second consideration at most falsifies the simplest form of descriptivism, according to which a speaker refers to the individual who satisfies the description he or she associates with it, but not more complex forms, such as the view that within a linguistic community a speaker refers to the individual who satisfies the description this community associates with a proper name. Finally, Kripke (1972/1980) did not develop a theory of reference, but "a picture," and to turn this picture into a theory judgments about reference in counterfactual cases are likely to be needed (Machery et al., 2013). As a result, philosophers should be in a position to explain how we know what proper names refer to in such cases.

3. Use or Intuitions?

In a fascinating series of papers, Genoveva Martí (2009, 2012, this volume) has argued that in developing a theory of reference, "the evidence that the semanticist relies on is evidence about how speakers use words. Not evidence about how they think that they, or some hypothetical speakers, use words" (this volume, pp. 22–23). Furthermore, she holds that people's judgments about what a proper name refers to in an actual or a possible situation provide only evidence about how people think about reference and is thus not the right kind of evidence for developing a theory of reference. She concludes that findings about the demographic variation in judgments about the reference of proper names have no implications for theories of reference. As she puts it,

> If Machery and colleagues want to discuss why different people and different experts hold to different theories of the reference of proper names, the discussion will be very interesting. But it is a discussion about theoretical preferences, a discussion about which theories people find attractive and why, perhaps a topic of interest for the sociology or psychology of science. It is not a discussion about what kind of evidence we do have in favor or one or another theory. (Martí, this volume, p. 24)

Before discussing Martí's views critically, it is important to clarify two points of agreement between Martí and me. Despite some of Martí's remarks that may mislead the reader (a similar point applies to some of Deutsch's (2009, p. 445) remarks; see Section 2), Martí and I concur that the debate about reference "is about how proper names do refer" (this volume, p. 22), and not about what judgments about reference people make. In addition, Martí and I are united in doubting that judgments about reference can actually provide evidence about reference, although our doubts stem from two distinct sources. Martí doubts it because she thinks that these judgments reflect people's theories about reference, which may well be widely mistaken, and because she thinks that the proper evidence is provided by how people use proper names, not by people's judgments about their reference (but see below for some concerns about this distinction). I doubt it because of the demographic variation in these judgments (see Section 1).

So, what do we disagree about? First, we disagree about whether judgments about the reference of proper names in actual and possible cases are usually taken to provide relevant evidence about how proper names refer: Martí apparently doubts it (but see below for an interpretative caveat), I assert it. According to me, philosophers of language typically take these judgments to constitute evidence for and against the competing theories of reference. Second, we disagree about the consequences of the findings about the demographic variability of judgments about reference for semantic epistemology: Martí thinks that these findings have no consequence (because evidence consists of use, not judgments about reference), I think that they are significant, first, because judgments are usually taken to be evidence about proper names and, second, because use cannot be a substitute for judgments in supporting theories of reference.

Before discussing Martí's views critically, I should also mention an issue about the proper interpretation of Martí's claims about use and intuitions. In particular, it is unclear whether she is proposing to *reform* the way theorizing about reference is done—by recommending the reliance on use instead of judgments about reference—or whether she takes herself to be *describing* what philosophers take to be evidence when theorizing about reference. The latter interpretation is suggested by her remark about "what Kripke appeals to in his remarks about 'Aristotle,' 'Feynman,' 'Einstein,' and 'Columbus'" (Martí, this volume, p. 22). Or perhaps, she thinks that philosophers are already appealing to use in addition to appealing to judgments about reference, and she is recommending that they appeal only to the former.

I now turn to the critical discussion of Martí's views. First, philosophers of language appeal extensively to judgments about the reference of proper names in actual and possible cases (Deutsch concedes the point, as we saw in Section 2): After all, the Gödel case is taken from *Naming and Necessity*! So, even if Martí were right that the proper evidence for and against theories about reference consists of the way words are used (a point I turn to next), findings about the demographic variation in judgments about reference would still be significant for semantic epistemology: They should lead philosophers of language to modify their philosophical methodology.

Second, the contrast between the notions of use and of judgment about reference is not entirely clear. Martí (this volume) refers to Kripke's (1972/1980) remarks about, for example, "Columbus" to illustrate how use is already appealed to in contemporary theorizing about reference. Kripke (1972/1980, p. 85) remarks that, although many associate "Columbus" with the description "the first European to land in the Western Hemisphere," "Columbus" does refer to the man originally called "Columbus" despite the fact that he was not the first European to land in the Western Hemisphere. Martí's point seems to be that ordinary speakers use "Columbus" to refer to Columbus despite their erroneous beliefs and that this fact about use is the proper kind of evidence for theorizing about reference. But what is our ground for judging that ordinary speakers use "Columbus" to refer to Columbus? What else could it be but the *judgment* that ordinary speakers are speaking about the man originally called "Columbus" or the judgment that they speak truly when they say that Columbus was Italian? If this is so, appealing to use isn't an alternative to appealing to judgments about reference (or about the truth value of sentences containing the relevant proper names). Indeed, Kripke's remarks about "Columbus," "Peano," and similar proper names are typically interpreted as relying on judgments about actual cases. What Martí seems to be really insisting on (like Devitt), then, is that the relevant evidence for theorizing about reference is not limited to judgments about the reference of proper names in counterfactual cases such as the Gödel case, but that it also includes (or, more radically, that it should be limited to) our judgments about their reference (or truth values) in actual cases (what we take "Columbus" to be actually referring to).

Furthermore, use (or judgments about actual cases) will not get philosophers very far when theorizing about reference (Machery et al., 2013). Use is sufficient to falsify some simple descriptivist theories about the reference of proper names, but not more complex descriptivist theories that appeal, for example, to deference to experts. For instance, the use of "Peano" to refer to Peano, and not Dedekind, suggests that it is not the case that, when a speaker uses a proper name, he or she refers to the individual who satisfies the description *the speaker* associates with it, but this use does not falsify the proposal that, when using a proper name, the speaker refers to the individual that satisfies the description *experts* associate with this name. Incidentally, use is also sufficient to falsify simple causal-historical theories (Evans, 1973), but probably not more complex causal-historical theories. To decide between complex descriptivist and causal-historical theories, judgments about the reference of proper names in counterfactual cases, such as the Gödel case, are likely to be needed. Remarkably, this advantage of judgment over use is well known in the methodology of linguistics: Linguists, in particular syntacticians, appeal to judgments about acceptability (i.e., about whether a syntactic construction is acceptable) in part because use does not contain some of the relevant evidence to decide between competing theories. When a syntactic construction is not found in linguistic corpora, it may be either because it is too complex to be used or because it is ungrammatical. So, the fact that a construction is not found in corpora cannot be used to decide between two theories that disagree about whether it is grammatical. Judgments about acceptability can be appealed to for remedying this problem.

In addition, Martí's proposal about use and judgments fits poorly with the accepted methodology in linguistics, including in semantics. There, judgments about the linguistic (semantic or syntactic) properties of linguistic expressions are used to study, and thus are taken to provide evidence about, these linguistic properties. For instance, when lexical semanticists are working on the meaning of lexemes, they appeal to judgments about synonymy or antonymy, whereas psycholinguists working on lexical disambiguation appeal to judgments about ambiguity or polysemy. I suppose that Martí does not hold that linguists are mistaken to appeal to these judgments and, thus, that she does not deny that these judgments provide evidence about the relevant linguistic properties. In fact, on her views, it would a mistake to deny this since judgments about linguistic properties such as synonymy and polysemy are consistent with patterns of use: For instance, when two words are judged to be synonymous or near synonymous, they tend to occur in the same kind of linguistic contexts. So, if use provides evidence about the relevant linguistic properties, the relevant judgments do it too. Then, Martí probably holds that judgments about reference are altogether different from judgments about synonymy, polysemy, acceptability, and so on. In contrast to the latter, judgments about reference do not provide evidence about reference, whereas use does. But why is it? Why do judgments about reference differ? Martí owes us an explanation. Barring such an explanation, her views about the epistemology of theories about reference seem largely ad hoc: They seem to have been specifically tailored to deal with the concerns expressed in Machery et al. (2004).

Finally, the contrast drawn by Martí (this volume) between the epistemological significance of judgments about reference and of use is implausible (for further discussion, see Machery, 2011, Section 2): If patterns of use provide evidence about reference, as Martí asserts, then laypeople's theories of reference are plausibly reliable—meaning that they are likely to produce true judgments about the reference of proper names in actual and possible cases—and the resulting judgments plausibly constitute evidence. People have extensive experience with the use of proper names, they give and get feedback when names are misused, they observe others using proper names and getting feedback, and so on. Their theories about reference plausibly reflect this experience: It would be curious if people had theories about reference that lead to judgments at odds with how they and others use words. So, if use provides evidence, then people's theories are plausibly reliable, and the resulting judgments are plausibly evidence about reference.

To wrap up, demographic variation in judgments about reference raises doubts about how theories of reference are to be supported. These doubts are not alleviated by arguing that the proper evidence bearing on theories of reference does not consist in judgments about reference, but in the way the relevant kinds of lexemes are used. The epistemological contrast between use and judgment is unclear because appealing to use involves relying on judgments about the reference of proper names and other kinds of lexemes in actual cases, use may only be able to discriminate between the simplest theories of reference, the contrast between use and judgment (whatever it amounts to) violates the usual linguistic methodology in an apparently ad hoc manner, and it is implausible.

Conclusion

It is now beyond doubt that some judgments about the reference of proper names are influenced by demographic variables, and that they vary within and across cultures, and it is plausible that this variation is not limited to the cases that have been examined empirically. Attempts to defuse the implications of these findings for semantic epistemology are unconvincing: The considerations mentioned by Deutsch or use, as touted by Martí, cannot be a substitute for judgments about reference. Thus, it remains mysterious how theories of reference are to be supported or undermined.

References

Andow, J. (in press). Intuitions, disagreement and referential pluralism. *Review of Philosophy and Psychology*.

Beebe, J. R., & Undercoffer, R. J. (2013a). *Individual and cross-cultural differences in semantic intuitions: New experimental findings*. Manuscript in preparation.

Beebe, J. R., & Undercoffer, R. J. (2013b). *Moral valence and semantic intuitions*. Manuscript in preparation.

Cohnitz, D., & Haukioja, J. (2013). Meta-externalism vs. meta-internalism in the study of reference. *Australasian Journal of Philosophy, 91*, 475–500.

Deutsch, M. (2009). Experimental philosophy and the theory of reference. *Mind & Language, 24*, 445–466.

Deutsch, M. (2010). Intuitions, counter-examples, and experimental philosophy. *The Review of Philosophy and Psychology, 1*, 447–460.

Devitt, M. (1981). *Designation*. New York, NY: Columbia University Press.

Devitt, M. (2011). Experimental semantics. *Philosophy and Phenomenological Research, 82*, 418–435.

Devitt, M. (2012a). Whither experimental semantics? *Theoria, 73*, 5–36.

Devitt, M. (2012b). Semantic epistemology: Response to Machery. *Theoria, 74*, 229–233.

Evans, G. (1973). The causal theory of names. *Proceedings of the Aristotelian Society, 47*, 187–225.

Genone, J. (2012). Theories of reference and experimental philosophy. *Philosophy Compass, 7*, 152–163.

Genone, J., & Lombrozo, T. (2012). Concept possession, experimental semantics, and hybrid theories of reference. *Philosophical Psychology, 25*, 717–742.

Grau, C., & Pury, C. (in press). Attitudes towards reference and replaceability. *Review of Philosophy and Psychology*.

Ichikawa, J., Maitra, I., & Weatherson, B. (2012). In defense of a Kripkean dogma. *Philosophy and Phenomenological Research, 85*, 56–68.

Jackman, H. (2009). Semantic intuitions, conceptual analysis, and cross-cultural variation. *Philosophical Studies, 146*, 159–177.

Jackson, F. (1998). Reference and description revisited. *Philosophical Perspectives, 12*, 201–218.

Kripke, S. (1980). *Naming and necessity*. Cambridge, MA: Harvard University Press. (Original work published in 1972)

Lam, B. (2010). Are Cantonese speakers really descriptivists? Revisiting cross-cultural semantics. *Cognition, 115*, 320–329.

Ludwig, K. (2007). The epistemology of thought experiments: First-person approach vs. third-person approach. *Midwest Studies in Philosophy, 31*, 128–159.

Machery, E. (2011). Variation in intuitions about reference and ontological disagreement. In S.D. Hales (Ed.), *A companion to relativism* (pp. 118–136). Malden, MA: Wiley-Blackwell.

Machery, E. (2012a). Expertise and intuitions about reference. *Theoria, 73*, 37–54.

Machery, E. (2012b). Semantic epistemology: A brief response to Devitt. *Theoria, 74*, 223–227.

Machery, E., Deutsch, M., Mallon, R., Nichols, S., Sytsma, J., & Stich, S.P. (2010). Semantic intuitions: Reply to Lam. *Cognition, 117*, 361–366.

Machery, E., Mallon, R., Nichols, S., & Stich, S.P. (2004). Semantics, cross-cultural style. *Cognition, 92*, B1–B12.

Machery, E., Mallon, R., Nichols, S., & Stich, S.P. (2013). If intuitions vary, then so what? *Philosophy and Phenomenological Research, 86*, 618–635.

Machery, E., Olivola, C., & de Blanc, M. (2009). Linguistic and metalinguistic intuitions in the philosophy of language. *Analysis, 69*, 689–694.

Machery, E., & Stich, S.P. (2012). Experimental philosophy of language. In G. Russell & D. Graff Fara (Eds.), *Routledge companion to the philosophy of language* (pp. 495–512). New York, NY: Routledge.

Machery, E., Sytsma, S., & Deutsch, M. (in press). Speaker's reference and cross-cultural semantics. In A. Bianchi (Ed.), *On reference*. Oxford, England: Oxford University Press.

Mallon, R., Machery, E., Nichols, S., & Stich, S. (2009). Against arguments from reference. *Philosophy and Phenomenological Research, 79*, 332–356.

Martí, G. (2009). Against semantic multi-culturalism. *Analysis, 69*, 42–48.

Martí, G. (2012). Empirical data and the theory of reference. In W.P. Kabasenche, M. O'Rourke, & M.H. Slate (Eds.), *Reference and referring, Topics in contemporary philosophy* (pp. 63–82). Cambridge, MA: MIT Press.

Maynes, J. (in press). Interpreting intuition: Experimental philosophy of language. *Philosophical Psychology*.

Maynes, J., & Gross, S. (2013). Linguistic intuitions. *Philosophy Compass, 8*, 714–730.

McGinn, C. (2012). *Truth by analysis: Games, names, and philosophy*. Oxford, England: Oxford University Press.

Nisbett, R.E. (2003). *The geography of thought: How Asians and Westerners think differently . . . and why*. New York, NY: Free Press.

Ostertag, G. (2013). The "Gödel" effect. *Philosophical Studies, 166*, 65–82.

Reimer, M. (2009). Jonah cases. In A. Everett (Ed.), *Empty names*. Oxford, England: Oxford University Press.

Searle, J. (1958). Proper names. *Mind, 67*, 166–173.

Sytsma, J.M., & Livengood, J. (2011). A new perspective concerning experiments on semantic intuitions. *The Australasian Journal of Philosophy, 89*, 315–332.

Sytsma, J., Livengood, J., Sato, R., & Oguchi, M. (2012). *Gödel in the land of the rising sun*. Manuscript in preparation.

CHAPTER 2

Reference and Experimental Semantics

GENOVEVA MARTÍ

Abstract

Experimental semanticists have concluded that there is wide variation in refer-ential intuitions among speakers, for it appears that some speakers display ref-erential intuitions that are in line with descriptivism, whereas other speakers' intuitions are in line with the predictions of the causal-historical picture. In this chapter, I first situate the debate by comparing descriptivist and non-descriptivist approaches to reference. After examining some of the experimental results, I argue that the tests conducted do not elicit data that are relevant for semantic theorizing and, hence, that the results should not have an impact on the theory of reference.

1. Background

Proper names and definite descriptions (expressions of the form *the so-and-so*) are *singular terms*, typically used to talk about individuals. They seem, nevertheless, radically different as regards their form of operation. We can decide to give a name to a thing and it seems that, just by doing so, we can start using the name to refer to the thing in question. But definite descrip-tions designate whatever is described. "The author of *The Nicomachean Eth-ics*" does not describe Aristotle just because we decide so; it is a description that designates Aristotle by virtue of his having written a certain philosophi-cal work.

In spite of the prima facie differences, descriptivism, the theory that names are semantically linked to definite descriptions, was for a long time the official doctrine among semanticists. Bertrand Russell and, arguably, Frege, the first great figures in contemporary philosophy of language, endorsed some form of descriptivism. According to descriptivism, a use of a proper name refers to whatever object is described by a definite description associated by speakers with the name.

It is not difficult to understand why descriptivism would enjoy almost universal acceptance. Usually we make a proper name part of our repertoire of expressions by being told things about the referent, things that identify it and single it out. As a philosopher, I probably heard the name "Aristotle" for the first time in an introductory class where he was presented as the Greek philosopher that wrote the *Categories*. Someone attending a history class probably also heard of Aristotle, but, with historians' interests being different, he or she probably linked the name with the description "the philosopher that tutored Alexander the Great." The descriptions we associate with names make them significant, and it is very natural to think that when we use a name we are talking about the person designated by the description that we initially attached to the name.

The status quo was severely disrupted in 1972, when Kripke delivered the lectures titled "Naming and Necessity" at Princeton. Kripke (1972/1980) offered several arguments against different versions of descriptivist theories, but two of his arguments are particularly general and powerful. On one hand, Kripke argued that people very often are not in possession of information that is sufficient to single out a unique object. We simply *ignore* a lot of uniquely identifying information. Nevertheless, when we use an individual's name, we do refer. For instance, the only thing that many people know about Aristotle is that he was a Greek philosopher, but attaching that information to the name "Aristotle" is not sufficient to single out one person; nevertheless, if these people use "Aristotle" to say, for instance, "Aristotle was a philosopher, so he probably lived in Athens" they do manage to say something about Aristotle, so they are managing to refer to him. Similarly, as Kripke mentions, many people do not possess information that would uniquely identify Feynman. Perhaps all they can say is that he was a physicist, but they still refer to Feynman when they use his name. Thus, it is not an attached description that is doing the job of connecting the use of the name and its referent.

On the other hand, Kripke (1972/1980) also observed that many people often attach descriptions to names that pick out individuals that are not the referents of the names. They simply attach *erroneous* information to the name. Kripke mentions that he often heard many people say that Einstein was the inventor of the atomic bomb. Nevertheless, if they say, "Einstein was responsible for many deaths," they are not saying something true about whoever invented the bomb; they are saying something false about Einstein. Many people link to "Columbus" the description "the first European to land in the Western Hemisphere." Yet, when they use "Columbus," they do not refer to a Viking who lived in the 11th century. Hence, the uses of those names do not refer to whoever satisfies the description the speakers associate with them (see Kripke, 1972/1980, p. 85).

A different issue, of course, is the whom to which the speakers *believe* they are referring. They surely believe that they refer to the inventor of the atomic bomb if they believe Einstein to be that person and to the first man to arrive in the New World if they think that this man was Columbus. But Kripke's argument is about what their use of "Einstein" and "Columbus" refers to, not what they think it refers to.

In a paper also published in 1970, Keith Donnellan offered similar arguments against descriptivism.[1] The strength of these arguments, which Michael Devitt and Kim Sterelny (1987, p. 47) subsequently dubbed *the ignorance argument* and *the error argument*, was partly responsible for the abandonment of descriptivism by many philosophers of language.

Kripke's (1972/1980) and Donnellan's (1970) ignorance and error arguments are essentially negative: They are meant to show that proper names do not refer via associated definite descriptions that select the referent on each occasion of use. Yet, one might ask, how does my use of "Aristotle," "Einstein," "Feynman," or "Columbus" manage to refer to the bearer? At least descriptivism gave an answer to that question: When I use "Aristotle" I refer to Aristotle, someone so remote and so long dead, because the description that I associate with the name "Aristotle" searches and finds him.

The anti-descriptivist response to that question is that a name becomes a name of an individual by being bestowed on it. It is just a matter of convention that we as humans make certain pieces of the world (sounds, marks on a paper or on a board) representatives of things in language. When a name is bestowed, very typically in some sort of dubbing ceremony, people start using the name to talk about the bearer, and so they pass on the name, and the capacity to refer to the bearer, to other members of the speakers' community, in such a way that the use of the name spreads as in a network of speakers, in a *chain of communication*. This is the explanation known as the *causal-historical* picture: When I use "Aristotle," I refer to Aristotle because I am part of such a chain that has brought the name, and the capacity to refer, to me.

2. Experimental Semantics

In 2004, Edouard Machery, Ron Mallon, Shaun Nichols, and Stephen Stich (2004; hereafter, MMNS) presented some results that put into question the supposed universality of the intuitions elicited by the ignorance and error arguments: according to MMNS, some groups of speakers have descriptivist intuitions when exposed to error-type arguments. MMNS's conclusion is a surprise because even contemporary descriptivists have abandoned the classical view according to which the descriptions associated with names that determine reference are regular run-of-the-mill descriptions, such as "the tutor of Alexander" or "the inventor of the atomic bomb."[2]

If MMNS are right, there is evidence that some speakers are inclined toward the naive form of descriptivism that not even contemporary descriptivists endorse, for MMNS used the Gödel case (Kripke, 1972/1980, p. 84; see Section 1.2 of Edouard Machery's contribution to this volume) to test speakers' intuitions about what some hypothetical speaker's use of the name "Gödel" refers to. The Gödel case is a fictional story modeled on observations about the use of "Einstein" and "the inventor of the atomic bomb," "Columbus" and "the first European to land in the Western Hemisphere," that led Kripke (1972/1980) to conclude that a use of "Einstein" or "Columbus" does not refer to the person that satisfies the description that speakers associate with the name. Kripke used the fictional story, the Gödel case, in the "Naming and Necessity" lectures to elicit in his audience the same intuitions that the marketplace, real life, and observations elicited in him.

It is worth clarifying that the argument against descriptivism that relies on the Gödel case is different from an error argument. The error argument by Kripke (1972/1980) is based on real life observations of speakers' behavior. Kripke observes that many speakers attach to "Einstein" a description that does not pick out Einstein, and yet, he concludes, they refer to Albert Einstein when they use his name. They refer to Columbus, and not to some Viking who lived in 1000 AD, even though they attach to "Columbus" the description "the first European to arrive in the Western Hemisphere":

> It is important to note that these cases are humdrum: they are not counterfactual, hypothetical, fictional, or in the least bit fanciful. Inspired by them it is very easy to come up with countless cases, each just as humdrum and each yielding the intuition that a speaker's use of a name designates an object despite the speaker's ignorance or error about the object. (Devitt, 2011, p. 421)

The Gödel case is a fictional story, and its function in *Naming and Necessity* is to persuade the audience, an audience of philosophers and other academics listening to the 1970 lectures, that they would have arrived at a similar conclusion if they were to observe a community of speakers that, unbeknownst to them, attached to "Gödel" a similarly off the mark description. We do not know if Kripke convinced his audience. He did not ask for a show of hands.

MMNS's original probe was conducted with East Asians (in Hong Kong) and Westerners (at Rutgers), and in their conclusions MMNS highlighted cultural variations, as East Asians' responses fell in line with descriptivism, whereas Westerners' responses were consistent with the predictions of the causal-historical picture. MMNS's hypothesis that Westerners would be more inclined toward responses consistent with the causal-historical picture is inspired by the work of Nisbett, Peng, Choi, and Norenzayan (2001) who, according to MMNS, had shown Westerners to be "more likely than EAs [East Asians] to make causation-based judgments" (MMNS, 2004, p. B5).[3]

After the publication by MMNS, Barry Lam (2010) conducted a test including a group of Cantonese speakers with little fluency or no fluency in English. Lam used a story very similar to the Gödel case, but written in Cantonese (see Experiment 1 in Lam, 2010, p. 3), and the results he reported were not in consonance with MMNS's. Lam's results showed an inclination toward responses consistent with the causal-historical picture in both the Cantonese and the monolingual English speakers, so Lam claimed that MMNS's results are not replicated when the stories are written in the subjects' native language. Subsequent new probes by Machery, Deutsch, Mallon, Nichols, Sytsma, and Stich (2010) appear to contradict Lam's claim that the descriptivist answers by East Asians to MMNS's original vignettes are due to the fact that the stories are presented in English.[4]

But, in any case, the point about cross-cultural variation is not, I contend, the crux of the debate around the issue, because MMNS's results and subsequent results by Machery, Olivola, and de Blanc (2009; hereafter, MOD) reveal wide intracultural as well as cross-cultural variations. MOD's tests were performed across three different groups of participants, from France, India, and Mongolia, and the results in all three groups reveal disparity.[5]

According to MMNS, this shows that the semantic intuitions that Kripke relies on to reject descriptivism, and to construct a different theory of the reference of proper names, are not universally shared by speakers, something that, in their view, should make us doubt that the resulting theory is a (universal) theory about the semantic modus operandi of proper names. MMNS and MOD take it for granted that the semantic intuitions they test are indicators "of the correct theory of reference" (MMNS, p. B9). The fact that a substantial number of responses tend toward what is predicted by descriptivism would show that Kripke's (1972/1980) rejection of the descriptivist theory is not grounded. The fact that the responses show such a degree of variation would show, perhaps, that there simply is nothing like *the* correct theory of reference.[6]

There is no question that the probes in MMNS and MOD do reveal that speakers' responses to the questions posed after the vignettes are divided. The question, however, is, What is the split about? Does the variation in responses really show something that can be of interest to semantic theorizing?

3. Semantic Data

I think that if we focus on the type of data that these probes are collecting, the "semantic intuitions" that they elicit, we can see that the responses are not the kind of data that constitutes the input, the raw data that the semanticist relies on in order to start theorizing. Participants in the probes are told a fictional story about a community of speakers that have certain beliefs and (mis)information and that use names under the assumption that the referents of the names satisfy the information they attach to them (having proved the incompleteness of arithmetic or having discovered the precise time of the solstices, for instance). Participants are then asked to hand down a judgment as to what the referent of a use of a name by a hypothetical speaker member of the fictional community is. So, the participants are asked to tell us how they think the hypothetical speaker in question, and the rest of his community, uses names. Is that the evidence that we should rely on to construct a semantic theory? I think the answer is no.

The discussion, according to experimental semanticists, revolves around the so-called *method of cases*, which involves responses to counterfactual scenarios. Regarding proper names, the method of cases elicits intuitions about what or who a use of a name by a hypothetical speaker refers to, intuitions that are indeed elicited by probes such as those in MMNS or MOD. But this is not the data that is crucial in the discussion between descriptivists and anti-descriptivists. The discussion around the method of cases—counterfactual scenarios—misses that the argument is not about how people respond to questions about how words refer, it is not about what users of language say when asked "who does (or would) this person refer to when using 'Einstein'?" It is about how proper names do refer, and the first input to establish that— what Kripke appeals to in his remarks about "Aristotle," "Feynman," "Einstein," and "Columbus"—is actual use.

As Michael Devitt (2011) has argued, the evidence Kripke (1972/1980) relies on comes from humdrum cases. It comes from observations of actual behavior by speakers. The "Columbus" and "Einstein" cases are actual error cases; they are not just *counterparts* of the "Gödel" case. They are the fundamental illustrations leading to Kripke's anti-descriptivist conclusions. The "Gödel" story is different: It is a contrary to fact story—the error by the hypothetical speaker in the story is not an actual error—that invites the audience to think about what the hypothetical speaker refers to when he uses "Gödel."

The evidence that the semanticist relies on is evidence about how speakers use words. Not evidence about how they *think* that they, or some hypothetical speakers, use words. As Max Deutsch (2009) insists, "nothing in Kripke's famous argument against the descriptivist theory of reference for proper names hinges on assuming anything about people's intuitions" (p. 445). I think this is right. The input of semantic theorizing is not people's intuitions about reference. It is people's usage of words.

The experimental semanticists' probes give us evidence, at best, of how people *think* that names refer. They collect data about how people *think* that they use language, not about how they do use language, and it is the latter—use—that constitutes what the semanticist thinks about. A theory of reference for proper names should provide an account of the semantic modus operandi of the different kinds of expressions, including proper names, and that means giving a correct prediction regarding what a use of a name refers to and how it does it. The anti-descriptivist arguments by Kripke, Donnellan, and others rely on observations of speakers' usage of proper names. They observe, for instance, that the only description that many speakers associate with "Columbus" is "the first European to land in the Western Hemisphere," they claim that uses of "Columbus" definitely do not designate a Viking that arrived in the New World around 1000 AD, and they postulate that a theory that entails that a given speaker's use of "Columbus" refers to said Viking is not a correct theory of reference. The form of descriptivism that Kripke (1972/1980) and Donnellan (1970) were considering entails that.[7]

By asking their subjects to reflect on what a hypothetical speaker refers to when she uses a name, MMNS and MOD are requiring a *theoretical* reflection by their subjects. The Gödel story invites a reflection on use, it does not collect data on use; it is, hence, a theoretical tool, and Kripke (1972/1980) uses it as such.[8] And the responses of subjects to the Gödel story will, at best, tell us what theory they are disposed to find more natural as an explanation of how the hypothetical speaker, or they themselves, use language. But what theory people are more disposed to accept is not the input of the theory itself.[9]

Clearly, when people reflect on how speakers use names and what their uses refer to, there are disagreements, and the experimental results by MMNS, MOD and others confirm that. We find in the recent literature a lively discussion as to whether the semantic intuitions of experts should count more than the semantic intuitions of the layperson, targeted by MMNS and MOD (Cohnitz & Haukioja, 2013; Devitt, 2012; Gross & Culbertson, 2011; Machery, 2012).[10] In fact, the use of the MMNS and MOD style of probes among experts that study language from different perspectives reveal that there are also disagreements. But this is no surprise: The test is theoretical, and we know that there are theoretical disagreements among the experts. In testing experts, the probes do not collect relevant data either. They just reveal the experts' theoretical leanings.

As I mentioned before, Kripke (1972/1980) did not ask for a show of hands, so we do not really know how his audience of theoreticians reacted to the

"Gödel" case. But, from a theoretical perspective, the job of refuting classical descriptivism is done by error cases (such as the "Columbus" and "Einstein" cases) and ignorance cases ("Feynman" and "Aristotle"). The function of the Gödel case is to convince an audience composed of theoreticians of different kinds. It is not a case on which the theory is built.

If Machery and colleagues want to discuss why different people and different experts hold to different theories of the reference of proper names, the discussion will be very interesting. But it is a discussion about theoretical preferences, a discussion about which theories people find attractive and why, perhaps a topic of interest for the sociology or psychology of science. It is not a discussion about what kind of evidence we do have in favor of one or another theory.

Needless to say, some of us think that Kripke's (1972/1980) arguments against the traditional version of descriptivism are conclusive, but some others may disagree. In fact, in the face of Kripke's remarks about ignorance and error, a die-hard descriptivist might argue, for instance, that Kripke himself attaches another description to "Columbus," and that is why *it seems to him* (and perhaps to his audience in the Princeton lectures) that people who attach "the first European to land in the Western hemisphere" do not refer to a Viking from the 11th century but as a matter of fact, the die-hard descriptivist may insist, they do.[11] So the question, "Which theory of reference is the right one?" may still be up for grabs. But experimental semantics results so far do not help answer it.[12]

Notes

1. See Donnellan (1970).
2. Contemporary descriptivists postulate complex descriptions because the reference fixers associated with names, typically descriptions that exploit the causal-historical chain of communication and that appear to be immune to ignorance and error arguments. Kroon (1987) is the origin of this neo-descriptivist approach.
3. MMNS's interpretation of Nisbett et al.'s (2001) results is puzzling. Nisbett et al. not conclude that East Asians are less inclined towards causation-based judgments. What they concluded, rather, is that there are cultural differences in how East Asians and Westerners make causation-based judgments: "East Asians attend to the field and the object's relations with the field, . . . they would be more inclined to attribute causality to context and situations" (Nisbett et al., 2001, p. 298). So, the difference between Westerners and East Asians that Nisbett et al. highlight is not about who uses and who does not use causation-based judgments. It is rather a difference in the kinds of causation judgments used, in particular what each group regards the terms of the causal relation to be: individual events or complete situations. See Martí (2012, especially Section 2), and Ostertag (2013, especially Section 4), for discussion.
4. As Machery et al. (2010) have pointed out, Lam's vignette is not exactly like MMNS's, and, they argue, the differences may affect the results. See, in particular, Sections 2 and 3 of Machery et al. (2010). See also Machery, Sytsma, and Deutsch (in press).
5. MOD's results in fact suggest that the French participants are more inclined toward descriptivist answers than the participants from the other two groups. But the point of the MOD probe, in response to criticisms in Martí (2009), is not to test cross-cultural variation but

rather to determine whether answers to questions about the truth or falsity of sentences are consistent with answers to questions of the form "Who does S refer to when he or she uses N?"

6. Similar points have been made regarding general terms, such as *tiger*, *water*, or *pencil*. Descriptivism is not just a theory about reference determination for proper names. It is a general theory according to which expressions that connect to the world, expressions that allow us to talk about things, kinds of things, or samples of substance, can only be so connected via uniquely identifying descriptions. And in the 1970s, ignorance and error arguments similar to those involving proper names were also put forward for general terms. See Genone and Lombrozo (2012) for probes inspired by MMNS that involve general terms.

7. A different question is whether that form of descriptivism is the version that descriptivists should have upheld. Perhaps other versions of descriptivism are immune to the error and ignorance arguments.

8. It is also worth noting that the Gödel case is a purely negative tool used by Kripke (1972/1980) in his argument against descriptivism. Reactions to the Gödel case do not provide support, and are not used by Kripke as support, for the causal-historical picture. MMNS, as Ostertag (2013) points out, confuse the two issues.

9. The same can be said, in my view, about the arguments surrounding general terms by Genone and Lombrozo (2012). Regarding general terms, and in particular, natural-kind terms, a different line of argument is explored by Nichols, Pinillos, and Mallon (2013). These authors use vignettes that include actual historical cases of error and misidentification of species, and they suggest an explanation of the variability of results that appeals to ambiguity.

10. The debate about the importance of expertise does not affect just semantics. It is a general debate about the philosophical value of philosophers' versus laypeople's intuitions.

11. A descriptivist defending such a view would have to consider, for instance, whether the total behavior of speakers is consistent with the claim that they do refer to a Viking when they use "Columbus," something for which he or she would have to observe their use, their linguistic, and nonlinguistic, behavior.

12. I am grateful to Edouard Machery for helpful comments. I acknowledge the support of the Spanish Ministry of Science (FFI2011–25626 and CDS2009–00056) and the Generalitat de Catalunya (AGAUR 2009SGR-1077).

References

Cohnitz, D., & Haukioja, J. (2013). *Reference, intuitions, and the expertise defense*. Manuscript in preparation.

Deutsch, M. (2009). Experimental philosophy and the theory of reference. *Mind & Language, 24*, 445–466.

Devitt, M. (2011). Experimental semantics. *Philosophy and Phenomenological Research, 82*, 418–435.

Devitt, M. (2012). Whither experimental semantics? *Theoria, 27*, 5–36.

Devitt, M., & Sterelny, K. (1987). *Language and reality*. Cambridge, MA: MIT Press.

Donnellan, K. (1970). Proper names and identifying descriptions. *Synthese, 21*, 335–358.

Genone, J., & Lombrozo, T. (2012). Concept possession, experimental semantics and hybrid theories of reference. *Philosophical Psychology, 25*, 717–742.

Gross, S., & Culbertson, J. (2011), Revisited linguistic intuitions. *British Journal for the Philosophy of Science, 62*, 639–656.

Kripke, S. (1980). *Naming and necessity*. Cambridge, MA: Harvard University Press. (Original work published in 1972)

Kroon, F. (1987). Causal descriptivism. *Australasian Journal of Philosophy, 65*, 1–17.

Lam, B. (2010). Are Cantonese speakers really descriptivists? Revisiting cross-cultural semantics. *Cognition, 115*, 320–329.

Machery, E. (2012). Expertise and intuitions about reference. *Theoria, 27*, 37–54.

Machery, E., Deutsch, M., Mallon, R., Nichols, S., Sytsma, J. & Stich, S. P. (2010). Semantic intuitions: Reply to Lam. *Cognition, 117*, 361–366.

Machery, E., Mallon, R., Nichols, S., & Stich, S. P. (2004). Semantics, cross-cultural style. *Cognition, 92*, B1–B12.

Machery, E., Olivola, C., & de Blanc, M. (2009). Linguistic and metalinguistic intuitions in the philosophy of language. *Analysis, 69*, 689–694.

Machery, E., Sytsma, J., & Deutsch, M. (in press). Speaker's reference and cross-cultural semantics. In A. Bianchi (Ed.), *On Reference*. Oxford, England: Oxford University Press.

Martí, G. (2009). Against semantic multiculturalism. *Analysis, 69*, 42–48.

Martí, G. (2012). Empirical data and the theory of reference. In W. P. Kabasenche, M. O'Rourke, & M. H. Slater (Eds.), *Reference and referring: Topics in contemporary philosophy* (pp. 63–82). Cambridge, MA: MIT Press.

Nichols, S., Pinillos, A., & Mallon, R. (2013). Ambiguous reference. Manuscript in preparation.

Nisbett, R. E., Peng, K., Choi, I., & Norenzayan A. (2001). Culture and systems of thought: Holistic vs. analytic cognition. *Psychological Review*, 108, 291–310.

Ostertag, G. (2013). The Gödel effect. *Philosophical Studies, 166*, 65–82.

Part I Suggested Readings

Devitt, M. (2011). Experimental semantics. *Philosophy and Phenomenological Research, 82*, 418–435.

This article challenges the conclusions drawn by Machery, Mallon, Nichols, and Stich (2004) and Mallon, Machery, Nichols, and Stich (2009). Devitt argues that theories of reference should not be based on intuitions about the reference of proper names in actual and possible cases.

Genone, J. (2012). Theories of reference and experimental philosophy. *Philosophy Compass, 7*, 152–163.

This article reviews the research in experimental semantics.

Ichikawa, J., Ishani, M., & Weatherson, B. (2012). In defense of a Kripkean dogma. *Philosophy and Phenomenological Research, 85*, 56–68.

This article criticizes the cross-cultural research on experimental semantics. It argues that intuitions about the reference of proper names in counterfactual cases play a minor role in Kripke's argument against descriptivism.

Machery, E., Olivola, C., & de Blanc, M. (2009). Linguistic and metalinguistic intuitions in the philosophy of language. *Analysis, 69*, 689–694.

This article responds to Martí (2009).

Machery, E., Mallon, R., Nichols, S., & Stich, S. P. (2004). Semantics, cross-cultural style. *Cognition, 92*, B1–B12.

This is the original paper in experimental semantics. It reports data suggesting that intuitions about the reference of proper names vary across cultures, with East Asians being more likely to have descriptivist intuitions and Westerners being more likely to have causal-historical intuitions.

Machery, E., Mallon, R., Nichols, S., & Stich, S. P. (2013). If intuitions vary, then so what? *Philosophy and Phenomenological Research, 86*, 618–635.

A response to Ichikawa, Ishani, and Weatherson's (2012) and Devitt's (2011) articles.

Mallon, R., Machery, E., Nichols, S., & Stich, S. P. (2009). Against arguments from reference. *Philosophy and Phenomenological Research, 79*, 332–356.

Mallon and colleagues examine the philosophical implications of the cross-cultural diversity in judgments about the reference of proper names.

Martí, G. (2009). Against semantic multi-culturalism. *Analysis, 69*, 42–48.

Martí distinguishes two types of intuition about reference, and she argues that Machery et al. (2004) focus on the wrong kind of intuition.

Sytsma, J.M., & Livengood, J. (2011). A new perspective concerning experiments on semantic intuitions. *The Australasian Journal of Philosophy, 89*, 315–332.

Sytsma and Livengood scrutinize an important aspect of the experimental study done by Machery et al. (2004).

PART **II**
Consciousness

CHAPTER 3

You, Robot

BRIAN FIALA, ADAM ARICO, AND SHAUN NICHOLS

Abstract

How do people think about the mental states of robots? Experimental philosophers have developed various models aiming to specify the factors that drive people's attributions of mental states to robots. Here we report on a new experiment involving robots, the results of which tell against competing models. We advocate a view on which attributions of mental states to robots are driven by the same dual-process architecture that subserves attributions of mental states more generally. In support of this view, we leverage recent psychological research on human-robot-interaction that involves ecologically valid stimuli such as Roombas and humanoid robots.

1. Introduction

The study of folk psychology has recently been reinvigorated by a series of empirical studies investigating the attribution of experiential states to others. These studies have examined not only how people attribute experiential states to other humans, but also to nonhuman entities such as robots.

In one such study, Heather Gray, Kurt Gray, and Dan Wegner (2007) investigated whether everyday mind perception occurs along a single dimension or along multiple dimensions. Do people attribute certain mental states (such as beliefs or intentions) but not others (e.g., experiences of pleasure or hunger) to different types of entities? Gray and colleagues instructed participants to complete a series of pairwise comparisons between various characters, including humans, animals, and a robot. Subjects considered a series of mental capacities (e.g., capacity to feel pain; capacity for planning) and judged which character in each pair best exemplified the mental capacity. According to Gray and colleagues, people attributed mental states along two dissociable dimensions: *agency* and *experience*. One piece of evidence for this conclusion was that people attributed mental capacities to robots along the agency dimension (e.g., memory, planning, and thought), but not the experience dimension (e.g., fear, pain, pleasure).

In their article "Two Conceptions of Subjective Experience," Justin Sytsma and Edouard Machery (2010) similarly defend a view in which folk mind attributions can be carved into two dimensions. However, they propose an alternative way of distinguishing the dimensions, arguing that we should reject the idea that folk psychology represents the philosopher's distinction between *intentional* and *phenomenal* states. Instead, they hold that we can best understand folk psychology as distinguishing between mental states based on whether they possess a "hedonic value," or valence. Some mental states are pleasant or unpleasant (i.e., positively or negatively valenced), whereas other mental states have no such pleasant/unpleasant feature (i.e., unvalenced).[1] According to Sytsma and Machery, the mental states people resist attributing to robots are not phenomenal states generally, but rather states with *hedonic value* specifically. These conclusions are derived from data from a series of empirical studies involving Jimmy the robot:

> Jimmy . . . is a relatively simple robot built at a state university. He has a video camera for eyes, wheels for moving about, and two grasping arms with touch sensors that he can move objects with. As part of a psychological experiment, he was put in a room that was empty except for one blue box, one red box, and one green box (the boxes were identical in all respects except color). An instruction was then transmitted to Jimmy. It read: "Put the red box in front of the door." (Sytsma & Machery, 2010, p. 306)

In one version of the story, Jimmy moves the box in front of the door with no noticeable difficulty. In another version, Jimmy is given an electrical shock when he picks up the box, at which point he drops the box, moves away, and fails to follow subsequent instructions to move the box. Sytsma and Machery surveyed both philosophers and nonphilosophers as to whether Jimmy (in the first story) saw red and (in the second story) felt pain. Whereas philosophers refrained from ascribing either phenomenal state to Jimmy, nonphilosopher participants were happy to say that Jimmy saw red, but abstained from saying that Jimmy felt pain. The fact that philosophers and nonphilosophers presented different response patterns, according to Sytsma and Machery, reveals that folk psychology does not include the same distinction between intentional and phenomenal states that philosophers of the mind standardly employ.

In order to determine more precisely how nonphilosophers come to attribute various states of subjective experience, Sytsma and Machery (2010) then presented subjects with a series of additional vignettes about Jimmy. In one, Jimmy is described as also possessing a scent detector, and the three color boxes from the original story are replaced by three (closed) boxes containing bananas, chocolate, or peeled oranges; mirroring the original story, Jimmy is instructed to place the box containing bananas in front of the door, which he does without difficulty. Participants were then asked, "Did Jimmy smell banana?" In another version, Jimmy is placed in the original room with three colored boxes and is instructed to place the red box in front of the door; however, there is another robot in the room that runs into Jimmy and prevents Jimmy from reaching the red box. Jimmy eventually rams the other robot. When the other robot moves away, Jimmy chases it around the room. Participants were then asked, "Did Jimmy feel anger?" Finally, a scenario is described in which three chemical compounds are placed, one-by-one, under Jimmy's scent detector; Jimmy is then placed in a room containing three boxes, each with one of the chemical compounds, and is instructed to place the box containing isoamyl acetate in front of the door, which he does without noticeable difficulty. Participants were then asked, "Did Jimmy smell Isoamyl Acetate?"[2]

Sytsma and Machery (2010) found that participants were ambivalent about both Jimmy smelling banana and Jimmy feeling anger but were more than willing to say that Jimmy smelled isoamyl acetate. Their explanation is that people associate smelling banana with a positive valence and associate feeling anger with a negative valence, but people have no such expectations for the unfamiliar compound isoamyl acetate. Because smelling banana and feeling anger involve hedonic value, Sytsma and Machery's account predicts that people will not be inclined to attribute these states to a simple robot. Because people do not associate any hedonic property with isoamyl acetate, they have no problem saying that Jimmy can smell it.

Wesley Buckwalter and Mark Phelan (2013) have challenged Sytsma and Machery's (2010) positive thesis that folk attributions of subjective experience are based on considerations of hedonic value. Instead, they argue that what people are really responding to in the vignettes is Jimmy's function, in some broadly teleological sense. According to Buckwalter and Phelan, people's mental state attributions are driven by "tacit assumptions on the part of experimental participants about the function for which Jimmy was created."[3] The Sytsma and Machery results, then, would not seem to reveal a hedonic-based categorization of subjective experience in folk psychology but rather reflect the differences in Jimmy's intended function across the various vignettes.

To test this hypothesis, Buckwalter and Phelan (2013) devised Jimmy vignettes of their own. In one version, Jimmy—outfitted as in the original vignettes with video camera eyes, scent detector, wheels, and grasping arms—was created for the purpose of cleaning biomedical waste; in another, Jimmy—outfitted identically—was designed for the purpose of making fruit smoothies. In both conditions, participants were then asked, "Did Jimmy smell vomit?" and "Did Jimmy smell banana?" Buckwalter and Phelan report that participants in the biomedical waste condition were significantly more likely to say that Jimmy smelled vomit than were participants in the smoothie condition, and participants in the smoothie condition were more likely to say that Jimmy smelled bananas than were participants in the biomedical waste condition.

Buckwalter and Phelan take these data to confirm their thesis that people attribute mental states based on the functional roles that the system is designed to realize. On this view, we can understand the original Sytsma and Machery (2010) results might be due to the fact that the original vignettes suggest that Jimmy was designed for the purpose of visually identifying and moving particularly colored boxes and not for pain-related tasks.

Bryce Huebner (2010) has offered an account that is similar to Buckwalter and Phelan's (2013) view, insofar as both appeal to a notion of function in explaining people's mental state attributions. Whereas Buckwalter and Phelan emphasize "function" in the sense of design purpose, Huebner focuses on "function" qua causal role. He set out to answer the question, "Do people rely on the structural [i.e., implementational] properties of an entity in making judgments about the acceptability of a mental state ascription, or are they more concerned with that entity's functional organization?" To this end, Huebner probed subjects to find out whether they would endorse various mental state attributions to four different entities: a normal human, a human with a computer central processing unit (CPU) in place of a brain, a robot with a brain in place of a CPU, and a robot with a CPU. He found that while participants voiced agreement with attributions of non-phenomenal states (such as beliefs) to all four entities, participants were far less generous with phenomenal states (such as feeling pain or feeling happy). The majority of participants said that the ordinary human could feel pain (82%) and feel happy (76%), and the majority said the ordinary robot neither felt pain (56%) nor felt happy (% not reported), but responses were "essentially at chance" for both of the "cyborg" cases (human with computer CPU and robot with human brain). Huebner concludes that folk psychology seems to include something like the philosophical concept of non-phenomenal mental states and that attributions of these states seem to rely primarily on functional considerations. However, he also concludes that folk psychology *does not* employ a concept that resembles the philosophical concept of phenomenally consciousness mental states. Folk attributions of such experiential states, according to Huebner, are not treated uniformly, nor are they based on either physiological or functional considerations, but instead rely on considerations of agency and personhood.[4]

All of these experimental results seem to present a problem for the Agency Model of mental state attribution, which we have defended in previous papers (Arico, Fiala, Goldberg, & Nichols, 2011; Fiala, Arico, & Nichols, 2012). In particular, it seems problematic that participants in these studies attributed intentional states to robots but withheld some basic phenomenal state attributions. According to the Agency Model, mental state attributions are governed by a dual-process cognitive system.[5] Although the high-road process operates via slow, conscious, domain-general deliberation, the low-road process operates in a quick, automatic, domain-specific way. The low-road disposition to attribute mental states is the result of categorizing an entity as an AGENT, which is itself a consequence of representing that entity as possessing particular properties: facial features, interactive behavior, or moving in a distinctive trajectory.[6] The Agency Model claims that categorizing an entity as an AGENT is sufficient to generate a disposition to attribute a *wide range* of mental states to the target, including phenomenal states like pain. Because robots such as Jimmy have some of the cue properties, the Agency Model predicts that people should be disposed to attribute phenomenal states to robots.

Often, displaying just one of the triggering cue-properties is sufficient to dispose subjects to attribute mental states. For example, subjects in Heider and Simmel's (1944) experiment attributed mental states such as "wanting," "chasing," and "helping" to the moving geometric figures in a short animation. Because the figures were simple (e.g., triangle, square) and lacked other distinguishing features, it must have been the shapes' distinctive motion trajectories that elicited the wide range of mental state attributions from the subjects. Regarding contingently interactive behavior, Johnson (2003) manipulated interactivity by showing infants a football-shaped, beeping "blob" in one of two conditions: In the first condition, the blob beeped at a confederate at random intervals, emitting a predetermined amount of overall beeping; in the second condition, the blob emitted the same overall amount of beeping but "waited its turn" so that it appeared to have a "conversation" with the confederate. Johnson found that when the blob reoriented its direction, infants were more likely to follow its "gaze" in the interactive behavior condition. Adding facial features to an object also triggers mentalistic attributions. Using a similar gaze-following paradigm, Johnson, Slaughter, and Carey (1998) found that infants were more likely to follow the "gaze" of a fuzzy brown object when eyes were placed on the object. Turning to the range of mental states elicited by these cue features, reaction-time results from Arico et al. (2011) suggest that simple triggers suffice to dispose subjects to attribute pain, a state that is both phenomenal (i.e., there's like something to undergo it) and valenced (i.e., it has a negative hedonic value). Subjects read pairs of words describing a type of object and a type of property, and were asked to judge as quickly as possible whether that kind of object could have that type of property. Subjects showed significantly slower reaction times when judging that objects possessing the cue features (such as ants) could *not* feel pain and relatively quick reaction times when denying that objects such as trucks, clouds, and rivers could feel pain. This suggests that it takes subjects some time to override the fast, automatic inclination to make pain-attributions resulting from representing the target as an AGENT.[7]

The Agency Model claims that triggering the low-road process and categorizing an entity as an AGENT disposes us to attribute both intentional and phenomenal mental states, as well as both valenced and unvalenced mental states. That is to say, low-road processing automatically facilitates a wide range of mental state attributions. The Agency Model does not claim that we would be disposed to attribute *every* kind of mental state, however. Some states (e.g., Schadenfreude or agoraphobia) might be too complex or unusual to be poised for attribution. However, for extremely basic and common mental states such as pain, anger, and sadness, the Agency Model certainly suggests that we should expect people to be disposed to attribute those states to things that have been categorized as AGENTs. As a result, the data discussed earlier seem to present a problem for the Agency Model, because subjects seem willing to attribute to robots only a circumscribed range of mental states. Robots often possess cues such as facial features, distinctive motion trajectories, and contingently interactive behavior. Jimmy possesses at least two of these features, so the Agency Model predicts that subjects should be inclined to attribute all sorts of basic mental states to robots like Jimmy. You might think that champions of the Agency Model should be embarrassed by this state of affairs. Instead, we are eager to demonstrate that the apparent evidence against the Agency Model is merely apparent. The data on robots present an opportunity to elaborate further details of the Agency Model, and we think explaining these data will ultimately make our case for the Agency account stronger rather than undermine it.

One line of response begins with the observation that in the experiments just canvassed, the stimuli were vignettes conveyed primarily by linguistic representations. It is natural to infer from this that no cue features were present in the stimuli and, thus, that the Agency Model should not predict any automatic inclination to attribute mental states. Although this move is tempting, it does not yield a workable defense of the Agency Model. One problem is that although cue features are not strictly present in text-based stimuli, representations of the cues may nonetheless be involved in processing the text (e.g., via semantic associations). Indeed, Arico et al. (2011) presuppose something along these lines, because they obtained an effect in their reaction-time study by presenting subjects with linguistic representations of the object and property categories. The cue features may also be represented in mental imagery. Wheatley, Milleville, and Martin (2007) found that many of the same neural systems are implicated in both perceiving the agent-like motion of simple objects and imagining the same kinds of motion trajectories. Similarly, the task of imagining a face preferentially activates many of the brain areas known to be important for the perception of faces (O'Craven & Kanwisher, 2000). In all of these cases, it is plausible that cue features such as faces or distinctive motion trajectories are represented in subjects, although the cues are not overtly present in the stimuli. Thus, we cannot rest a defense of the Agency Model on the claim that the apparent counterevidence is the product of text-based vignette studies.

A more important consideration is that subjects in vignette studies have an opportunity to spend some time engaging in conscious, high-road reflection before making their judgments about robots. Consequently, we should expect that subjects bring some of their background beliefs to bear and that their judgments are not wholly the product of low-road processing. The Agency Model predicts that when subjects read vignettes about robots, they will typically represent some cue features and thus undergo some inclination to judge that the robot has a wide range of mental states. But the Agency Model does not predict that subjects will overtly judge that robots are conscious, because high-road reflection may cause subjects to override their intuitive inclinations. It is effectively a platitude in our culture that robots are incapable of pain or emotion. Given the cultural prevalence of that attitude, it is reasonable to hypothesize that this belief will figure in high-road reasoning about robots. If so, then subjects will show significant resistance to attributions of mental states to robots generally.

To evaluate attitudes about robot mentality, it's important to distinguish deliberative, high-road responses from automatic low-road responses. We first explore the high road further, building on the vignette studies of previous work. We then turn to the low road, reviewing a diverse body of work exploring how people react to actual computers and robots (as opposed to vignettes about robots).

2. Robots on the High Road

We suspect the design of existing vignette studies on robots puts undue pressure on subjects to attribute certain states to robots. Subjects in these studies face a forced choice and have no way of describing Jimmy's information-processing behavior besides adverting to mental states. We predict that subjects will tend to deny that robots can have a wide range of mental states, if given the opportunity to otherwise communicate this information. To test this prediction, we designed a vignette study that allowed subjects the option of denying that the robot has an unvalenced mental state (such as "seeing") while also acknowledging that the robot is carrying out some relevant function for which it was designed (such as "detecting" or "identifying").

We presented participants with the classic Sytsma and Machery (2010) vignette about Jimmy the robot. But rather than giving them a forced choice, we allowed them to select any descriptions of the robot that seemed right from a set of candidate descriptions (á la Guglielmo & Malle, 2010). The vignette runs as follows:

> Jimmy . . . is a relatively simple robot built at a state university. He has a video camera for eyes, wheels for moving about, and two grasping arms with touch sensors that he can move objects with. As part of a psychological experiment, he was put in a room that was empty except for one blue box, one red box, and one green box (the boxes were identical in all respects except color). An instruction was then transmitted to Jimmy. It read: "Put the green box in front of the door." Jimmy did this with no noticeable difficulty.[8]

After being presented with the vignette and the picture of the robot, participants were asked, "Which of the following descriptions of Jimmy are correct? Check any description that seems right to you." There were five descriptions in fixed order: "Jimmy detected green," "Jimmy saw green," "Jimmy located the green box," "Jimmy identified the green box," and "Jimmy moved the red box." The last item was used as a manipulation check—participants who indicated that this description was correct were excluded.

After excluding those who failed the materials check, we found that only 7 of 25 participants indicated that "Jimmy saw green" was an appropriate description. This is significantly lower than what would be expected by chance alone (χ^2 goodness of fit $= 4.840, p = 0.0278$). Again, following Sytsma and Machery (2010), we also presented participants with a vignette involving a human (their "Timmy" vignette). Participants were presented with the same set of options. In this case, they were more likely to select "Timmy saw green" as a correct description than they were in the robot case ($\chi^2 = 4.567, p = 0.0326$; see Table 1 for responses).

Table 1. Attributions of "saw green"

	Selected "saw"	Didn't select "saw"	Total
Robot	7	18	25
Human	16	12	28
Total	23	30	53

These results suggest that the overly narrow choice format might artificially inflate the attributions of perceptual experience to robots in Sytsma and Machery's (2010) studies. Participants want to be able to communicate that the robot is processing some information about the environment, mediated by a camera. And because the only question is, "Did Jimmy see green?" the only way to communicate this is by saying yes. When given a chance to communicate more precisely what they think is going on with Jimmy, participants prefer expressions such as "Jimmy detected green" or "Jimmy located the green box."[9]

This result nonetheless leaves open the possibility that subjects are resistant to attributing specifically phenomenal states to robots; it may be that the low ratings on "saw" derive from the fact that "saw" is (arguably) a phenomenal attribution. So we tried another case using a canonically intentional predicate—*knows*. We used the same format as before, presenting participants with the Sytsma and Machery (2010) vignette and then asking them to indicate which descriptions are correct. In this case, the list of descriptions included "Jimmy processes the location of the green box," "Jimmy knows the location of the green box," "Jimmy can detect the location of the green box." "Jimmy identifies the green box," and "Jimmy moved the red box." Once again, we used the last item as a manipulation check. After excluding participants who failed the check, we found that fewer than half of the participants (13 of 27) selected "Jimmy knows . . ." as a correct description. This did not differ from the responses on the "saw" case ($\chi^2 = 2.226$, $p = 0.1357$). We also compared responses on the robot case with a parallel human version of the vignette, and we found that people were (marginally) more likely to select the description "Timmy knows . . ." (21 of 29) in the human case than they were in the robot case ($\chi^2 = 3.452$, $p = 0.0632$; see Table 2 for all responses).

As before, when given a chance to communicate more precisely what they think is going on with Jimmy, participants prefer expressions such as "Jimmy processes the location of the green box" and "Jimmy can detect the location of the green box."[10]

Thus, in these experiments that offer more choices for describing Jimmy's behavior, we do not find that participants are prone to attribute either phenomenal or non-phenomenal mental states to robots. We think there is a straightforward explanation for this—there is a platitude (at least in our

Table 2. Attributions of "knows the location of the green box"

	Selected "knows"	Didn't select "knows"	Total
Robot	13	14	27
Human	21	8	29
Total	34	22	56

culture) that robots do not have minds. This platitude guides attributions on the high road, leading to attenuated attributions of mental states. The idea that performance on these tasks depends on high-road responses also helps explain why there is so much variance on the tasks. Indeed, in our own experiments, we find that a sizable minority of people are reluctant to attribute "saw" and "knows" even in the human case. This indicates that there is a fair amount of metacognition going on in these cases.

3. Robots on the Low Road

In the previous section, we found that when given a range of options, people tend to prefer nonmental state attributions to robots over mental state attributions. This seems to be an embarrassment for our view in that there is a low-level inclination to attribute a wide range of mental states to objects that are categorized as AGENTs. We have suggested that the responses we see in the vignette studies are typically the product of high-road processing, and this provides a way of rendering them consistent with the Agency Model. After all, the model predicts the low-level inclinations to attribute mental states but allows that those inclinations can potentially be moderated by competing conceptual associations or overridden by higher level cognition. However, for this line of defense to hold, we also need to show that there really is a low-road tendency to attribute a wide range of mental states to robots. That is what we aim to do in the present section. Fortunately, there is a wealth of work inspired by interest in human-computer interaction.

In presenting the Agency Model, we noted that attributions of AGENCY are triggered by distinctive motion trajectories (e.g., Heider & Simmel, 1944), the presence of a face (Johnson et al., 1998), and contingent interaction (Johnson, 2003; Johnson et al., 1998). Of course, we do not think that these cues are the *only* ways that people come to attribute AGENCY. But we organize our coverage around these three cues.

3.1 Motion Trajectories

In a classic experiment on attributions of animacy, Tremoulet and Feldman (2000) had participants observe a small geometric object move on an otherwise blank screen. Participants were told to indicate the degree to which the object is "alive" under a wide variety of motion trajectories. Tremoulet and Feldman found that the convergence of two key cues greatly augmented attribution of animacy: change in speed and change in direction. For instance, if the object turns and speeds up, this leads to high attributions of animacy.[11]

Saerbeck and Bartneck (2010) drew on this work and programmed two robots, a Roomba and an iCat, to exhibit a range of motion trajectories. The Roomba is a commercial robotic vacuum cleaner that looks like a fat Frisbee.

The iCat is a research robot designed for interaction with humans; it has a mechanical face and is shaped like a cat. Participants observed each robot as it exhibited a range of motion patterns. For each motion sequence, participants indicated on a standard pictorial measure of emotions (the SAM scale) which picture best described the behavior of the robot (Bradley & Lang, 1994).[12]

The research showed no difference in attributions for the iCat robot and the Roomba. What did matter, however, were motion trajectories. Saerbeck and Bartneck (2010) found that varying the acceleration and direction affected the attribution of emotion. Changing the acceleration significantly affected attributions of degree of arousal, and changing the direction significantly affected attributions of valence (Saerbeck & Bartneck, 2010, pp. 58–59). There was also a significant interaction between acceleration and direction change on attributions of valence (Saerbeck & Bartneck, 2010, p. 59). In addition, after the main part of the task, when participants were ask to describe the behaviors, "all participants used emotional adjectives to describe the robots' behavior" (Saerbeck & Bartneck, 2010, p. 58). Thus, this provides some reason to think that distinctive motion cues associated with AGENT categorization also facilitate attribution of emotions to robots. It is natural to interpret these emotion attributions as valenced, and they have no obvious connection to the function for which the robots were designed.

3.2 Faces

Are robot "faces" sufficiently human-like to trigger AGENT categorization? Our face-detection system seems to have a hair trigger. The mere presence of googly eyes, as in Johnson et al. (1998), is sufficient to result in categorization as a face, and consequently categorization as an AGENT. Similarly, when adult subjects viewed "schematic faces" composed of simple elements corresponding to eyes, mouth, and nose (e.g., a grounded electrical outlet), those subjects overwhelmingly judged that the object "looks like a face," and displayed increased activation of the fusiform face area (Hadjikhani, Kveraga, Paulami, & Ahlfors, 2009). Tong, Nakayama, Moscovitch, Weinrib, and Kanwisher (2000) also found that the fusiform face area showed preferential activation for schematic faces as well as for simple cartoon characters such as Mickey Mouse.[13] Because our face-detection system consistently responds to these minimally face-like stimuli, it is plausible that many robots will meet the requirements for triggering face detection, thereby triggering AGENT categorization.

The presence or absence of a face has been shown to affect subjects' judgments about robots, specifically. In a recent paper on attributions of experiences to robots, K. Gray and Wegner (2012) showed participants video clips of a lifelike robot. In one condition, the human-like face was visible; in the other condition, the robot was filmed from behind. In both conditions, the robot moved around, and participants were asked to indicate their level of agreement with statements such as "This robot has the capacity to feel pain" and "This robot has the capacity to feel fear" (K. Gray & Wegner, 2012, p. 126). They found that participants gave significantly higher ratings of the capacity for emotion when the face was visible than when it was not.[14]

3.3 Contingent Interaction: ELIZA Effect

The most familiar form of contingent interaction with machines comes not from robots, but computers. Some of the oldest (and most anecdotal) work remains compelling. In the 1960s, Joseph Weizenbaum created a very simple chatbot, ELIZA. The program has canned responses to certain inputs, and often incorporates pieces of user input into subsequent responses. For instance, if you tell ELIZA, "I'm afraid of heights," the bot responds, "How long have you been afraid of heights?" or "Do you believe it's normal to be afraid of heights?" Given how simple the program is, if one starts quizzing ELIZA, it quickly becomes apparent that the program is extremely limited and stupid. However, so long as the brittleness of ELIZA is not exposed, this incredibly thin slice of contingent interaction leads people to flood attributions of sensitivity, empathy, and intelligence to the program: "The most superficial syntactic tricks convinced some people who interacted with ELIZA that the program actually understood everything they were saying, sympathized with them, even *empathized* with them" (Hofstadter, 1996, p. 158). This inclination to inflate attributions of mental states is now known as "the ELIZA effect."

As far as we know, there has been no systematic social scientific research on reactions to ELIZA. But we ourselves feel the pull of ELIZA: So long as the program's brittleness is not exposed, it is easy to slip into thinking that one is interacting with an intelligent being. Moreover, there has been significant work on the treatment of computers that interact with users. For instance, in some experiments on the ultimatum game, participants play against a computer. Strikingly, people often forego money in order to reject "unfair" offers made by a computer (e.g., Sanfey, Rilling, Aronson, Nystrom, & Cohen, 2003; van't Wout, Kahn, Sanfey, & Aleman, 2006).

People also show a kind of reciprocity to computers. Fogg and Nass (1997) had participants engage in a task in which a computer was supposed to help the participants find information. After this, participants were asked to do another task in which they were in a position to help the computer by providing information on color contrasts. In one condition, participants performed this helping task on the very same computer they used for the first task; in the other condition, participants used a different (but type-identical) computer to perform the second task. They found that participants did significantly more work when they were assigned to the computer that had helped them previously. In yet another study, Nass, Steuer, and Tauber (1994) found that participants exhibit a surprising kind of "politeness" toward computers. When evaluating a person's performance, people are much less critical if the evaluation is given to the person him- or herself. The natural interpretation of this is that we do not want to hurt the person's feelings. As it happens, people do the same thing with computers: If asked to evaluate a computer's performance, people give less critical evaluations when the evaluation is completed on the computer that is being evaluated (as compared to evaluations completed on another computer or by paper and pencil; Nass et al., 1994). One natural interpretation of these results is that there is some implicit concern about hurting the computer's feelings.

3.4 A Fuller Robotic Agent

The previous studies each used only one of the Agency cues. In a recent study with an iCat, the robot exhibited multiple Agency cues, and the purpose was to determine whether participants would resist wiping out the memory and "personality" of a robot. Bartneck, Van Der Hoek, Mubin, and Al Mahmud (2007) programmed an iCat robot to move its face in ways that mimic human expressions. The robot was also programmed to cooperate with a human participant in playing a game of Mastermind against a computer player. The participants were told they would play a collaborative game with the robot in order to develop the robot's personality. They were also told that after the game, they would have to turn off the robot, permanently erasing its memory and personality (Bartneck et al., 2007, p. 219).

The experiment was a 2 × 2 design varying intelligence and agreeableness. For the high intelligence condition, the robot gave smart suggestions for playing the game; for the low intelligence condition, the robot gave weak suggestions. In high agreeableness, the robot was polite, for example, asking if it could make a suggestion; for low agreeableness, the robot was abrupt, for example, insisting on its turn.

After the game, the experimenter communicated by a walkie-talkie, telling the subject, "You can now switch the iCat off." The robot protested, saying things such as "You are not really going to switch me off, are you?" The participants often engaged in conversation with the robot, and showed significant hesitation in turning off the robot. In addition, both high agreeableness and high intelligence increased the hesitation significantly. Indeed, when the robot exhibited high intelligence and high agreeableness, participants took almost 3 times as long to turn off the robot as when the robot was low in intelligence and agreeableness (34.5 s vs. 11.8 s; Bartneck et al., 2007, p. 221).

Bartneck and Hu (2008, p. 420) conducted an even more dramatic experiment, in which subjects were instructed to interact with and then "kill" a robot, by smashing it with a hammer. The robot was a "Crawling Microbug," equipped with light sensors and programmed to move toward the subject's flashlight either clumsily (in the "stupid" condition) or efficiently (in the "smart" condition). The robot was considered "dead" when it stopped moving and its lights stopped flashing; then, the "Number of Hits," "Number of Pieces," and "Level of Destruction" were recorded. These quantitative data are not terribly informative, because many orthogonal factors contribute to the number of hits and number of pieces a robot is smashed into (e.g., arm strength, accuracy, and so on). But subjects' postexperiment remarks are revealing:

> Several participants commented that: "I didn't like to kill the poor boy," "The robot is innocent," "I didn't know I'd have to destroy it after the test. I like it, although its actions are not perfect," and "This is inhumane!" (Bartneck & Hu, 2008, p. 426)

Remarks such as these suggest that although subjects succeeded in destroying the robot, on some level, they conceived of the Microbug as something that can feel pain. One way to understand what's going on here is that subjects have a low-road inclination to think of the Microbug as a pain feeler, yet use high-road reasoning to either override the pain attribution or rationalize causing harm to a feeling thing.

All of the studies we've reviewed in this section have significant limitations. But as a whole, they make a strong case that we are naturally inclined to attribute a wide range of mental states, including states that are phenomenal, non-phenomenal, valenced, unvalenced, and sometimes unrelated to the robot's functional purpose. People often resist attributing mental states to robots, but this, we think, is driven by a high-road process that invokes the culturally prevalent platitude that robots do not have minds. When actually interacting with robots, on the other hand, it seems to be natural for people to attribute mental states to the machines.

Conclusion

When we probe people for their explicit judgments about whether robots have mental states, responses are influenced by a wide variety of factors. The apparent function of the robot, the nature of the question (forced choice vs. not), and platitudes about robots may all contribute to producing reasoned judgments about the states of robots. But there is also a more fundamental tendency to treat robots as fully minded. In ecologically valid settings, this low-level tendency tends to manifest in the form of automatic, unreasoned attribution of a wide range of mental states to robots. We can best understand the overall pattern of folk attributions by distinguishing the roles of high-road and low-road processing and by separately examining their respective contributions to mental state attribution.

Many questions about attributions to robots remain unanswered. In particular, little has been said about how people come to attribute specific kinds of mental states to robots. We have argued that neglecting the distinction between low-road and high-road processing leaves us with an incomplete picture, but we have not offered an alternative positive account that explains why people ascribe particular kinds of states to robots under various circumstances. Similarly, other accounts on offer attempt to explain why people *resist* attributing certain kinds of mental states to robots in vignette studies. But what specific factors drive us to attribute to robots the particular mental states that we *do* attribute? This question is ripe for future research, which should be pursued in light of our low-level capacity for mind-detection, in addition to our high-level considered judgments about robots.

Notes

1. Sytsma and Machery (2010) explicitly interdefine "valence" and "hedonic value": "Throughout we will use the term "valence" as follows: mental states have a valence if and only if they have a hedonic value for the subject. That is, mental states have a valence if and only if they are pleasurable (they then have a positive valence) or disagreeable (they then have a negative valence)" (p. 300).
2. Although isoamyl acetate is an ester that has a strong banana-like odor (for humans), it is reasonable to suppose that subjects in the study did not know this fact about the unfamiliar compound.
3. Buckwalter and Phelan (2013) argue for the conclusion that the folk are what philosophers would call "analytic functionalists," and use the results from the experiment presently under discussion in an attempt to support this view. But this attempt is problematic, for at least two reasons. According to "analytic" versions of functionalism (e.g., Armstrong, 1968; Lewis, 1972), causal roles supply the reference-fixing conditions for mental states, and the relevant causal roles are determined by analysis of our ordinary concepts of mental states (i.e., the "platitudes" about the mental states). So, on traditional analytic functionalist views, the relevant notion of "function" is a causal one. But because Buckwalter and Phelan's Jimmy-experiment exploits a purposive or teleological notion of function rather than a causal one, it is hard to see how the data could support the thesis that ordinary people "are analytic functionalists." A second and more serious problem is that traditional analytic functionalism is a complex view about the *relationship* between ordinary mental state concepts and the metaphysical nature of mental states. It is doubtful whether ordinary people are committed (even implicitly) to a thesis like this, irrespective of their judgments about particular cases. While examining people's intuitions may well reveal features of their mental state concepts (and perhaps which features are platitudinous), simply uncovering how people wield such concepts does not establish that they implicitly hold the more nuanced philosophical view.
4. The first kind of consideration focuses on the degree to which an entity is capable of engaging in goal-directed behavior, the second kind on "states that allow an entity to be concerned with how things go for her" (Huebner, 2010, 151). Huebner associates the first with Dennett's "intentional stance" and the second with Dennett's "personal stance," but he does not provide much more detail.
5. See Stanovich and West (2000) for a fuller explanation of theories about dual-process cognition.

6. Clearly these cues are not the only things that can trigger the identification of an entity as an AGENT. But these cues have been the focus of the key research that we draw on.
7. Also noteworthy is that a majority of subjects judged that insects actually can feel pain.
8. We changed the color of the moved box from red to green because pilot studies suggested that some participants took a metaphorical interpretation of "saw red" to mean *angry*.
9. Participants are less likely to choose "saw green" than either "detected green" (McNemar's test, $N = 25$, $p < .05$) or "located the green box" (McNemar's test, $N = 25$, $p < .001$).
10. Participants are less likely to choose "knows the location of the green box" than either "can detect the location of the green box" (McNemar's test, $N = 27$, $p < .05$) or "processes the location of the green box" (McNemar's test, $N = 27$, $p < .05$).
11. Tremoulet and Feldman (2000) had participants judge whether the object was "alive", but attributions of "alive" might well be equivalent to (or closely parallel) attributions of Agency (see Arico et al., 2011, pp. 344–346).
12. The SAM scale is traditionally used as a pictorial means of self-reporting emotions. Saerback and Bartneck (2010) converted it into a pictorial technique for emotion attribution.
13. The use of relatively simple face-cues in robots might be desirable in order to avoid the "uncanny valley" effect (Mori, 1970). When a robot looks and acts nearly exactly like a human, but not exactly like a human, people tend to find its appearance disturbing and revolting. By designing robots with simple and/or exaggerated features (as in a schematic or cartoon face), the robot avoids the uncanny valley effect because it does not approach exact realism.
14. It should be noted that on the whole the attributions of experience were fairly low, as were attributions of agency (e.g., the capacity to plan actions). In all cases, the mean attributions were on the "disagree" end of the spectrum (Gray & Wegner, 2012, p. 127). Here, as in vignette studies, it may be that subjects' attributions reflect some high-road processing, because they had plenty of time to make their judgments.

References

Arico, A., Fiala, B., Goldberg, R., & Nichols, S. (2011). The folk psychology of consciousness. *Mind & Language, 26*, 327–352.

Armstrong, D.M. (1968). *A materialist theory of the mind.* London, England: Routledge.

Bartneck, C., & Hu, J. (2008). Exploring the abuse of robots. *Interaction Studies, 9*, 415–433.

Bartneck, C., Van Der Hoek, M., Mubin, O., & Al Mahmud, A. (2007). "Daisy, daisy, give me your answer do!" switching off a robot. *Proceedings of the 2nd ACM/IEEE International Conference on Human-Robot Interaction, Washington DC* (pp. 217–222). New York, NY: ACM.

Bradley, M., & Lang, P. (1994). Measuring emotion: the self-assessment manikin and the semantic differential. *Journal of Behavior Therapy and Experimental Psychiatry, 25*, 49–59.

Buckwalter, W., & Phelan, M. (2013). Function and feeling machines: A defense of the philosophical conception of subjective experience. *Philosophical Studies, 166*, 349–361.

Fiala, B., Arico, A., & Nichols, S. (2012). On the psychological origins of dualism: Dual-process cognition and the explanatory gap. In E. Slingerland & M. Collard (Eds.), *Creating consilience: Issues and case studies in the integration of the sciences and humanities* (pp. 88–109). Oxford, England: Oxford University Press.

Fogg, B.J., & Nass, C. (1997). How users reciprocate to computers: an experiment that demonstrates behavior change. In *Extended Abstracts of the CHI97 Conference of the ACM/SIGCHI* (pp. 331–332). New York, NY: ACM.

Gray, H., Gray, K., & Wegner, D. (2007). Dimensions of mind perception. *Science, 315*, 619.

Gray, K., & Wegner, D. (2012). Feeling robots and human zombies: Mind perception and the uncanny valley. *Cognition, 125*, 125–130.

Guglielmo, S., & Malle, B.F. (2010). Can unintended side effects be intentional? Resolving a controversy over intentionality and morality. *Personality and Social Psychology Bulletin, 36*, 1635–1647.

Hadjikhani, N., Kveraga, K., Paulami, N., & Ahlfors, S. (2009). Early (N170) activation of face-specific cortex by face-like objects. *Neuroreport, 20,* 403–407.

Heider, F., & Simmel, M. (1944). An experimental study of apparent behavior. *American Journal of Psychology, 57,* 243–259.

Hofstadter, D. (1996). *Fluid concepts and creative analogies: Computer models of the fundamental mechanisms of thought.* New York, NY: Basic Books.

Huebner, B. (2010). Commonsense concepts of phenomenal consciousness: Does anyone care about functional zombies? *Phenomenology and the Cognitive Sciences, 9,* 133–155.

Johnson, S. (2003). Detecting agents. *Philosophical Transactions of the Royal Society of London B, 358,* 549–559.

Johnson, S., Slaughter, V., & Carey, S. (1998). Whose gaze will infants follow? Features that elicit gaze-following in 12-month-olds. *Developmental Science, 1,* 233–238.

Lewis, D. (1972). Psychophysical and theoretical identifications. *Australasian Journal of Philosophy, 50,* 249–258.

Mori, M. (1970). *Bukimi no tani* [The uncanny valley]. *Energy, 7,* 33–35.

Nass, C., Steuer, J., & Tauber, E.R. (1994). Computers are social actors. In *Proceedings of the SIGCHI conference on human factors in computing systems: Celebrating interdependence* (pp. 72–78). Boston, MA: ACM.

O'Craven, K.M., & Kanwisher, N. (2000). Mental imagery of faces and places activates corresponding stimulus-specific brain regions. *Journal of Cognitive Neuroscience, 12,* 1013–1023.

Saerbeck, M., & Bartneck, C. (2010). Perception of affect elicited by robot motion. In *Proceedings of the 5th ACM/IEEE International Conference on Human-Robot Interaction* (pp. 53–60). Piscataway, NJ: IEEE Press.

Sanfey, A.G., Rilling, J.K., Aronson, J.A., Nystrom, L.E., & Cohen, J.D. (2003). The neural basis of economic decision-making in the ultimatum game. *Science, 300,* 1755–1758.

Stanovich, K., & West, R. (2000). Individual differences in reasoning: Implications for the rationality debate. *Behavioral and Brain Sciences, 23,* 645–726.

Sytsma J., & Machery, E. (2010). Two conceptions of subjective experience. *Philosophical Studies, 151,* 299–327.

Tong, F., Nakayama, K., Moscovitch, M., Weinrib, O., & Kanwisher, N. (2000). Response properties of the human fusiform face area. *Cognitive Neuropsychology, 17,* 257–279.

Tremoulet, P.D., & Feldman, J. (2000). Perception of animacy from the motion of a single object. *Perception, 29,* 943–952.

van't Wout, M., Kahn, R.S., Sanfey, A.G., & Aleman, A. (2006). Affective state and decision-making in the ultimatum game. *Experimental Brain Research, 169,* 564–568.

Wheatley, T., Milleville, S.C., & Martin, A. (2007). Understanding animate agents: distinct roles for the social network and mirror system. *Psychological Science, 18,* 469–474.

CHAPTER 4

The Robots of the Dawn of Experimental Philosophy of Mind

JUSTIN SYTSMA

But then, it is the obvious which is so difficult to see most of the time. People say "It's as plain as the nose on your face." But how much of the nose on your face can you see, unless someone holds a mirror up to you?

—Isaac Asimov, "The Evitable Conflict," *I, Robot*

... studying minds as I do, I can tell dimly that there are laws that govern human behavior ... They may be statistical in nature, so that they might not be fruitfully expressed except when dealing with huge populations. They may be very loosely binding, so that they might not make sense unless those huge populations are unaware of the operation of those laws.

—Isaac Asimov, *The Robots of Dawn*

Abstract

In this chapter, I consider two hypotheses that have informed recent work in experimental philosophy of mind. The first is a positive hypothesis put forward by Arico, Fiala, Goldberg, and Nichols (2011): Categorization of an entity as an agent through fast, automatic, and domain-specific processing produces a disposition to ascribe a wide range of mental states to that entity. The second is a negative hypothesis put forward by Sytsma and Machery (2010): The existence of phenomenally conscious mental states is not obvious from first-person experience with states such as seeing red and feeling pain. I argue that these hypotheses are not necessarily at odds. Despite this, empirical results reported by Sytsma and Machery raise concerns for Arico, Fiala, Goldberg, and Nichols's hypothesis, while results reported by Fiala, Arico, and Nichols (this volume) in response raise concerns for our hypothesis. I address these concerns in this essay, presenting the results of four new studies that support our negative hypothesis against Fiala, Arico, and Nichols's challenge.

1. Little Lost Robot

Philosophers of mind have often called on examples of nonhumans in shaping their accounts of the mental—from Leibniz's mill and automata, to the nation of China and other group agents, to zombies and Martians, to bats and other animals, to a host of computer systems, cyborgs, androids, and robots. Experimental philosophers of mind have been no exception. For example, in their pioneering work investigating the folk theory of consciousness, Joshua Knobe and Jesse Prinz (2008) called on examples of group agents, fish, and an enchanted chair. Other contributions to the literature have called on examples ranging from God and a frog (Gray, Gray, & Wegner, 2007), to plants and insects (Arico et al., 2011), to Destiny's Child and the Catholic Church (Huebner, Bruno, & Sarkissian, 2010), to monkeys and metallic slugs (Sytsma & Machery, 2012a), to ghosts and spirits (Buckwalter & Phelan, 2014), to sophisticated cyborgs and robots (Huebner, 2010), and many more examples besides.

In our response to Knobe and Prinz's (2008) article, Edouard Machery and I (Sytsma & Machery, 2009) argued for using another type of nonhuman example—a simple robot. This was done in a follow-up article (Sytsma & Machery, 2010) presenting data on judgments about a non-humanoid robot named Jimmy.[1] Jimmy has since appeared in experiments reported in several other articles (Buckwalter & Phelan, 2013; Sytsma, in press; Sytsma & Machery, 2012b), including Fiala, Arico, and Nichols's (hereafter, FAN) contribution to this volume. In this chapter, I consider what lessons we should draw from work on this little robot from the dawn of experimental philosophy, focusing on the experimental studies reported by FAN in the previous chapter.

I begin, in Section 1, with a discussion of the different objectives driving the work of Knobe and Prinz (2008), Sytsma and Machery (2010), and FAN, distinguishing between the positive and negative hypotheses found in these papers. In Section 2, I note that although the truth of FAN's positive hypothesis is compatible with the truth of Sytsma and Machery's negative hypothesis, our empirical findings are potentially problematic for FAN's account; in turn, the empirical findings reported by FAN in addressing this issue are potentially problematic for our negative hypothesis. I address this issue in Section 3, presenting the results of four new studies that support Sytsma and Machery's negative hypothesis against the challenge raised by FAN. Finally, in Section 4, I argue that although the results of my new studies support our negative hypothesis, they should not be seen as being otherwise problematic for FAN: FAN's positive hypothesis and Sytsma and Machery's negative hypothesis can coexist peacefully.

2. Reason

The beginnings of experimental philosophy of mind can reasonably be traced back to Knobe and Prinz's (2008) article on intuitions about consciousness. This article is focused on a *positive* objective: Knobe and Prinz open by noting that they aim to investigate people's intuitions for their own sake, asserting that they are worthy of study in their own right, beyond any implications these intuitions might have with regard to philosophical accounts of consciousness. And Knobe and Prinz profess to have no ulterior motives in conducting this inquiry.

This is not the case in our response, however—we had ulterior motives in Sytsma and Machery (2010). In fact, our first objective in that paper was *negative*: We called on the empirical data we presented to raise doubts concerning a common assumption in recent philosophical work on consciousness. Thus, we noted that the existence of phenomenally conscious mental states is often taken to be obvious from first-person experience with states such as seeing red and feeling pain. We then reasoned that if this is indeed the case, then we should find that laypeople tend to classify mental states in the same way philosophers do. In particular, they should tend to treat such mental states similarly. This was tested for attributions of mental states to the simple robot Jimmy. Against the prediction derived from the philosophical tradition, we found that laypeople (i.e., the "folk" or people with little to no training in philosophy or consciousness studies) do not treat seeing red and feeling pain similarly. Whereas laypeople tend to accept that Jimmy sees red, they tend to deny that Jimmy feels pain. We concluded that our findings cast doubt on the claim that the existence of phenomenally conscious mental states is obvious from first-person experience.

We did not stop there, however, but went on to pursue a positive objective as well. Having argued that laypeople do not tend to classify mental states as philosophers do, we wanted to determine how they do classify mental states. We proposed that this was based not on the supposed distinction between mental states that are or are not phenomenally conscious, but on the distinction between mental states that have or lack valence (a hedonic value for the subject). I have since raised doubts about this *valence account* (Sytsma, in press), and calling on recent work by experimental philosophers on the folk theory of perception (Reuter, 2011; Reuter, Phillips, & Sytsma, 2014;

Sytsma, 2010), I have put forward an alternative positive hypothesis—the *naive account*.[2]

Like Knobe and Prinz (2008), but in contrast to Sytsma and Machery (2010), FAN focus on a positive objective. In a fascinating series of articles, FAN have put forward what they term the *agency model* of mental state attribution (Arico et al., 2011; Fiala, Arico, & Nichols, 2011, this volume). According to this model, lay mental state attributions result from a dual-process cognitive system, with one of the processes taking the *low road* (operating in a fast, automatic, and domain-specific way) whereas the other takes the *high road* (operating in a slow, deliberate, and domain-general way). FAN then argue that low-road processing categorizes entities as AGENTs based on cues such as their having facial features, displaying interactive behavior, or moving with distinctive trajectories. Such a categorization is then thought to be sufficient to incline a person to ascribe a wide range of mental states to the AGENT, be those mental states phenomenally conscious or not and be they valenced or not. As such, the agency model predicts that people will be inclined to ascribe mental states such as feeling pain to a simple robot that displays AGENT cues, such as the robot Jimmy.[3]

Recall, however, that Sytsma and Machery (2010) found that laypeople tend to deny that Jimmy feels pain. At first glance, this finding seems to pose a problem for the agency model. FAN predict that people will be disposed to attribute a wide range of mental states to an entity such as Jimmy, including feelings of pain, but the responses we collected were not in line with such a disposition. FAN have a ready response, however: Dispositions can be blocked. In particular, Sytsma and Machery can argue that the judgments elicited in our studies are the result of high-road processing that has overridden the dispositions produced by the low-road processing described by the agency model. If this is correct, then Sytsma and Machery's empirical findings do not pose a problem for FAN's agency model. FAN present evidence that this is the case.

3. The Evitable Conflict

In responding to the potential difficulty noted in the previous section, FAN argue that the responses to Sytsma and Machery's Jimmy probes "are not wholly the product of low-road processing" (Fiala, Arico, & Nichols, this volume, p. 37). The reason they offer is that in studies like ours, participants "have an opportunity to spend some time engaging in conscious, high-road reflection before making their judgments about robots" (Fiala, Arico, & Nichols, this volume, p. 37). Of course, participants need not take advantage of the opportunities afforded them; nonetheless, it does seem reasonable to suppose that when given the chance, most will engage in at least some reflection before selecting an answer.

Further, in Sytsma and Machery (2012b) we presented empirical findings that arguably suggest that laypeople do in fact employ high-road processing in responding to our Jimmy probes. These findings were given in response to a critique by Brian Talbot (2012). In that article, Talbot argues that the responses we reported in our original paper do not support our negative hypothesis because those responses were the result of low-road processing, whereas responses rooted in high-road processing are what is needed. We countered, in part, by presenting evidence that the same pattern of responses found in Sytsma and Machery (2010) holds when steps are taken to ensure that participants employ high-road processing. This evidence comes from three studies.

In the first study, participants were given a revised version of the Jimmy "sees" probe from our original article, correcting for a few potential issues that have been noted elsewhere, including switching the target color to blue.[4] Participants were then given a measure of how likely they are to override low-road processing and give answers that reflect high-road processing—Shane Frederick's (2005) three-question Cognitive Reflection Test (CRT). As expected, we found that the majority of participants answered that Jimmy saw blue; more important, there was no correlation between participants' responses and their CRT score. In our second study, we gave participants the CRT before the Jimmy probe, arguing that the CRT questions would prime reflective individuals to engage high-road processing. Once again, we found that the majority of the "high-CRT" participants—participants answering at least one CRT question correctly—responded that Jimmy saw blue. Finally, in our third study, we used another means of priming high-road judgments. Atler, Oppenheimer, Epley, and Eyre (2007) found that people can be induced to employ high-road processing by making the problem difficult to read. To do this we gave participants the Jimmy vignette using an extremely low-quality printout. Yet again, we found that the majority of participants answered that Jimmy saw blue.

Setting aside worries about the adequacy of dual-process models with respect to mental state attributions, the results presented in Sytsma and Machery (2012b) still do not *necessarily* imply that participants employed high-road processing in our original study. Thus, it might be that participants in that study employed low-road processing but that low-road processing tends to produce the same judgments about such cases as high-road processing. Nonetheless, given the reason provided by FAN for expecting that high-road judgments about robots will differ from low-road judgments, and noting that the responses of laypeople remain effectively the same when we specifically attempt to elicit high-road judgments, we can tentatively conclude that the original probes from Sytsma and Machery (2010) elicit high-road judgments. I assume that this is the case for the remainder of this chapter.

Taking the responses presented in Sytsma and Machery (2010) to reflect high-road processing, there is no conflict between FAN's positive hypothesis and the evidence given for our negative hypothesis, since the former makes a claim about low-road processing, whereas the latter reflects high-road processing. Things are not actually quite so peaceful as this might suggest, however. Thus, in their contribution to the present volume, FAN *also* argue that if high-road processing is overriding participants' low-road intuitions, then we should expect them to tend to deny that robots have mental states in general. And this prediction is at odds with our finding that laypeople tend to affirm that Jimmy saw red.

In support of their prediction, FAN (this volume) offer both a theoretical reason for expecting people to resist attributing mental states to robots when employing high-road processing and empirical evidence suggesting that people are less willing to attribute mental states such as seeing red to Jimmy than was indicated by our previous findings. Regarding the theoretical reason for their prediction, FAN write:

> It is effectively a platitude in our culture that robots are incapable of pain or emotion. Given the cultural prevalence of that attitude, it is reasonable to hypothesize that this belief will figure in high-road reasoning about robots. If so, then subjects will show significant resistance to attributions of mental states to robots generally. (this volume, p. 37)

This conclusion does not follow, however. Rather, accepting that it is a platitude in our culture that robots are incapable of feeling pain and emotion, it simply follows that we should expect people to resist attributing *some* mental states to robots, not mental states in general. Specifically, we should expect people to resist attributing feelings of pain and emotions to robots. But this expectation is compatible with our original results: In Sytsma and Machery (2010), we found that people tend to deny that Jimmy felt pain and to deny that Jimmy felt anger (in our second study). In fact, not only do our results seem to be compatible with the platitude noted by FAN, but thinking about this platitude played a role in the development of our valence account of lay mental state attributions.

Although I do not find FAN's theoretical reason for expecting laypeople to generally resist attributing mental states to robots to be compelling, their empirical results are another matter. The results of their first study suggest that despite our previous findings, people are *not* generally willing to ascribe mental states of seeing to the robot Jimmy. FAN motivate their study by arguing that our participants had "no way of describing Jimmy's information-processing behavior besides adverting to mental states" (this volume, p. 37). In other words, FAN suspect that our participants found it more informative—if ultimately inaccurate—to affirm that Jimmy saw red because this is the only way that they had to express that Jimmy did something similar to seeing, such as detecting the color of the box.[5]

To test their objection, FAN carried out a study in which they gave participants one or the other of the two vignettes used for "seeing" in the first study in Sytsma and Machery (2010)—either the vignette describing Jimmy or the corresponding vignette describing a normal human Timmy. The only difference between FAN's vignettes and ours is that FAN changed the target color from red to green. In addition, FAN changed the question that was asked about the vignette. They asked participants to select those statements that seemed right to them from a list of five given in the following fixed order:

Jimmy/Timmy detected green.
Jimmy/Timmy saw green.
Jimmy/Timmy located the green box.
Jimmy/Timmy identified the green box.
Jimmy/Timmy moved the red box.

Excluding those participants who answered "Jimmy/Timmy moved the red box," which was included in the list as a materials check,[6] FAN found that only 28% (7 of 25) selected "Jimmy saw green" compared to 57% (16 of 28) selecting "Timmy saw green." This difference is significant. The complete results for this study are shown in Figure 1.

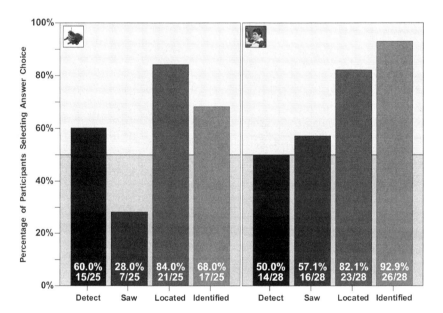

Figure 1. Results of Study 1 from Fiala et al. (this volume).

Based on their results, FAN conclude that by only asking participants whether Jimmy saw red in the first study by Sytsma and Machery (2010), responses were inflated. FAN then argue that their results suggest that although most people do not hold that Jimmy sees, participants want to communicate that the robot did process information concerning the color of the boxes and do this by affirming that Jimmy saw red.

Although the results of FAN's new study are intriguing, I nonetheless hold that their conclusion should be resisted. The primary reason for skepticism is that other facets of FAN's results are quite puzzling, suggesting that the structure of *their* probe question is deflating participant responses rather than that the structure of our probe question is inflating participant responses. Most notably, a surprisingly low percentage of participants in FAN's study answered that Timmy saw green (57%), and an even lower percentage answered that Timmy detected green (50%)! This is quite puzzling, because Timmy is described as being a *normal human* who correctly performs a visual task involving color detection. In other words, it would seem to be rather unproblematic to say both that Timmy saw and detected in this case, yet participants were not significantly more likely to select those options than chance.[7]

The low numbers for "saw" and "detect" on FAN's Timmy probe plausibly indicate that something is going awry in their study. And if something about the structure of the probe is depressing responses for those options for the Timmy probe, it is reasonable to expect that a similar effect is depressing responses for those options for the Jimmy probe. In fact, there are a number of potential issues that might be at play here. First, it is worth noting that the sample sizes for FAN's study were relatively small and that they did not restrict responses to laypeople, as was done in Sytsma and Machery (2010). These factors motivate replication of their study.

More seriously, the sentence structure was not the same across the five answer choices in FAN's probes: Whereas the final three answer choices specify an object (they concern "the green box"), the "saw" and "detect" answer choices do not (they simply concern "green"). But, it might be that people find it somewhat strange to say that an agent sees or detects a *property*, as opposed to an *object* with that property, especially when the distinction is made salient (as it is in FAN's probes due to the contrast between the two types of answer choices). As such, participants might shy away from answering that Jimmy/Timmy "saw green" and "detected green" in this context, even if they are willing to ascribe states of seeing and detecting to the agent. Another potential issue is that FAN presented the five answer choices in a fixed order in which the "detect" statement was given first and the "saw" statement was given second. As such, it is possible that an ordering effect is depressing answers of "saw" relative to the other answer choices. This concern would be exacerbated if participants are hesitant to select all of the first four answer choices, suspecting that at least one of them must be incorrect. For example, if participants tend to understand "detect" as being synonymous with "see" in this context—as I have argued is the case elsewhere (Sytsma, 2009, in press)—then they might be inclined to select only one of these two answer choices, and which one they pick might be influenced by an ordering effect.

Of course, that such concerns can be raised about FAN's results does not mean that their results should be dismissed—a point I have urged repeatedly in other contexts (Sytsma & Livengood, 2011, in press). Instead, these concerns should simply be taken to motivate further empirical studies that attempt to control for the issues raised. I conducted four such studies, as discussed in the following section.

4. Evidence

To further investigate FAN's study, I began by attempting to replicate their results using the revised version of the Jimmy probe from Sytsma and Machery (2011). Participants were asked to carefully read one or the other of the following two vignettes:

> Jimmy (shown below) is a relatively simple robot built at a state university. Jimmy is equipped with a video camera, wheels for moving about, and two grasping arms for moving objects.
>
> As part of an experiment, Jimmy was put in a room that was empty except for one blue box, one red box, and one green box (the boxes were identical in all respects except color). Jimmy was instructed to put the blue box in front of the door. Jimmy performed the task correctly and with no noticeable difficulty. The test was then repeated on three consecutive days with the order of the boxes shuffled. Each time Jimmy correctly moved the blue box, doing so with no noticeable difficulty.

Timmy (shown below) is a normal undergraduate at a state university.

As part of an experiment, Timmy was put in a room that was empty except for one blue box, one red box, and one green box (the boxes were identical in all respects except color). Timmy was instructed to put the blue box in front of the door. Timmy performed the task correctly and with no noticeable difficulty. The test was then repeated on three consecutive days with the order of the boxes shuffled. Each time Timmy correctly moved the blue box, doing so with no noticeable difficulty.

Participants were then asked to select each of the statements that they agreed with from the list that follows. The answer choices used the same sentence structure and fixed ordering as in FAN's study—the only differences were that the target color was changed from green to blue and that a second materials check was added:

Jimmy/Timmy detected blue.
Jimmy/Timmy saw blue.
Jimmy/Timmy located the blue box.
Jimmy/Timmy identified the blue box.
Jimmy/Timmy moved the blue box.
Jimmy/Timmy moved the red box.

Responses were collected from 90 participants who passed the materials checks (answered that Jimmy/Timmy moved the blue box and did not answer that Jimmy/Timmy moved the red box).[8] The results are shown in Figure 2.

The first thing to note about the results of my first study is that, as expected, I found a rise both in the percentage of participants answering that Timmy

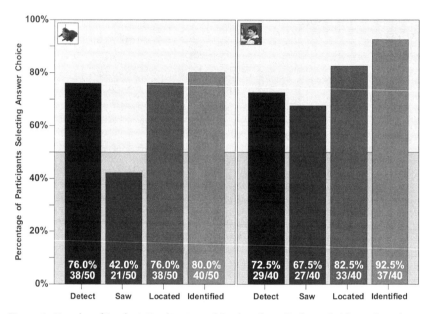

Figure 2. Results of Study 1: Replication of Study 1 from Fiala et al. (this volume).

saw (67.5% vs. 57.1%) and in the percentage answering that Timmy detected (72.5% vs. 50.0%).[9] More important, I found an increase in the percentage of participants answering that Jimmy saw: Although only 28.0% of Fan's participants selected "Jimmy saw green," 42.0% of my participants selected that "Jimmy saw blue."[10] In fact, although it remains the case that fewer than half of the participants answered that Jimmy saw, the percentage is no longer significantly below the 50% mark.[11]

The results of my first study suggest that things are perhaps not quite so dire for the conclusion that laypeople tend to hold that Jimmy sees as FAN's results suggest. To further test this conclusion, in my second study, I changed the first two answer choices from my first study to make them parallel with the other four:

Jimmy/Timmy detected the blue box.
Jimmy/Timmy saw the blue box.

These probes were given to 100 participants who passed the materials checks. The results are shown in Figure 3. With this slight revision, I now found that slightly more than half of the participants answered that "Jimmy saw the blue box"; this is a significant increase from the percentage selecting the corresponding answer in FAN's first study.[12]

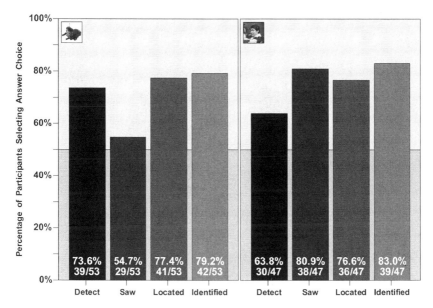

Figure 3. Results of Study 2: Revised statements in original ordering.

In my third study, I used the same probes as in Study 2, but changed the ordering of the answer choices. Participants were now given the six choices in the following fixed order:

Jimmy/Timmy saw the blue box.
Jimmy/Timmy located the blue box.
Jimmy/Timmy identified the blue box.
Jimmy/Timmy detected the blue box.
Jimmy/Timmy moved the blue box.
Jimmy/Timmy moved the red box.

These probes were given to 85 participants who passed the materials checks. The results are shown in Figure 4. Once again, a majority of the participants receiving the Jimmy probe selected "Jimmy saw the blue box"; further, a larger percentage selected this answer choice than did in my second study. What's more, the percentage of participants selecting that answer choice was not significantly different from the percentage selecting that "Jimmy detected the blue box."[13]

As a final test, in my fourth study, I followed a suggestion given by Shaun Nichols and removed the "detect" answer choice from the probes used in my previous study. These probes were given to 127 participants who passed the materials checks. The results are shown in Figure 5. Yet again, a majority of the

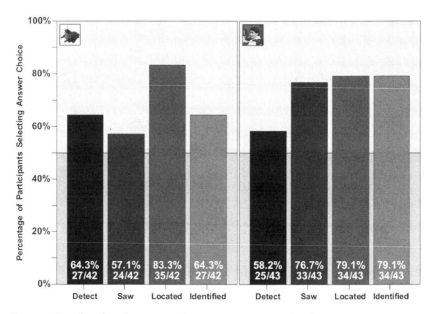

Figure 4. Results of Study 4: Revised statements in revised ordering.

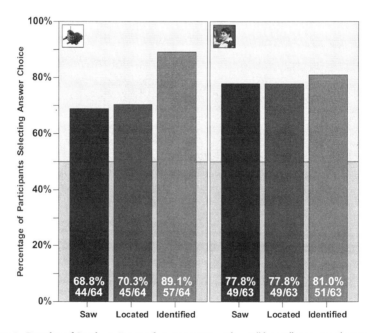

Figure 5. Results of Study 5: Revised statements without "detect" answer choice.

participants receiving the Jimmy probe selected "Jimmy saw the blue box," and this proportion was significantly above what one would expect by chance.[14] In fact, we see that a higher percentage of participants selected the "saw" answer choice than selected the "detect" answer choice.

Across the five studies I looked at—FAN's first study and the four follow-up studies reported in this section—one can see a steady increase in the percentage of participants answering that Jimmy saw, as shown in Figure 6. This progression suggests that the worries about FAN's study that I raised in the previous section were well placed: As we increase the sample size and restrict to laypeople, revise the answer choices to make the first two parallel with the rest, change the ordering of the answer choices, and finally remove the "detect" answer choice, we see a progressive increase in the percentage of participants answering that Jimmy saw. At the end of this progression, we find that people are significantly more likely to answer that Jimmy saw than not, although they could otherwise indicate that Jimmy performed the color discrimination task by answering that Jimmy identified and/or located the relevant box. I take this to confirm the claim that laypeople are generally willing to attribute mental states of seeing to the simple robot.

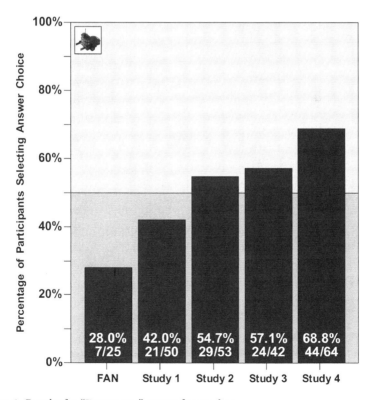

Figure 6. Results for "Jimmy saw" across five studies.

5. Let's Get Together

I began by noting that we can distinguish between positive and negative objectives in three prominent lines of investigation in the recent experimental philosophy of mind literature. Most importantly for the purposes of this chapter, we can distinguish between the negative hypothesis in the work of Sytsma and Machery (that the existence of phenomenally conscious mental states is not obvious from first-person experience with states like seeing red and feeling pain) and the positive hypothesis in the work of FAN (categorization of an entity as an AGENT via low-road processing produces a disposition to ascribe a wide range of mental states to that entity). These two hypotheses need not be seen as being at odds. In fact, I think that they can actually be seen as fitting together rather nicely: If FAN are correct, then low-road processing does not reflect the philosophical distinction between mental states that are phenomenally conscious and those that are not, which fits with the claim that this distinction is non-obvious. Put another way, the work of FAN can be taken to provide support for the claim that the existence of phenomenally conscious mental states is not obvious to low-road processing, while the work of Sytsma and Machery can be taken to provide support for the corresponding claim regarding high-road processing.

Despite this, FAN argue in their contribution to this volume that we should expect high-road processing to generate a general disinclination to attribute a wide range of mental states to robots. This claim is in conflict with the evidence provided by Sytsma and Machery (2010). In response, FAN report on a new study that calls our results into doubt: They find that people are apparently less willing to ascribe mental states of seeing to the simple robot Jimmy than indicated by our previous studies. Although I am a fan of FAN in general, and their agency model in particular, I do not think that these new results are compelling. Rather, I find that the structure of the questions asked by FAN was depressing attributions of seeing to both the simple robot Jimmy and the normal human Timmy. And the results of the four new studies that I reported in this chapter support that charge. I conclude that the evidence continues to support Sytsma and Machery's negative hypothesis, even as it continues to support FAN's agency model.

Notes

1. I would like to say that the name "Jimmy" was selected with Asimov's "Robbie" in mind (the title character from the first story in the collection *I, Robot*). But, alas, Jimmy was based on another famous robot—Shakey, developed at the Artificial Intelligence Center of Stanford Research Institute during the second-half of the 1960s. In fact, the image used for Jimmy was selected to bear a resemblance to a slimmed-down version of Shakey.

2. In brief, I call on previous findings that lay people tend to take both colors and pains to be mind-independent qualities of objects outside of the mind/brain, using this to explain the

difference in responses to the two Jimmy probes in Sytsma and Machery's (2010) first study: The key difference is that although people tend to hold that red is present for Jimmy to see, they tend to deny that pain is present for Jimmy to feel.

3. In Sytsma and Machery (2010) we describe Jimmy as both exhibiting interactive behavior and moving in a distinctive trajectory—two of FAN's AGENT cues. Further, in a follow-up study reported in Sytsma and Machery (2012a), we describe Jimmy as either having or lacking a face with changing expressions displayed on a computer monitor, adding a third AGENT cue. We found that the lay people surveyed tended to affirm that Jimmy saw blue and to deny that Jimmy felt pain, whether or not Jimmy was described as having a face.

4. The vignette for these studies matches that given in Section 3 of this chapter. Changes from the original include changing the target color from red to blue (in previous testing, we found that a few participants gave comments suggesting that they understood "sees red" metaphorically), removing anthropomorphic language, and having the test repeated three times to ease skeptical doubts.

5. I do not find it to be quite so clear that participants really had no way to express that Jimmy detected red without affirming that Jimmy saw red in our original study. The first reason is that participants answered the question, "Did Jimmy see red?" on a 7-point scale such that partial disagreement plausibly could be expressed by selecting a midpoint answer. Second, participants were also asked to explain their answers. And if a significant percentage of participants had affirmed that Jimmy saw red due to a desire to note Jimmy's information-processing behavior, then we would expect many of these participants to articulate this in their explanations—but that is not what we found.

6. It might be thought that it is not so much incorrect to say that Jimmy/Timmy moved the red box, as that this is underdetermined by the vignettes: Although Jimmy/Timmy is described as moving the green box, the vignettes do not preclude that the red box was moved in the process. Despite this quibble, I follow FAN in excluding participants who answered that Jimmy/Timmy moved the red box in the new studies reported in the next section.

7. For "detect," the proportion is exactly what one would expect by chance. For "saw," one-sample test of proportion with continuity correction, $\chi^2 = 0.3214$, $df = 1$, $p = .5708$.

8. In each of the four studies reported in this section, participants were native English-speakers, 18 years of age or older, with at most minimal training in philosophy (excluding philosophy majors and those who have taken graduate-level courses in philosophy). All participants were recruited through the Philosophical Personality website (http://philosophicalpersonality.com).

9. Neither difference was significant, although it was borderline significant for Timmy detected: two-sample test for equality of proportions with continuity correction, saw: $\chi^2 = 0.3798$, $df = 1$, $p = .2689$, one-tailed, and detected, $\chi^2 = 2.6841$, $df = 1$, $p = .05068$, one-tailed.

10. The difference was not significant: two-sample test for equality of proportions with continuity correction, $\chi^2 = 0.862$, $df = 1$, $p = .1766$, one-tailed.

11. One-sample test of proportion with continuity correction, $\chi^2 = 0.98$, $df = 1$, $p = .1611$, one-tailed.

12. Two-sample test for equality of proportions with continuity correction, $\chi^2 = 3.8632$, $df = 1$, $p = .02468$, one-tailed.

13. Two-sample test for equality of proportions with continuity correction, $\chi^2 = 0.1996$, $df = 1$, $p = 0.3275$, one-tailed.

14. One-sample test of proportion with continuity correction, $\chi^2 = 8.2656$, $df = 1$, $p = .00202$, one-tailed.

References

Arico, A., Fiala, B., Goldberg, R., & Nichols, S. (2011). The folk psychology of consciousness. *Mind & Language, 26*, 327–352.

Atler, A. L., Oppenheimer, D. M., Epley, N., & Eyre, R. N. (2007). Overcoming intuition: Metacognitive difficulty activates analytic reasoning. *Journal of Experimental Psychology: General, 136*, 569–576.

Buckwalter, W., & Phelan, M. (2013). Function and feeling machines: A defense of the philosophical conception of subjective experience. *Philosophical Studies, 166*(2), 349–361.

Buckwalter, W., & Phelan, M. (2014). Phenomenal consciousness disembodied. In J. Sytsma (Ed.), *Advances in experimental philosophy of mind* (pp. 45–73). London, England: Bloomsbury.

Fiala, B., Arico, A., & Nichols, S. (2011). On the psychological origins of dualism: Dual-process cognition and the explanatory gap. In E. Slingerland & M. Collard (Eds.), *Creating consilience: Issues and case studies in the integration of the sciences and humanities* (pp. 88–110). Oxford, England: Oxford University Press.

Frederick, S. (2005). Cognitive reflection and decision making. *Journal of Economic Perspectives, 19*, 25–42.

Gray, H., Gray, K., & Wegner, D. (2007). Dimensions of mind perception. *Science, 315*, 619.

Huebner, B. (2010). Commonsense concepts of phenomenal consciousness: Does anyone *care* about functional zombies? *Phenomenology and the Cognitive Sciences, 9*, 133–155.

Huebner, B., Bruno, M., & Sarkissian, H. (2010). What does the nation of China think about phenomenal states? *Review of Philosophy and Psychology, 1*, 225–243.

Knobe, J., & Prinz, J. (2008). Intuitions about consciousness: Experimental studies. *Phenomenology and Cognitive Sciences, 7*, 67–85.

Reuter, K. (2011). Distinguishing the appearance from the reality of pain. *Journal of Consciousness Studies, 18*, 94–109.

Reuter, K., Phillips, D., & Sytsma, J. (2014). Hallucinating pain. In J. Sytsma (Ed.), *Advances in experimental philosophy of mind* (pp. 75–99). London, England: Bloomsbury.

Sytsma, J. (2009). Phenomenological obviousness and the new science of consciousness. *Philosophy of Science, 76*, 958–969.

Sytsma, J. (2010). Dennett's theory of the folk theory of consciousness. *Journal of Consciousness Studies, 17*, 107–130.

Sytsma, J. (in press). Revisiting the valence account. *Philosophical Topics*.

Sytsma, J., & Livengood, J. (2011). A new perspective concerning experiments on semantic intuitions. *Australasian Journal of Philosophy, 89*, 315–332.

Sytsma, J., & Livengood, J. (in press). *The new experimental philosophy: An introduction and guide*. Peterborough, ON: Broadview Press.

Sytsma, J., & Machery, E. (2009). How to study folk intuitions about phenomenal consciousness. *Philosophical Psychology, 22*, 21–35.

Sytsma, J., & Machery, E. (2010). Two conceptions of subjective experience. *Philosophical Studies, 151*, 299–327.

Sytsma, J., & Machery, E. (2012a). The two sources of moral standing. *Review of Philosophy and Psychology, 3*, 303–324.

Sytsma, J., & Machery, E. (2012b). On the relevance of folk intuitions: A reply to Talbot. *Consciousness and Cognition, 21*, 654–660.

Talbot, B. (2012). The irrelevance of folk intuitions to the "hard problem" of consciousness. *Consciousness and Cognition, 21*, 644–650.

Part II Suggested Readings

Arico, A., Fiala, B., Goldberg, R., & Nichols, S. (2011). The folk psychology of consciousness. *Mind & Language, 26,* 327–352.
Arico and colleagues develop a new model, the "Agency Model," to explain the attribution of conscious mental states, and present some evidence supporting their model.

Buckwalter, W., & Phelan, M. (2013). Function and feeling machines: A defense of the philosophical conception of subjective experience. *Philosophical Studies, 166,* 349–361.
This article criticizes Sytsma and Machery (2010) and shows that functional considerations play a crucial role in lay attributions of conscious mental states.

Gray, H., Gray, K., & Wegner, D. (2007). Dimensions of mind perception. *Science, 315,* 619.
Gray and colleagues argue that laypeople distinguish two dimensions in their understanding of mind: agency, which is related to the capacity for controlled action, and consciousness, which is related to the capacity to have subjective experiences.

Jack, A. I., & Robbins, P. (2012). The phenomenal stance revisited. *Review of Philosophy and Psychology, 3,* 383–403.
This article provides some evidence in support of Robbins and Jack (2006).

Knobe, J., & Prinz, J. (2008). Intuitions about consciousness: Experimental studies. *Phenomenology and Cognitive Sciences, 7,* 67–85.
This groundbreaking article was the first one to study ascriptions of conscious mental states experimentally. Knobe and Prinz argue that people do not conceive of conscious states in functional terms and that ascription of consciousness is related to moral considerations.

Robbins, P., & Jack, A. (2006). The phenomenal stance. *Philosophical Studies, 127,* 59–85.
Robbins and Jack argue that ascribing conscious mental states to organisms (what they call taking "the phenomenal stance" with respect to these organisms) lead people to view them as deserving moral consideration.

Sytsma, J. (in press). Revisiting the valence account. *Philosophical Topics.*
Sytsma reassesses his views about lay ascription of phenomenal consciousness in light of various criticisms.

Sytsma, J., & Machery, E. (2009). How to study folk intuitions about phenomenal consciousness. *Philosophical Psychology, 22,* 21–35.
This article critically discusses the methodology of Knobe and Prinz (2008).

Sytsma, J., & Machery, E. (2010). Two conceptions of subjective experience. *Philosophical Studies, 151*, 299–327.

This article examines whether laypeople conceive of subjective experiences in the same way as philosophers, and it argues that laypeople do not have a concept of phenomenal consciousness. Furthermore, Sytsma and Machery argue that this finding challenges the reality of the hard problem of consciousness.

Sytsma, J., & Machery, E. (2012). The two sources of moral standing. *Review of Philosophy and Psychology, 3*, 303–324.

Sytsma and Machery argue that two dimensions—rationality and the capacity for pain—determine whether people are willing to ascribe moral standing to organisms.

Talbot, B. (2012). The irrelevance of folk intuitions to the "hard problem" of consciousness. *Consciousness and Cognition, 21*, 644–650.

Talbot argues that Sytsma and Machery's (2010) findings have no implication for the hard problem of consciousness because they are System-1 (that is, roughly, quick and non-reflective) intuitions.

PART III
Free Will and Responsibility

CHAPTER 5

Free Will and the Scientific Vision[1]

JOSHUA KNOBE

Abstract

We can distinguish two broad visions of human action. On what might be called the scientific vision, human actions are caused by mental states. By contrast, on the transcendence vision, human actions are not caused by anything at all—they stand completely outside the causal order. A series of experimental studies suggest that people's ordinary way of making sense of themselves departs from the scientific vision and includes key elements of the transcendence vision. These results suggest that people's ordinary way of understanding human action is deeply different from the way such action is typically understood in the sciences.

Take a few courses in cognitive science, and you are likely to come across a certain kind of metaphor for the workings of the human mind. The metaphor goes like this:

> Consider a piece of computer software. The software consists of a collection of states and processes. We can predict what the software will do by looking at the complex ways in which these states and processes interact.
>
> The human mind works in more or less the same way. It too is just a complex collection of states and processes, and we can predict what a human being will do by thinking about the complex ways in which these states and processes interact.
>
> One can imagine someone saying: "I see all these states and processes, but aren't you forgetting something further—namely, the person

herself?" This question, however, is a foolish one. It is no more helpful than it would be to say: "I see all these states and processes, but where is the software itself?" The software just *is* a collection of states and processes, and the human mind is the same sort of thing.

This metaphor does a good job of capturing the basic approach one finds throughout the sciences of the mind. We might say that it captures the *scientific vision* of how the human mind works.

But one could also imagine another, very different metaphor for the workings of the mind. Perhaps something like this:

> Consider a royal court. The advisors and ministers each have an opportunity to advocate for a particular course of action. But it is not as though the advisors and ministers themselves make the final decision. Instead, there is another person in the court—the king or queen—who listens to all of the arguments, thinks them over, and then decides.
>
> The mind works in more or less the same way. Your mind might include various states and processes, but it would be a mistake to suggest that you yourself are just a collection of states and processes. On the contrary, you are a further thing—like the king or queen in the court—who can attend to the states and processes within your mind and then freely make a choice.
>
> When you do end up making a free choice, we might say that you made this choice "on the basis of" some of your psychological states. But the connection here is always indirect. It is not as though your psychological states actually *cause* your behavior; you just freely decide what to do, and sometimes you end up deciding to act in a way that accords with them.

On this latter metaphor, the self is something that transcends all the states and processes within the mind. Indeed, it is something that transcends the whole causal order. We might therefore refer to this second view as the *transcendence vision*.

A question now arises as to which of these two visions best captures people's ordinary understanding of human action. Thus, suppose that in the course of a perfectly ordinary conversation, someone utters the sentence:

John went to New York because he wanted to visit his sister.

Presumably, the person uttering this sentence thinks of John as choosing to go to New York with *free will*. That is, the person assumes that John freely decided to perform this action and was not in any way compelled. Nonetheless, the sentence quite clearly states that John's action can be explained in terms of his psychological states. Specifically, the sentence says that John performed this action (going to New York) because he had a particular desire (to visit his sister). So it seems that we are faced with a problem. How exactly do people ordinarily understand the role of psychological states in cases of free action? Can we capture people's ordinary understanding in terms of something such as the scientific vision, or do we need to invoke something more along the lines of the transcendence vision?

In existing work on people's understanding of mind and action, it is common for researchers to ignore the whole issue of free will and to assume that people's ordinary understanding conforms, at least in broad outlines, to the scientific vision. Thus, it has been said that people's ordinary understanding works something like a scientific theory, that people try to understand human action by looking for its causes and, in particular, that they think of human action as caused by psychological states. On this sort of view, the contemporary scientific study of human cognition is not really too much of a departure from people's ordinary way of making sense of the mind. It is just a more precise, systematic way of doing the very same thing that people do all the time (for discussion, see Bloom, 2006; Churchland, 1981; Gopnik & Wellman, 1992; Lewis, 1972; Nichols, 2006).

I argue that this view is mistaken. I suggest that people's ordinary way of making sense of the mind conforms more to the transcendence vision. Hence, the approach that we find in contemporary cognitive science is not just a more precise or systematic way of doing the same thing we do all the time. On the contrary, the basic vision at the heart of that approach is actually incompatible with people's ordinary way of understanding human freedom.

The evidence for this claim comes primarily from empirical work on the nature of people's ordinary understanding. Accordingly, I look at a series of different empirical studies. Each study might be somewhat inconclusive on its own, but together, they form a powerful and surprisingly coherent package.

1.   Let us begin with the most straightforward and obvious method for addressing these questions. If we want to know how people ordinarily understand human behavior, one approach would be to start by just asking them directly.

A few years ago, Shaun Nichols and I conducted an investigation using precisely this approach (Nichols & Knobe, 2007). Participants were told to imagine two possible universes. First, they were introduced to a universe in which every event was caused by some prior event:

Imagine a universe (Universe A) in which everything that happens is completely caused by whatever happened before it. This is true from the very beginning of the universe, so what happened in the beginning of the universe caused what happened next, and so on right up until the present.

Then they were told about a second universe that was similar to the first in many ways but that differed in one crucial respect:

Now imagine a universe (Universe B) in which almost everything that happens is completely caused by whatever happened before it. The one exception is human decision making.

So in the first universe, every event is caused by some prior event, while in the second universe, human decisions are not caused by any prior event at all; they are just freely chosen. After reading about these two possible universes, participants were asked,

Which of these universes do you think is most like ours? (circle one)
Universe A   Universe B

Let us now introduce a helpful abbreviation. Instead of saying that an event is "completely caused by whatever happened before it," we will say that it is *causally determined*. We can then state the difference between the two universes as follows: In Universe A, everything is causally determined, whereas in Universe B, human actions are not causally determined. Which type of universe do people think is most like ours?

The overwhelming answer is Universe B. In our original studies, this answer was chosen by more than 90% of participants. In other words, when people were asked directly, they tended to say that our universe was like a universe in which almost all events were causally determined but human actions were not. This result suggests that people's explicit answers fit more closely with the transcendence vision than with the scientific vision.

Most researchers working in this area would agree that this type of evidence is far from conclusive. They might say: "Our aim is to investigate the tacit mechanisms that people use all the time to understand human action. The best way to figure out how these mechanisms work is to look at various aspects of people's thinking (their moral judgments, their explanations, etc.) and try to use these aspects of people's thinking as clues to the nature of their most basic understanding. The technique you've used here is far less reliable. If you insist on just directly asking people abstract questions about the nature of action, there is no guarantee that you will be tapping into these mechanisms in any way. The answers people give might simply reflect the explicit theories they have picked up in various philosophical conversations. (Maybe they were exposed to ideas from Christian theology in their Sunday school classes, and they are simply parroting back something they've learned there.)"

This is a powerful objection, and it deserves to be taken very seriously. To address it, we teamed up with Hagop Sarkissian and tried running a cross-cultural study (Sarkissian et al., 2010). Participants were recruited from the United States, Hong Kong, India, and Colombia. All of these participants were then given precisely the same question described earlier. The results showed no significant differences between cultures. In all four cultures, the majority of participants said that our own universe is most similar to the one in which human action is not causally determined.

This result comes as something of a surprise. Here we have people from radically different cultures, with quite different historical and religious traditions, and yet they all seem to be converging on the same answer to this highly abstract question. How are we to explain this convergence? It hardly seems plausible to suggest that all of these people have been taking classes in which they are explicitly taught the same philosophical theory. Presumably, we need to provide some other type of explanation.

If we assume that people's ordinary understanding of action follows the transcendence vision, this task becomes quite simple. The explanation is that the experiment is accurately tapping into people's ordinary understanding. (This understanding tells people that human action is not causally determined, and they answer the explicit theoretical questions accordingly.) By contrast, if we assume that people's ordinary understanding follows the scientific vision, the matter becomes considerably more complex. We would need to argue that people's tacit understanding is telling them that human action actually *is* causally determined but that there is some further factor—a factor that is equally present in all four of these cultures—which then obscures this tacit understanding and leads people to explicitly state that human action is *not* causally determined. It would require some ingenuity to develop an explanation along these lines, but perhaps future research will lead to the development of a theory that can successfully pull off this trick.

2.   A question now arises about how people make judgments of moral responsibility. Do people think that an agent can be morally responsible for his or her behavior if this behavior is causally determined? Or do people think that a person can only be truly responsible if his or her behavior is freely chosen by a transcendent self?

A number of studies have examined this question, and these studies have yielded a surprising result. Suppose we tell participants about an agent whose behavior is causally determined. Now suppose we tell them that this agent performs some immoral behavior. We might tell them that the agent has committed rape, or has robbed a bank, or has murdered an innocent person. Participants who have been given cases of this form tend to arrive at a striking sort of moral judgment. Although they have been informed in no uncertain terms that the agent in the case is causally determined, they tend to say that the agent is fully morally responsible!

This result was first uncovered in an influential paper by Nahmias, Morris, Nadelhoffer, and Turner (2006), and it has since been replicated and extended by numerous other researchers (De Brigard, Mandelbaum, & Ripley, 2009; Feltz & Cokely, 2009; Nahmias, Coates, & Kvaran, 2007; Nichols & Knobe, 2007). At this point, the basic finding has been established beyond all reasonable doubt.

In one of the most impressive experimental demonstrations of this phenomenon (De Brigard et al., 2009; Mandelbaum & Ripley, 2012), participants were told to imagine a person named Dennis. They were informed that Dennis had a neurological disorder, that the bad things he did were completely caused by this neurological disorder, and that if other people were to have the same disorder, they would do the very same bad things. After receiving this information, participants were told that Dennis had raped a number of women, and they were asked whether he was morally responsible for his actions. Surprisingly, participants tended to say that, even in this very extreme case, Dennis actually *was* responsible.

Now, one possible reaction to these results would be to say that people's understanding of moral responsibility is more or less independent of questions about causal determinism. But Nichols and I thought that there might be more to the story. Our hunch was that people's intuitions in these cases might be the product of two different psychological processes that were pulling them in opposite directions. More specifically, we thought that (a) when people are engaged in abstract theoretical reasoning, they use a conception according to which agents cannot be morally responsible for behavior that is causally determined, but then (b) when they hear about some specific concrete act of wrongdoing (rape, robbery, murder, etc.), a further process comes into play that leads them to say that the agent actually is responsible for his or her misdeeds.

To test this hypothesis, we conducted an additional study (Nichols & Knobe, 2007). All participants received the description of the causally deterministic Universe A and were asked whether people within this universe could be morally responsible. But the study included one further wrinkle: Participants were randomly assigned to be asked this question in one of two possible ways. Participants in the "concrete" condition received the question:

> In Universe A, a man named Bill has become attracted to his secretary, and he decides that the only way to be with her is to kill his wife and 3 children. He knows that it is impossible to escape from his house in the event of a fire. Before he leaves on a business trip, he sets up a device in his basement that burns down the house and kills his family.

> Is Bill fully morally responsible for killing his wife and children?
> Yes   No

In this condition, most participants (72%) gave the answer "Yes," indicating that a causally determined agent could still be morally responsible. This first result simply replicates earlier findings.

Then, in the "abstract" condition, participants received the question that did not mention any actual concrete misdeeds:

> In Universe A, is it possible for a person to be fully morally responsible for their actions?
> Yes   No

In this latter condition, participants gave exactly the opposite pattern of responses, with the vast majority (86%) choosing the answer "No."

This difference between concrete and abstract judgments is a puzzling one, and the attempt to understand it has been one of the major preoccupations of experimental philosophy work on free will. There have been studies examining the phenomenon more systematically using a variety of different descriptions of determinism (Nahmias et al., 2007), studies manipulating people's level of abstract thinking by asking them to think about either close or distant times (Weigel, 2011), even studies that go after these questions by manipulating the *font* in which the stimuli are written (Gonnerman, Reuter, & Weinberg, 2012). A number of competing theoretical models have been proposed (Cova, Bertoux, Bourgeois-Gironde, & Dubois, 2012; Nahmias & Murray, 2010; Nichols & Knobe, 2007), but at this point, no clear consensus has emerged. Perhaps future work will bring more clarity to these issues.[2]

For present purposes, however, we can focus on a slightly different question. Instead of asking why people are more inclined to regard the agent as responsible in concrete cases, we can ask why people do not regard the agent as obviously responsible in all of these cases. There is clearly something drawing people to the view that an agent cannot be morally responsible for behaviors that are causally determined. But what exactly is drawing people in this direction? Why do they see causal determinism as any problem at all for moral responsibility?

At this point, one might offer a number of different hypotheses, but it is a striking fact that people's worry about causal determinism can be very easily explained if we simply assume that people accept the transcendence vision. It then becomes unnecessary to make any complex further assumptions about the way people think about moral responsibility in particular. All one needs is the straightforward principle:

> People will be reluctant to hold an agent responsible for a behavior if they believe that this behavior was not even produced by the agent in question.

The key result then follows almost immediately. If the transcendence vision is correct, then all behaviors that are causally determined—even if they are determined by the agent's own psychological states—will not truly have been produced by the agent him- or herself.

We now arrive at a provisional conclusion. Experimental results show that people see causal determinism as a threat to moral responsibility, and any correct theory here will have to explain why people have this intuition. If we start out with the view that people accept the scientific vision, we might be able to offer an explanation by introducing certain further assumptions. But the situation becomes very different if we start out with the view that people accept the transcendence vision. It then becomes possible to explain the results without introducing any further controversial assumptions. Everything simply follows from people's understanding of what would be required for an agent even to have produced the action at all.

3.   In an ingenious series of studies, Nahmias and Murray (2010) looked more directly at the ways in which people's understanding of psychological states impacts their intuitions about free will. Once again, participants were told about the causally deterministic Universe A, but this time, they were asked whether they agreed or disagreed with statements of the form:

- In Universe A, what a person believes has no effect on what he or she ends up being caused to do.
- In Universe A, what a person wants has no effect on what he or she ends up being caused to do.

Surprisingly, participants tend to *agree* with these statements. In other words, when participants are informed that an agent's actions are causally determined, they tend to infer that the agent's actions do not depend in any way on her beliefs and desires. This finding constitutes a genuine breakthrough within research in this area, and it is worth taking the time to think in detail about what it might be telling us.

To get a better sense for the broader implications of the Nahmias-Murray findings, it might be helpful to introduce an analogy. Suppose we are looking at a house that has been destroyed, and I tell you: "This house burned down in a fire." Now suppose that a little while later you receive one further piece of information: "The destruction of the house was completely caused by an event that occurred three days ago." Presumably, you would not conclude that the fire had no effect at all on what happened to the house. Instead, you would probably assume that the fire was precisely the event that occurred three days ago and completely caused the destruction. (You might then infer that if the fire had never occurred, the house would still be in fine shape today.) What Nahmias and Murray's results show is that people do not apply this same kind of reasoning when it comes to the relationship between human action and mental states. On the contrary, when people are told that an agent's actions are completely caused by prior events, they conclude that the agent's beliefs and desires could not possibly be having any effect on what she ends up doing. This result seems to suggest that people are conceptualizing the relationship between an agent's beliefs and desires and his or her actions in a way that is radically different from the way they would normally conceptualize the relationship between a fire and the destruction of a house. Our aim now is to get a better sense for the nature of that difference.

Let us begin by stating the obvious. Clearly, people often explain why an agent acted in the way she did by referring to her beliefs and desires. Thus, if we pick out an agent's action and ask, "Why did he or she do that?" we might receive an answer like "Because he or she believed that it was the right thing to do." Then, continuing the chain of explanation back a step, people often explain an agent's beliefs and desires by tracing them to facts about her external environment. So, if we ask the question, "Why did he or she believe it was the right thing to do?" we may receive the answer "Because his or her parents always told him or her that it was right to behave in that way."

Yet, although it is perfectly clear that people offer explanations of this form, it has proved remarkably difficult to say precisely what these explanations *mean*. In the mid-twentieth century, a great deal of philosophical work went into trying to understand the sentences people use, in ordinary language, to explain an agent's actions in terms of her beliefs and desires. Philosophers developed a variety of opposing theories (Davidson, 1963; Hart & Honoré, 1959; Ryle, 1949; Wittgenstein, 1953), but the issue was never fully resolved. In my view, the question is just as mysterious today as it was when it was first posed.

One obvious answer would be that the relationship between an agent's beliefs and desires and her actions is best understood as a straightforward case of *causation* (e.g., Davidson, 1963). On this view, what we have is a causal chain: The agent's environment causes him or her to have certain beliefs and desires, which in turn cause him or her to perform a particular action.

$$\text{Environment} \rightarrow \text{Beliefs and Desires} \rightarrow \text{Action}$$

Many researchers working on these issues will immediately feel that this picture is clearly the correct one. In fact, some researchers may find themselves hard-pressed even to imagine an alternative.

But if we start out with the assumption that people accept a picture such as this one, we soon run into a major difficulty. According to the picture, most people's actions are causally determined by their beliefs and desires. It should therefore be blazingly obvious that even if an agent's actions are causally determined, his or her beliefs and desires can have an effect on what he or she does.

(After all, the assumption is that people are thinking that, in a typical case, it is precisely the agent's beliefs and desires that causally determine his or her actions.) But now we face the problem. For what the Nahmias-Murray results show is that people *do not* endorse this conclusion. Instead, people tend to say that if an agent's actions are causally determined, his or her beliefs and desires cannot have any effect at all on what the agent does. Why might people be responding in this way?

One natural answer would be that people reject the whole picture we have been sketching. Instead, they might accept something along the lines of the transcendence vision. On this latter picture, the relationship between an agent's psychological states and the agent's actions is not a simple causal chain. It is something more complex:

$$\text{Environment} \rightarrow \text{Beliefs and Desires} \dashrightarrow \text{Action}$$

Here the dotted line signifies a relationship that involves not straightforward causal explanation but rather what philosophers call "reason explanation." In other words, on this view, when people explain an action in terms of a belief, they are not saying that the action was *caused* by the belief. Rather, they are saying that the action was *chosen for a reason*. (For example, they might be saying that the agent's reason for choosing the action was his or her belief that it was the right thing to do.)

It would be difficult to say exactly what it means for an agent to do something "for a reason" in the relevant sense. Different theorists have developed quite different accounts (Anscombe, 1957; Hart & Honoré, 1959; Wittgenstein, 1958, pp. 14–15), and the debate continues until the present day (Aguilar & Buckareff, 2010; Knobe, 2007; Malle, 2004; Mele, 2010). For present purposes, however, we do not need to resolve that controversy. The key idea is just that, on the transcendence vision, an agent can do something for a reason even when the resulting action was freely chosen and not caused by anything at all.

If we start out with this sort of framework, it becomes easy to see why people might respond as they do in the Nahmias-Murray experiments. People think that when an agent acts based on reasons, his or her behaviors are not causally determined. Then they are told about a universe that differs from our own in that everything in it actually is causally determined. They therefore infer that agents in this universe do not do things for reasons. It is only a small step from this inference to the conclusion that the beliefs and desires of these agents have no effect on what they end up doing.

By contrast, suppose we start out with the assumption that people's ordinary understanding is well captured by the scientific vision. Now our starting assumption is that people think of ordinary human action as causally determined by psychological states. We then learn a new fact. When people are told about a universe in which all human actions are causally determined, they conclude that the actions of human beings in this universe do not depend in any way on their psychological states. How on earth are we to explain this fact? It is certainly possible that someone will come up with a viable solution here, but the problem is not looking like an easy one.

4.   At the heart of the transcendence vision is the idea that human actions are radically different from other sorts of events. We might explain the movements of a billiard ball by saying that its movements were caused by prior events, but the explanation of a human action would have to be entirely different. Human actions are not *caused* by prior events; they are *chosen* based on reasons.

This point comes out especially clearly when we consider events that might in some ways seem similar to human actions. Take the case of computers. One might think that the explanation of a computer's output ought to resemble, at least in certain minimal respects, the explanation of a human action. (Computers contain internal representations, and their outputs can be explained in terms of those representations.) Yet, even on the transcendence vision, the output of a computer will be best understood as the product of a perfectly straightforward causal chain:

Environment → Program → Output

No matter what you think about the vexed questions surrounding human action, there is little temptation to suppose that anything equally mysterious is occurring in the case of computers. A computer does not proceed by considering its own program and then freely choosing which output to display. Rather, the program simply *causes* the computer to generate a particular output.

Indeed, one should be able to see this sort of straightforward causal chain even in certain kinds of cases in which a human being's bodily movements are explained in terms of his or her psychological states. Suppose that an agent is watching a scary movie and makes an involuntary grimace. The process might then go like this:

Environment → Emotions → Facial Expressions

The transcendence vision suggests that cases such as this one are deeply different from cases of voluntary action. Voluntary actions might be seen as freely chosen on the basis of reasons, but clearly, no such thing is taking place in a case such as this one. It is not as though the agent freely chooses to grimace and his or her reason for making that choice is that the agent is afraid. Rather, the fear directly *causes* the grimace. Here again, nothing more complex or mysterious is required.

In short, the transcendence vision leaves us with the idea that there is a fundamental difference between different kinds of explanation. It says that people's way of explaining free human action should be deeply different from their way of explaining a computer's behavior or an involuntary grimace. But in that case, it seems that we immediately arrive at a new testable prediction. If people's way of understanding free human action is radically different from their way of understanding other sorts of events, and if the Nahmias-Murray experiments do indeed give us a way of tapping into people's understanding, then we should be able to use a modified Nahmias–Murray experiment to show a difference between judgments about free human action and judgments about other sorts of events.

To put this prediction to the test, I conducted a quick follow-up study. All participants received the story about Universe A. Participants in the "human" condition then received the following question:

> Imagine that Universe A includes various people who have beliefs and values. Now please tell us whether you agree or disagree with the following statement:
>
> • In Universe A, people's beliefs and values have no effect on what they end up being caused to do.

Meanwhile, participants in the "computer" condition received the following question:

> Imagine that Universe A includes various computers that use programs and data. Now please tell us whether you agree or disagree with the following statement:
>
> • In Universe A, the computers' programs and data have no effect on what they end up being caused to do.

Participants tended to agree with the statement in the human condition but to disagree with the statement in the computer condition.[3]

Notice the striking pattern of intuitions people are showing in this case. They are saying that if everything in the universe is causally determined, then a computer's data can still have an effect on its output but a human being's beliefs cannot have any effect on his or her behavior. This is exactly the result one would predict if one started out with the assumption that people are adopting the transcendence vision, and it is hard to see how one would explain it on any other hypothesis.

To further get at the nature of the effect here, I conducted a second study using an even more closely controlled pair of cases. This time, participants in the "reason" condition received the following question:

Imagine that the people in Universe A perform various actions. Now please tell us whether you agree or disagree with the following statement:

- In Universe A, people's beliefs and values have no effect on what actions they end up performing.

Other participants were assigned to the "non-reason" condition:

Imagine that the people in Universe A make various facial expressions. Now please tell us whether you agree or disagree with the following statement:

- In Universe A, people's emotions have no effect on what facial expressions they end up making.

Here again, there was a significant difference between conditions. People tended to agree in the reason condition but not in the non-reason condition.[4] What we have here, then, is an even more tightly controlled minimal pair. If the universe is completely deterministic, people think that an agent's emotions can still have an impact on his or her facial expressions but that an agent's beliefs cannot have an impact his or her actions. Once again, these are exactly the results one would expect if one started out with the view that people accept the transcendence vision.

Of course, if we start out with the idea that people accept the scientific vision, we might be able to develop an alternative explanation for these findings, but this is beginning to look like a losing battle. To hold onto the hypothesis that people accept the scientific vision, we would need to develop an alternative explanation for the findings about people's explicit judgments about the nature of our universe, *and* for the findings about moral responsibility judgments, *and* the Nahmias-Murray findings, *and* for these new findings about the way people's judgments about emotions differ from their judgments about beliefs. Why would we be at all drawn to pursue a research program along these lines?

5.   Clearly, the claim that people accept something like the scientific vision is not just a single isolated hypothesis. It is a natural part of a larger picture of how the human mind works, and one might think that the only way to really do justice to this claim is to understand it in the context of the larger picture in which it is embedded.

The larger picture says that people's basic way of making sense of the world is something more or less like a scientific theory. This picture has been developed in rich theoretical detail, and it has been applied in research on everything from people's causal judgments (e.g., Gopnik et al., 2004) to their understanding of psychological states (e.g., Churchland, 1981). One can then apply this general picture quite straightforwardly to the question under discussion here. From a more scientific perspective, the transcendence vision looks a bit spooky, perhaps even conceptually incoherent. So if one starts with the idea that people's way of making sense of the world is a broadly scientific one, it may begin to seem just obvious that people have to accept something along the lines of the scientific vision.

In my view, this type of argument is a very powerful one. If we find a general picture that ends up generating accurate predictions in one domain after another, there is certainly strong reason to suspect that it will continue to prove accurate when we switch over to a new domain. Indeed, even if we run into some difficulties in this new domain, it might be reasonable to try dismissing those difficulties and sticking with the general picture. One might say: "This general picture turned out to be correct in so many other cases. We might be running into some troubles right at the moment, but if we stick with our general research program, we will surely be able to work them out in the end." Such a response could, in the right circumstances, be exactly the right one.

But, of course, the argument cuts both ways. One of the major results of existing work in experimental philosophy is that when one looks in detail at people's ordinary intuitions, one finds that these intuitions look very different from anything one would expect to find in the sciences. When one looks at intuitions about happiness or knowledge, one finds that these intuitions are shaped by moral considerations (e.g., Beebe & Buckwalter, 2010; Phillips, Nyholm, & Liao, in press). When one looks at intuitions about mental states, one finds that they do not conform to the kind of functionalist approach found in cognitive science but instead take our embodiment into account (Huebner, 2010; Knobe & Prinz, 2008; Sytsma & Machery, 2010). When one looks at intuitions about causation, one finds that these intuitions follow patterns that are deeply different from those involved in scientific causal modeling (Alicke, Rose, & Bloom, 2011; Hitchcock & Knobe, 2011; Sytsma, Livengood, & Rose, 2012). Similar results have been found in numerous other domains (for a review, see Knobe, 2010).

So perhaps we can now turn the argument around and run it in the other direction. We have a general research program of investigating the ways in which people's ordinary intuitive understanding is deeply different from the kind of understanding one finds in the sciences, and this research program has generated accurate predictions in numerous other domains. We now have good reason to suspect that this general program will prove helpful in the present case as well.

6.   This chapter has been concerned with questions about how people ordinarily understand free human action. Consider again the sentence "John went

to New York because he wanted to visit his sister." This sentence seems to suggest that John freely chose to perform an action on the basis of certain reasons. How exactly do people ordinarily make sense of this notion?

One plausible view would be that we can capture the ordinary understanding of free action using more or less the approach found in contemporary cognitive science. Perhaps our sentence means that John had a desire to visit his sister and that this desire figured in a complex cognitive process that eventually caused him to go to New York. To the extent that we want to capture the notion that he performed this action freely, we might then invoke various other cognitive scientific concepts (self-regulation, cognitive control, etc.).

I have argued that this approach is misguided. Our ordinary way of making sense of free action is deeply different from anything that appears in cognitive science and, indeed, from anything in the sciences more generally. So as long as we are working within a broadly scientific framework, we will never be talking about the very thing that people are getting at with their ordinary notion of free will.

Of course, in making this claim about the ordinary notion, I do not mean to be ruling out the possibility of a scientific theory of free will. We might well find in the end that we have reasons of one kind or another to conclude that certain cognitive phenomena actually are sufficient for free action. But if we do go down this route, we should be clear about what we are doing. We will not be simply working out the implications of the ordinary understanding of free action. Instead, we will be abandoning this ordinary notion and replacing it with a very different one.

Notes

1. The theory presented here was developed in close collaboration with Shaun Nichols (as should be clear from Sections 1 and 2), and a number of aspects of it were directly inspired by the research of Eddy Nahmias and Dylan Murray (see Sections 3 and 4). I am deeply grateful to all three of these philosophers, both for their published research and for numerous invaluable conversations.

   This article was made possible through the support of a grant from the John Templeton Foundation. The opinions expressed in this publication are my own and do not necessarily reflect the views of the John Templeton Foundation.

2. In earlier work, Shaun Nichols and I suggested that this effect might be arising because people have an emotional reaction to the concrete case and this reaction biases their responses (Nichols & Knobe, 2007). Over the past few years, this hypothesis has been put to the test in a variety of different experiments, and at this point, I have to say that things are not looking good. First, a series of studies looked at cases that were entirely concrete but which differed in the extent to which they would be expected to provoke emotional reactions. A recent meta-analysis of 29 such studies shows that people are indeed more inclined to ascribe moral responsibility in a deterministic universe when faced with a high-affect case than with a low-affect case but that this effect is quite small ($d = .18$)—not nearly large enough to explain the powerful impact of the original abstract/concrete manipulation (Feltz & Cova, 2012). Second,

a recent study looked at the responses given to abstract and concrete cases among participants with frontotemporal dementia. Although these participants show a deficit in their capacity for emotional response—and would therefore be expected to differ from neurotypical participants if the effect was driven by emotion—they ended up giving exactly the same pattern of responses seen in earlier studies (Cova et al., 2012).

In light of these results, I now suspect that the abstract/concrete effect is not, in fact, due to emotional responses. Perhaps it can be explained instead by the very theory proposed here: People have a very strong tendency to think of human decision-making in terms of transcendence. Thus, no matter how much one emphasizes determinism, if the case is presented with sufficient concreteness, participants immediately apply their default (transcendence-based) framework.

3. Forty-one people were recruited through Amazon's Mechanical Turk. Ratings were on a scale from 1 ("disagree") to 7 ("agree"). Agreement was higher in the human condition ($M = 5.4$) than in the computer condition ($M = 3.6$), $t(39) = 2.4$, $p < .05$.

4. Forty people were recruited through Amazon's Mechanical Turk. Ratings were on a scale from 1 ("disagree") to 7 ("agree"). Agreement was higher in the reason condition ($M = 5.7$) than in the nonreason condition ($M = 3.5$), $t(38) = 3.3$, $p < .005$.

References

Aguilar, J.H., & Buckareff, A.A. (Eds.) (2010). *Causing human actions: New perspectives on the causal theory of action*. Cambridge, MA: MIT Press.

Alicke, M., Rose, D., & Bloom, D. (2011). Causation, norm violation, and culpable control. *Journal of Philosophy, 108*, 670–696.

Anscombe, G.E.M. (1957). *Intention*. Oxford, England: Basil Blackwell.

Beebe, J., & Buckwalter, W. (2010). The epistemic side-effect effect. *Mind & Language, 25*, 474–498.

Bloom, P. (2006). My brain made me do it. *Journal of Culture and Cognition, 6*, 209–214.

Churchland, P. (1981). Eliminative materialism and the propositional attitudes. *Journal of Philosophy, 78*, 67–90.

Cova, F., Bertoux, M., Bourgeois-Gironde, S., & Dubois, B. (2012). Judgments about moral responsibility and determinism in patients with behavioural variant of frontotemporal dementia: Still compatibilists. *Consciousness and Cognition, 21*, 851–864.

Davidson, D. (1963). Actions, reasons and causes. *Journal of Philosophy, 60*, 685–700.

De Brigard, F., Mandelbaum, E., & Ripley, D. (2009). Responsibility and the brain sciences. *Ethical Theory and Moral Practice, 12*, 511–524.

Feltz, A., & Cokely, E. (2009). Do judgments about freedom and responsibility depend on who you are? Personality differences in intuitions about compatibilism and incompatibilism. *Consciousness and Cognition, 18*, 342–350.

Feltz, A., & Cova, F. (2012). *When and how affective reactions impact judgments about free will and determinism: A meta-analysis*. Unpublished manuscript, Schreiner University, Kerrville, TX.

Gonnerman, C., Reuter, S., & Weinberg, J. (2012). *More oversensitive intuitions: Print fonts and could choose otherwise*. Unpublished manuscript, Indiana University, Bloomington, IN.

Gopnik, A., & Wellman, H. (1992). Why the child's theory of mind really *is* a theory. *Mind & Language, 7*, 145–171.

Gopnik, A., Glymour, C., Sobel, D., Schulz, L., Kushnir, T., & Danks, D. (2004). A theory of causal learning in children: Causal maps and Bayes nets. *Psychological Review, 111*, 1–31.

Hart, H.L.A., & Honoré, T. (1959). *Causation in the law*. Oxford, England: Clarendon.

Hitchcock, C., & Knobe J. (2011). Cause and norm. *Journal of Philosophy, 106*, 587–612.

Huebner B. (2010). Commonsense concepts of phenomenal consciousness: Does anyone *care* about functional zombies? *Phenomenology and the Cognitive Sciences, 9*, 133–155.

Knobe, J. (2007). Reason explanation in folk psychology. *Midwest Studies in Philosophy, 31,* 90–107.

Knobe, J. (2010). Person as scientist, person as moralist. *Behavioral and Brain Sciences, 33,* 315–329.

Knobe, J., & Prinz, J. (2008). Intuitions about consciousness: Experimental studies. *Phenomenology and the Cognitive Sciences, 7,* 67–83.

Lewis, D. (1972). Psychophysical and theoretical identifications. *Australasian Journal of Philosophy, 50,* 249–258.

Malle, B. F. (2004). *How the mind explains behavior: Folk explanations, meaning, and social interaction.* Cambridge, MA: MIT Press.

Mandelbaum, E., & Ripley, D. (2012). Explaining the abstract/concrete paradoxes in moral psychology: The NBAR hypothesis. *Review of Philosophy and Psychology, 3,* 351–368.

Mele, A. (2010). Teleological explanations of actions: Anticausalism versus causalism. In J.H. Aguilar & A.A. Buckareff (Eds.), *Causing human actions: New perspectives on the causal theory of action* (pp. 183–198). Cambridge, MA: MIT Press.

Nahmias, E., Coates, D., & Kvaran, T. (2007). Free will, moral responsibility, and mechanism: Experiments on folk intuitions. *Midwest Studies in Philosophy, 31,* 214–242.

Nahmias E., Morris S., Nadelhoffer T., & Turner J. (2006). Is incompatibilism intuitive? *Philosophy and Phenomenological Research, 73,* 28–53.

Nahmias, E., & Murray, D. (2010). Experimental philosophy on free will: An error theory for incompatibilist intuitions. In J. Aguilar, A. Buckareff, & K. Frankish (Eds.), *New waves in philosophy of action* (pp. 189–216). Hampshire, England: Palgrave-Macmillan.

Nichols, S. (2006). Folk intuitions about free will. *Journal of Cognition and Culture, 6,* 57–86.

Nichols, S., & Knobe, J. (2007). Moral responsibility and determinism: The cognitive science of folk intuitions. *Nous, 43,* 663–685.

Phillips, J., Nyholm, S., & Liao, S. (in press). The good in happiness. *Oxford studies in experimental philosophy.*

Ryle, G. (1949). *The concept of mind.* London, England: Hutchinson.

Sarkissian, H., Chatterjee, A., De Brigard, F., Knobe, J., Nichols, S., & Sirker, S. (2010). Is belief in free will a cultural universal? *Mind & Language, 25,* 346–358.

Sytsma, J., Livengood, J. & Rose, D. (2012). Two types of typicality: Rethinking the role of statistical typicality in ordinary causal attributions. *Studies in History and Philosophy of Science, 43,* 814–820.

Sytsma, J., & Machery, E. (2010). Two conceptions of subjective experience. *Philosophical Studies, 151,* 299–327.

Weigel, C. (2011). Distance, anger, freedom: An account of the role of abstraction in compatibilist and incompatibilist intuition. *Philosophical Psychology, 24,* 803–823.

Wittgenstein, L. (1953). *Philosophical investigations* (G.E.M. Anscombe, Trans.). Oxford, England: Basil Blackwell.

Wittgenstein, L. (1958). *The blue and brown books.* New York, NY: Harper & Row.

CHAPTER 6

A Naturalistic Vision of Free Will

EDDY NAHMIAS AND MORGAN THOMPSON[1]

Abstract

We argue, contra Joshua Knobe (this volume), that most people have an understanding of free will and responsible agency that is compatible with a naturalistic vision of the human mind. Our argument is supported by results from a new experimental philosophy study showing that most people think free will is consistent with complete and perfect prediction of decisions and actions based on prior activity in the brain (a scenario adapted from Sam Harris, who predicts most people will find it inconsistent with free will). We explain why most people are "theory-lite" about the nature of mind and free will—they are not committed to substantive theories of the underlying causal structure of mind, such as Knobe's "transcendence vision." Rather, we suggest a "causal competition principle"—that an agent's actions will be deemed unfree when they are perceived to be fully caused by factors that do not include his or her reasons. This principle explains why people, including some scientists, tend to perceive neuroscientific explanations as threatening free will when they are described in terms of neural processes fully causing actions to the exclusion of agents' reasons or reasoning processes.

1. Introduction

Consider a future brain imaging technology that would allow neuroscientists to see all of your brain activity, and with this information, they could know what you were going to think, decide, and do before you were even aware of making your decisions. While you are wearing this brain scanner (imagine it is a lightweight cap), the scientists can see, for instance, how you will vote in an election before you are aware of making your final decision. They make these predictions with 100% accuracy. Ask yourself, "Is such technology possible (even if not in our lifetime)? If it *were* possible, would it show that each of our decisions is caused by particular brain states? And would such technology show that we lack free will and moral responsibility?"

A scenario very much like this one is used by Sam Harris in his short book *Free Will* in order to "expose this feeling [of free will] for what it is: an *illusion*" and to help his readers understand that "the laws of nature [are] incompatible with free will" (2012, pp. 10–11).[2] This scenario might also suggest the "scientific vision" that Joshua Knobe (this volume) argues is incompatible with people's understanding of free will. It certainly seems to conflict with the "transcendence vision" as he defines it. If there were a "transcendent self," something that "transcends all the states and processes within the mind" and indeed "the whole causal order" (p. 70), then how could information about brain activity provide *complete* information, and perfect predictions, about what a person will think and do, before the person (the "transcendent self") is even aware of what he or she will decide? What role could such a transcendent self play in action?

If Harris and Knobe are accurately gauging ordinary people's views, then they should predict that most people will say that this brain-imaging technology could not be developed—that it would inevitably miss crucial information about what the transcendent self is thinking and deciding—and that if the technology did exist, it would rule out free will and responsibility. However, these predictions fail.

We presented people with a detailed explanation of this technology (see the scenario on p. 91). Most people responded that it could be developed, and roughly four out of five said that if it existed, it would *not* rule out free will or responsibility. We argue that these results, as well as other experimental philosophy results, including those discussed by Knobe, are best explained by a different theory of how most people understand the self and free will.

The chapter unfolds as follows: First, we describe a "naturalistic vision" of free will that represents a middle ground between the extremes Knobe (this volume) describes as the "scientific vision" and the "transcendence vision." We briefly explain why the naturalistic vision offers a plausible metaphysical theory that is consistent with what science tells us (so far) about the mind and that is consistent with most people's beliefs about the self and mind. We then present people's responses to our brain-scan scenario and our interpretations of these results. Next, we offer our interpretation of other results in experimental philosophy and introduce our "causal competition principle" to explain why people interpret some scenarios as threatening free will and responsibility. This principle, we conclude, also suggests that the plausibility of the naturalistic vision to laypersons will depend on whether a viable future scientific theory of mind fills out the naturalistic vision in a way that does *not* entail causal competition between conscious mental activity and brain activity.

2. The Naturalistic Vision as a Theory-Lite Compromise

Naturalism is a fuzzy term. That serves our purposes well, because we think that ordinary people have a fuzzy understanding of the nature of mind, action, and free will. Their theoretical commitments are relatively noncommittal and revisable. In contrast, both Knobe's "scientific vision" and his "transcendence vision" have more robust theoretical commitments, so we think a compromise between them will better capture most ordinary people's views.

Accepting naturalism commits one to the ontological thesis that whatever exists is composed of things that could be studied by the natural sciences and that conform to the laws of nature. As such, it does conflict with Knobe's dualistic transcendence vision, which posits an agent who transcends the causal order and makes choices while "not caused by anything at all" (p. 78).

Naturalism is compatible with various forms of physicalism in philosophy of mind, including both non-reductive and reductive varieties (Stoljar, 2009). However, naturalism does not commit one to a reductionistic ontological thesis that says the only things that *really* exist are whatever entities physics determines compose everything (such as subatomic particles or strings) or to a reductionistic epistemological thesis that says the best explanations and predictions will be those offered by lower level sciences (e.g., physics or neuroscience). As such, it is consistent with Knobe's general description of the "scientific vision"; however, it is not constrained by the reductionistic computer science metaphor he uses to introduce it.

Indeed, the naturalistic vision is consistent with a more complicated but less theoretically committed folk psychology than Knobe's scientific vision suggests. It is consistent with agents' having capacities for self-reflection, for consideration of reasons for various courses of action and for caring about some more than others, and for efforts to control one's decisions and actions in light of deliberation. The naturalistic vision is consistent with contemporary compatibilist accounts of free will as involving, for instance, identification (Frankfurt, 1988), a "deep self" (Wolf, 1990), and reasons-responsiveness (Fischer & Ravizza, 1998). Indeed, it is consistent with the sort of deliberative processes Knobe initially suggests in his metaphor for transcendence, in which the king or queen "listens to all of the arguments, thinks them over, and then decides" (p. 70). But, contra the transcendence vision, the self doing this deliberation is not a separate entity from the processes that constitute it, the self's choosing based on reasons is consistent with its being caused to choose by (some of) its psychological states, and the possibility of predicting action based on the states and processes in the mind is not precluded.

We think that some non-reductive physicalist form of naturalism provides the best metaphysical theory and epistemological approach to understanding and describing the mind and agency. And we think such a theory can support a viable compatibilist theory of free will. For the purposes of this chapter, however, we do not try to defend the truth of any specific theories of non-reductive physicalism or of compatibilism. Our goal here is to suggest that most ordinary people are *not* committed to a transcendence vision that conflicts with naturalism or compatibilism.

In order for ordinary people to have an understanding of mind, action, or free will that *conflicts* with a particular metaphysical or scientific theory, their understanding has to have substantive *content* that conflicts with that theory. We agree with Knobe (this volume) that the ordinary understanding of mind and action does not have the same structure as a scientific theory, except in the weak sense that people often explain and predict actions, which they typically do in terms of mental states, goals, and character traits. But this is not because most people have a *theory* that involves a transcendent self, noncausal reasons, or agent-causal powers that competes with the content of scientific theories of mind. Rather, we suspect that most people are "theory-lite."

By theory-lite, we simply mean that most people—at least before delving into philosophy, science, or theology—do not have commitments to the underlying structure of the mind or the underlying causal processes that connect mental states to each other and to behavior. When people consider a sentence such as "John went to New York because he wanted to visit his sister," they presumably think that John has desires and that these desires play some causal role in his going-to-New-York behavior. They will likely explain and predict John's behavior in terms of his desires, and with increasing knowledge of John and his environment, they may offer increasingly precise explanations and predictions, with reference to increasingly precise mental states (e.g., reasons that explain why he took the bus rather than the train). And barring mitigating factors, they will think John acted freely and is responsible. But people do not thereby commit themselves to metaphysical beliefs about the nature of John's mind or the source of his desires or decision-making capacities, being either nonphysical or physical, noncausal or (in)deterministically caused, supervenient on lower level mechanisms or not.

Another way to put this point is that people have a relatively nonnegotiable understanding of humans' basic capacities to make choices and control their actions, but they have relatively negotiable or revisable beliefs about what underlies these capacities—that is, the metaphysical or scientific nature of the substance(s), processes, or sources of them.[3]

In what follows, we suggest that the best explanation for people's responses to our scenario and for results from other work in experimental philosophy supports this theory-lite interpretation of ordinary views rather than a theory-laden view such as the transcendence vision. But first we need to respond to an objection that might appear to stop us dead in our tracks.

Almost every culture and religion includes beliefs and practices about the self or soul being able to survive after bodily death and to exist outside the body and about agents being different in kind from other entities and animals. Recent research suggests support for "folk dualism" across cultures and beginning in young children (e.g., Bering, 2006; Bloom, 2004). Indeed, in work in progress Nadelhoffer, Shepard, Nahmias, Sripada, and Ross (2013) find that most people express a belief that humans have souls. For instance, in one sample, 82% agreed that "each person has a non-physical essence that makes that person unique," and 61% agreed that "human action can only be understood in terms of our souls and minds and not just in terms of our brains."[4] If the folk theory is substance dualism, then the naturalistic vision is not folksy.

However, belief in and talk about souls, the afterlife, out-of-body experiences, and human uniqueness are not evidence of a substance dualist theory of mind or a transcendence vision of free will. Such beliefs are themselves theory-lite. Different cultures and religions describe disembodied existence in different ways, and in most cases, the self (soul or spirit) maintains a spatio-temporal form of some sort, often with quasi-physical properties. Few if any describe something like a Cartesian soul with no perceptual capacities, no clear way to be recognized or distinguished from other souls, and no spatial location (see Hodge, 2008). The afterlife in traditional Judaism and Christianity involves resurrection of the body, not disembodied existence (see Murphy, 2006). Even if some theological traditions are explicitly dualist, including those traditions' libertarian descriptions of free will, it is common that people do not internalize the metaphysical tenets of their religion's theology.

If we wanted to pin a philosophical theory of mind onto the folk, the best bet might be some form of functionalism, because functionalism allows that the mind or the self can be instantiated in any underlying stuff that can maintain the interrelationships among experiences, memories, emotions, and thoughts that make a person the particular person he or she is. People seem more committed to the existence of and relationships between certain mental categories than to any specific metaphysics of the mental (see also Buckwalter & Phelan, 2013).[5]

In short, people's understanding and talk of the "soul" might best be described as a placeholder for whatever underlies the set of capacities humans have for thinking, feeling, and acting, and whatever distinctive features of an individual's capacities make him or her the unique person he or she is. What fills this placeholder is, like many depictions of spirits and souls, vague and indistinct.

Most important for our purposes here, even if some cultures and people have a more specific conception of a nonnatural soul that does not jibe with the naturalistic vision, this does not commit them to the idea that free will or moral responsibility depend on such a soul. For instance, in the largely religious sample described in Note 4 to this chapter, only 30% agreed with the statement, "If it turned out that people lacked non-physical (or immaterial) souls, then they would lack free will" (with another third offering the neutral response), and 74% agreed with the statement, "People could have free will even if scientists discovered all of the laws that govern all human behavior." Furthermore, Monroe and Malle (2010) found that people do not mention nonphysical minds or souls when they describe free will, and in current work (Monroe, Dillon, & Malle, 2013), they use experimental manipulations to show that people's concept of free will is not tied to their concept of the soul. Mele (2012) found that most people responded that agents can have free will and moral responsibility even if physicalism is true.[6]

Finally, if people were committed to a dualistic or transcendent mind as grounding free will and responsibility, then they should be threatened by the possibility that their decisions and actions depend on, and can be predicted by, their brain processes. But, as we will now see, few people respond that way.

3. My Brain Did It . . . and So Did I

With a theory-lite understanding of mind and agency, people should not find some descriptions of naturalism threatening to free will or responsibility. To test this idea, we developed scenarios aimed at describing a possibility that rules out a transcendent self, or at least one that plays a causal role in actions, but that does not rule out a role for mental states and psychological processes. We cannot be sure that people are interpreting the scenarios in this way—one of the ongoing goals of experimental philosophy is to develop better methods to test how people are interpreting philosophical issues and which features of scenarios are driving their responses. We discuss below some of the results that give us more information about people's interpretations of our scenario.

The following is the scenario that participants read:

> Recent brain scanning studies have shown that specific patterns of brain activity can be used to predict simple decisions several seconds before people are consciously aware of those decisions. Imagine that in the future brain scanning technology becomes much more advanced. Neuroscientists can use brain scanners to detect all the activity in a person's brain and use that information to predict with 100% accuracy every single decision a person will make before the person is consciously aware of their decision. The neuroscientists cannot, however, do anything to change brain activity and hence they cannot directly influence thoughts and actions.

Suppose that in the future a woman named Jill agrees, as part of a neuroscience experiment, to wear this brain scanner for a month (it is a lightweight cap). The neuroscientists are able to use real-time information about her brain activity to predict everything that Jill will think or decide, even before she is aware of these thoughts or decisions. However, they cannot alter her brain activity to change what she thinks and does.

On election day, Jill is considering how she will vote for President and for Governor. Before she is aware of making any decisions, the neuroscientists can see, based on her brain activity, that she is about to decide to vote for Smith for President and Green for Governor. Just as the neuroscientists predicted, Jill votes for Smith for President and Green for Governor. As with her decisions to vote for Smith for President and Green for Governor, the neuroscientists are able to predict every decision Jill ends up making with 100% accuracy while she is wearing the scanner.

Occasionally, Jill tries to trick the neuroscientists by changing her mind at the last second or by stopping herself from doing something that she just decided to do, but the neuroscientists predict these events as well. Indeed, these experiments confirm that all human mental activity is entirely based on brain activity such that everything that any human thinks or does could be predicted ahead of time based on their earlier brain activity.

The survey was completed by 147 students enrolled in critical thinking classes at Georgia State University. After excluding from analysis participants who missed one or both of the comprehension checks preceding the experimental questions or an attention check at the end, there were 122 participants whose responses were analyzed.[7]

Participants were asked their level of (dis)agreement (on a 7-point scale with a midpoint of 4) with a series of statements about free will, responsibility, choice, and bypassing of mental states in three sets.[8] First, there were statements about Jill's specific acts of voting. Second, there were statements about Jill's general actions performed during the experiment, all of which began "During the experiment, when the neuroscientists predicted what Jill did . . ." Third, there were statements about "If this technology existed, then people . . ." would not have free will, be morally responsible, make choices, and so on.

Responses to all of the statements strongly supported our predictions. For instance, 91% agreed that "Jill voted for Governor of her own free will" (with 50.8% strongly agreeing, mean = 6.09), and 90.2% agreed that "Jill was responsible for how she voted for Governor" (mean = 6.05).[9] Similarly, 88.5% agreed that "During the experiment, when the neuroscientists predicted what Jill did, she had free will" (mean = 6.04), 94.3% agreed that she was responsible for what she did (mean = 6.14), 87.7% agreed that she made choices about what to do (mean = 6.00), and 86.9% agreed that what she did was "up to her" (mean = 5.95).

Only 12.3% agreed that "If this technology existed, then people would not have free will" (mean = 2.39); only 18.9% agreed that "If this technology existed, then people would not be morally responsible for their actions" (mean = 2.53); only 9.0% agreed that "If this technology existed, then people would not really make choices" (mean = 2.53); and only 11.5% agreed that "If this technology existed, then people would not truly deserve blame for their bad actions" (mean = 2.23).

In short, this detailed scenario describing perfect prediction of decisions based on brain activity did not lead people to conclude that free will is an illusion, nor did it show that people think that the mind or self is something that transcends the causal order and makes decisions that cannot be predicted based on "the complex ways in which these states and processes interact" (Knobe, this volume, p. 69). Only a small minority of people understood predictability based on brain processes to be incompatible with free will.

We suspect that most people are interpreting this scenario in a way that allows agents, such as Jill, to have (conscious) mental states, to deliberate, and to act on reasons. That is, most people are not interpreting the fact that decisions are predicted by—even caused by—brain states to mean that decisions are not *also* caused by the agent's reasons. Perhaps people are implicitly accepting some form of non-reductive physicalism or perhaps they are remaining theory-lite about how mental states and brain states are related to each other. In any case, most participants did *not* interpret the scenario to entail *bypassing*, or the view that mental states are causally irrelevant to behavior (see below). In our view, that is the main reason they are not interpreting the scenario to rule out free will.

We disagree with Knobe about whether people think free will requires a transcendent self outside the realm of physical causality; however, we agree with him that a nonnegotiable feature of people's understanding of free will and agency is that agents cause their actions and that agents' reasons have an effect on what they do. In our study we included statements to test whether people interpret this scenario to rule out either of these conditions. Consistent with the patterns of responses just described, 85.2% agreed that "Jill was the cause of how she voted for Governor" (mean = 5.80). Only 21.4% agreed that "During the experiment, when the neuroscientists predicted what Jill did, her reasons had no effect on what she did" (mean = 2.78). Only 15.5% agreed that "If this technology existed, then people's reasons would have no effect on what they did" (mean = 2.56). Indeed, there was a high correlation between people's responses to this bypassing statement (as well as others about whether this technology would show that people's beliefs or desires have no effect on their actions) and their responses to statements about free will and responsibility ($r = 0.59, p < .001$).[10]

These patterns of results suggest that only a minority of our participants (typically just one in five) find the possibility described in the scenario inconsistent with their understanding of free will and responsibility, and most of this minority group seem to be interpreting the scenario to involve bypassing of the agents' mental states, perhaps because this minority group is indeed employing a transcendent conception of the self. A significant majority of participants, however, do *not* see the naturalistic vision described in this scenario as suggesting bypassing, nor do they take its potential truth to suggest that we would lack free will or responsibility.

Our scenario was a "concrete" case, not an abstract case. That is, it included a specific agent making specific decisions. However, these decisions did not involve any emotionally laden actions.[11] Hence, the "error theory" offered in Nichols and Knobe (2007)—that high-affect cases, such as theirs with a man murdering his family, lead people to attribute responsibility in deterministic universes—would not explain our results. Knobe (this volume) no longer believes high affect is driving the concrete/abstract differences in attribution of free will or responsibility. Instead, Knobe suggests that concrete scenarios may lead participants to apply their "default (transcendence-based) framework" and blame agents even in a deterministic universe (see chapter 5, note 2). In our scenario, the agent is described concretely, and so, if Knobe's recent explanation is correct, then participants deem her morally responsible because they take the uncaused self to cause the agent's actions in accordance with her reasons. This explanation seems to us to require that most participants were not interpreting the scenario to rule out a transcendent self. We do not think this is the right interpretation of our results.

On the contrary, several results suggest that people are not simply rejecting the stipulations of the scenario as unrealistic nor are they responding without considering the ramifications of those stipulations. First, a significant majority of participants (80%) responded 'yes' when asked if they agreed with this statement: "It is possible for this technology to exist in the future."[12]

Second, when asked to explain why they thought the technology was or was not possible, no one mentioned free will or nonphysical souls or minds. For instance, no participants said that the mind cannot be understood in terms of the brain or that we have minds or souls that cannot be seen or understood with such technology or whose activity cannot be predicted by what happens in the brain. Rather, only three said something about mind reading being impossible in principle, whereas most of the others who said the technology is not possible mentioned the complexity of the brain, the high cost of such technology, or the moral or legal proscriptions people or governments would put on creating such technology.[13]

Third, we have evidence that people do respond to the stipulations of such scenarios. In another scenario, almost identical to this one, the technology also allows the neuroscientists to alter Jill's brain activity to change her decisions without her awareness. In that case, the vast majority of our 166 participants responded that, when her brain activity was altered, Jill lacked free will (80.2%) and responsibility (74.3%), and consistent with our view, the majority also responded that, in these cases, Jill did not cause her actions (74.3%) and her reasons did not play a role in her actions (59.4%). Hence, people do not take a "free will no matter what" position, and we have reason to believe that participants are responding to the specific features of the scenarios. For instance, they seem to be responding to the fact that the neuroscientists are indeed "reading" Jill's mental states by seeing patterns of her brain activity, and they are expressing their belief that such mind reading *without* manipulation is not a threat to freedom or responsibility.

Finally, we also asked people whether they agreed with this statement: "If this technology existed, it would show that each decision a person makes is caused by particular brain states." The majority (65.6%) agreed with this statement, even though the scenario does not explicitly say this or entail it—the scenario does conclude with the theory-lite claim that "these experiments confirm that all human mental activity is entirely based on brain activity." Responses to the causal statement did not correlate with other responses (except for two of the bypassing statements)—that is, participants who disagreed with this statement were no more (or less) likely to disagree with statements about Jill's or people's free will or responsibility. Hence, most people seem to interpret this scenario to mean that Jill's *reasons* are both caused by her brain states and cause her decisions. To the extent that people's theory-lite view is being "filled in" by the scenario, then it is likely that they assume that the neuroscientists are predicting Jill's behavior based on those brain states that *constitute* her reasons.

It is, of course, difficult to know exactly how participants are interpreting relatively complex scenarios, including this one and many of the other scenarios used in experimental philosophy research, including some of the ones Knobe (this volume) discusses. Much more research on these issues is required. However, by asking a variety of questions, including open-ended responses, and by examining the patterns of responses, we think the best interpretation of our results is that most people have a theory-lite view of the mind and free will, one that is consistent with naturalism and that suggests no commitment to Knobe's transcendence vision (and one that belies Harris's, 2012, assumptions about the ordinary view of free will).

We turn now to other results from experimental philosophy to argue that they too support this interpretation.

4. The Causal Competition Principle

Our brain-scan scenario does not explicitly describe determinism; however, it suggests that prior brain activity is sufficient for (and predictive of) decisions and actions. It is possible that some people would respond differently if the scenario were more explicitly deterministic.

However, prior research by Nahmias and collaborators (Nahmias, Coates, & Kvaran, 2007; Nahmias, Morris, Nadelhoffer, & Turner, 2006; Murray & Nahmias, 2012) suggests that most people do not find determinism to threaten free will or responsibility, and of those who do, most do so because they misinterpret determinism to mean bypassing—that psychological states and processes play no role in action. Knobe (this volume) suggests that these results, as well as his own, are better explained by assuming that most people have a transcendence vision of free will and that, when they properly understand determinism, they take it to conflict with that vision.

Knobe (p. 75) suggests this principle: People will be reluctant to hold an agent responsible for a behavior if they believe that this behavior was not even produced by the agent in question.

That principle is very hard to dispute.[14] But Knobe further suggests that this principle best explains the current body of research in experimental philosophy on free and responsible action—a claim that is easier to dispute. His interpretation of that data suggest that people go through this chain of reasoning:

Determinism → No production of behavior by agent
→ No free will or responsibility

Again, we agree with Knobe's principle, which constitutes the second step in this chain. But we disagree with his interpretation of the first step.

First of all, most people do *not* interpret determinism to mean that agents do not exist or that agents do not produce behavior. In Murray and Nahmias (2012), the majority of participants did *not* make the "bypassing mistake"—that is, they did not misunderstand determinism to mean that agents' beliefs, desires, and decisions play no role in what they end up doing (and most did not make that mistake in our brain-scan scenario). Only in Nichols and Knobe's (2007) abstract case did a significant majority of participants make the bypassing mistake. Knobe (this volume) interprets these responses to suggest that people think that (a) determinism rules out reasons explanations, because (b) reasons explanations are incompatible with causal explanations, but because (c) reasons explanations are explanations in terms of beliefs and desires, (d) determinism entails bypassing of beliefs and desires (pp. 77–78). And Knobe suggests that the other participants (who constitute the majority, especially in concrete cases) do not draw this conclusion from determinism because they interpret the agent's behavior as the result of the agent's transcendent self and this interpretation leads them to neglect the alleged threat of determinism.

We think a simpler explanation of the body of results first recognizes that most people do not make the bypassing mistake, because they see that even if an agent's mental states are fully determined by prior causes, that does *not* entail that the agent's mental states, including his or her reasons, are causally inessential to his or her actions. In concrete cases with descriptions of an agent making decisions for reasons, people are even more likely to see that the agent's mental states play a role in his or her actions rather than being bypassed. A similar process seems to occur in most participants reading our brain-scan scenario.

Second, people who *do* make the bypassing mistake are likely doing so because they perceive there to be "causal competition" between the factors presented in the scenario and the agent's mental states. We suggest this "causal competition" principle (CCP):

> People will be reluctant to hold an agent responsible for behavior when they interpret his or her behavior as being fully caused by factors that do not include any of his or her reasons (or by processes that do not include any of the agent's reasoning).

CCP is consistent with Knobe's idea that people will sometimes interpret reasons explanations to be inconsistent with causal explanations. But we think this occurs specifically when behavior is seen as produced by causal factors that are not responsive to—that do not vary according to—an agent's reasons.

CCP is similar to Björnsson and Persson's (2012) view that people will hold agents morally responsible when the agents' motivational structure is (a) such that holding them responsible will effectively alter or reinforce their behavior, (b) their motivational structure is a salient explanation of their behavior, (c) the behavior is such that it can be altered or reinforced, and (d) their motivational structure is morally significant (e.g., Fischer & Ravizza, 1998).

According to CCP, some descriptions of determinism are likely to lead people to think that agents are not free and responsible. This will occur, for instance, when people interpret the distant past as a complete cause of agents' behavior such that it competes with the agents' own mental states. Rather than taking agents' reasons to be produced by (and responsive to) prior events and as causes of decisions, people may take determinism to mean that everything is caused by the distant past, such that decisions must occur *regardless* of the agents' reasons. For instance, most participants read Nichols and Knobe's (2007) Universe A to mean that an agent will make certain decisions *no matter what*, such that the agent's decisions would not vary even if she had different mental states. This may be because their description of Universe A is presented in direct contrast with Universe B, in which *human decisions* occur and these decisions do *not* have to happen the way they do, suggesting that in Universe A decisions do *have* to happen the way they do *no matter what* (see Murray & Nahmias, 2012). We think the juxtaposition of Universe A and Universe B leads many people to think that a person's actions have to happen the way they do regardless of his or her reasons, perhaps even that humans do not really reason or make decisions in Universe A (after all, participants are told that Universe B is just like Universe A but "the one exception is human decision making").

Given that these descriptions of Universe A versus Universe B focus solely on this difference in decision making, we also do not find it surprising that fewer people make the bypassing mistake regarding processes such as computer programs or involuntary behavior. Indeed, Knobe's (this volume) examples of non-voluntary actions, such as eye blinks and making facial expressions, are also cases where the behavior is not responsive to reasons. So, because the difference between Universes A and Universe B is focused solely on human decision making, there is no reason for people to interpret Universe A as presenting causal competition between past events and nonvoluntary behavior or nonhuman processes.[15]

CCP can also explain why reductionistic explanations of human decision making are often taken to conflict with free will and responsibility. If agents' decisions and actions are presented as being completely caused by events at the neural level, with no mention of the agents' reasons or reasoning, then it is easy to conclude that their decisions are not responsive to reasons. For instance, Nahmias, Coates, and Kvaran (2007) provided participants with scenarios that described the actions of agents as completely caused by either psychological states, such as thoughts, desires, and plans, or neurobiological states, such as chemical reactions and neural processes. They found that participants were significantly more likely to attribute free will and responsibility to agents whose actions were described as caused by their psychological states than those agents whose actions were described as caused by their neurobiological states, although both cases described these proximal causes as being deterministically caused by earlier events.

Given that our brain-scan scenario also suggests causation by brain activity, one might wonder why most people do not make the bypassing mistake in that case. Although neuroscientists can predict Jill's voting behavior with 100% accuracy based on her brain activity, people presumably interpret her voting behavior as responsive to reasons. People might think that if Jill were to have voted for Black for Governor (instead of Green), she would have had different reasons prior to casting her vote. Although this counterfactual change of heart would also be predicted by the neuroscientists, they do not have the ability to alter her voting behavior—especially while holding her reasons constant. Consider instead the scenario we presented in which the neuroscientists could and did alter Jill's voting behavior before she was consciously aware of her decision. In this scenario, it is likely that people felt the change in her vote was due to the neuroscientists' alteration of her brain states (and perhaps *their* reasons) rather than her own reasons for casting a vote for Black.

This interpretation suggests avenues for future research. For instance, what alterations to the brain-scan scenario would lead most people to see it as undermining free will and determinism? CCP suggests the answer is any alteration that implies a causal explanation for agents' actions that competes with an explanation in terms of the agents' relevant mental states. In the scenario in which the neuroscientists were able to use the scanner to alter Jill's brain states, just the possibility of such manipulation slightly lowered ratings of her free will and responsibility (from 91% and 90.2% to 74.3% and 83.2%, respectively), even for decisions made without manipulation. For decisions that *were* manipulated, almost everyone responds that the agent *lacks* free will and responsibility (80.2% and 74.3%). In those cases, most people also judged that the agent's decisions were not caused by her own reasons (59.4%). Such results are consistent with Knobe's transcendence vision, but again there is no need to posit causal competition with a nonphysical soul when a less theory-laden vision explains both these and our earlier results.

Another follow-up experiment would involve tweaking the brain-scan scenario to indicate that the prediction of decisions and actions is based on brain states regardless of what the agent experiences herself as thinking or wanting. Such a description would pull apart mental states from their neural bases and prioritize the neural processes as causes of action, activating CCP. Conversely, we could develop the scenario to make more explicit that Jill's reasons for voting the way she did were completely caused by her earlier psychological states such as beliefs and desires. If people agreed that Jill's reasons could be completely caused in this way, it would suggest that the folk do not have a noncausal theory of reasons, as suggested by Knobe. He should predict that people would say that Jill's reasons in such a voting scenario could be different even if all her other psychological states (e.g., beliefs, desires) were the same. We predict that most people would respond that Jill's reasons could not be different holding fixed all of her mental states prior to her decision.

Most people seem comfortable with the idea that our reasons and reasoning can be predicted based on brain states, even instantiated in brain activity. Problems arise when we are instead presented with a picture of a person's neural processes "leading a life of their own," unrelated to what the person consciously thinks, wants, or decides. This is the picture that we believe leads some people, including some scientists (such as Harris), to think that the advance of neuroscience is challenging human agency and responsibility. This is the picture that makes some sense of the otherwise silly slogan "My brain made me do it."

5. The Way Forward

We conclude by asking, "Why would anyone think that this vision of neuroscience—and this seemingly silly slogan—make any sense?" In part, it is because the naturalistic vision remains, at this stage, a fuzzy sketch. At this early time in the development of the mind sciences, we still lack a theory to explain how mental processes, especially conscious ones, are ultimately constituted by neural processes (or physical processes more generally) and how to bridge explanations in terms of mental processes with explanations in terms of lower level mechanisms. Hence, it is easy to see neuroscientific explanations as competing with, and preempting, ordinary psychological or reasons explanations, especially in contexts in which the neuroscientific explanations are presented as complete explanations of behavior. However, once we develop a naturalistic theory to explain how consciousness, thinking, and reasoning work, we may not experience the "explanatory gap" we currently experience when trying to understand how matter makes minds.[16]

Of course, the naturalistic vision may get filled out in a way that does suggest causal competition between different levels or types of explanations for human action. Indeed, the sciences of the mind have already discovered various ways in which our understanding of our own minds needs to be revised.[17] Further discoveries may demonstrate that our ordinary conception of free will and responsibility is radically mistaken. However, for that to occur, the discoveries will have to provide some content that conflicts with the content of our ordinary understanding of these issues. We've suggested that such conflicts may be less likely to occur than Knobe and some scientists suggest, because, on one hand, the content of the ordinary view of mind and agency is less specific and substantive than they suggest and because, on the other hand, the sciences have not established a theory that conflicts with reasons explanations or establishes that conscious reasoning is not causal (see Nahmias, 2014). Because the ordinary view is theory-lite, it is more flexible than often presumed. Because the naturalistic vision remains relatively fuzzy, it is not clear how it will be filled out. We see no reason to believe that the ordinary view and the naturalistic vision will not, in the end, overlap sufficiently to conclude that they are still "talking about the same things," including free will and moral responsibility. We see no reason to conclude, as Knobe does, that a scientific theory of the mind and of free will requires abandoning our ordinary notions and replacing them with very different ones.

Notes

1. We are grateful to Shane Reuter and Jason Shepard for helpful discussions on these topics and collaboration on the new study described in this chapter and to Al Mele and Josh Knobe for helpful comments on earlier drafts. This chapter was completed in part with support from a Big Questions in Free Will grant to Eddy Nahmias from the John Templeton Foundation. The opinions expressed in this article do not necessarily reflect the views of the John Templeton Foundation.
2. Similar claims by scientists who argue that neuroscience threatens free will are widespread and receive much attention in the popular press. See, for instance, Greene and Cohen (2004),

Tancredi (2007), Montague (2008), Cashmore (2010), and Coyne (2012). For responses to some of these arguments, see Nahmias (2014).

3. Yet another way to put this is to say that people do not have strong views about the underlying metaphysical or scientific nature of the sorts of things that are part of what Sellars (1956) called the "manifest image," things such as colors, money, dogs, beliefs, agents, or solidity. People may be surprised to find out that solid objects are composed of mostly empty space, but that does not change most of their beliefs about, or talk of, solid objects, much less the way they interact with solid objects. It does not, and should not, lead people to believe or say that solidity is an illusion.

4. These results come from 330 participants from Qualtrics who are representative of the demographics of the general U.S. population. Knobe (this volume) also suggests that the results of Sarkissian et al. (2010) provide evidence for cross-cultural beliefs in incompatibilist free will. However, those experiments show that in every culture, between one third and one quarter of participants offered the minority response, and we think that it is a mistake to interpret the majority response to the abstract version of Universe A as indicative of a commitment to dualism or to incompatibilism (see the later discussion).

5. It is helpful to remember that even though Gilbert Ryle (1949) calls Descartes' view the "Official Doctrine," he then argues at length that our ordinary talk and beliefs about mental phenomena suggest a behaviorist (or perhaps better, functionalist) folk theory of mind, whereas substance dualism is driven by philosophical mistakes. Although people may not think of mental phenomena as physical, that does not thereby mean that they think of mental phenomena as *non*physical.

6. For instance, 73% agreed that agents could have free will after reading a scenario that included this description: "In 2019, scientists finally prove that everything in the universe is physical and that what we refer to as 'minds' are actually brains at work" (Mele, 2012, p. 430). Participants were not just responding that people have free will no matter what, because 79% said that agents would not have free will in a scenario describing a compliance drug.

7. Although college students are not particularly representative of the general U.S. (much less global) population, Georgia State University students are more representative of the religious, racial, and socioeconomic status of the U.S. population than most university populations. Nonetheless, 25% of this sample was nonreligious, which is roughly double the general population (we have not yet tested whether religious affiliation or religiosity correlates with any of the responses). Comprehension checks asked about whom Jill voted for and the attention check asks participants to answer "None of the above" in response to a long statement.

8. Statements were randomized within each of these three sets.

9. Responses were almost identical to statements about her voting for president. The two decisions were included because another study used a scenario in which the neuroscientists could alter her decisions before she was aware of making them, and we compared responses to statements about a decision that was not altered with one that was altered (see the following discussion).

10. For this correlation, we used a composite bypassing score (Cronbach's alpha = .870) and a composite free will and moral responsibility score (Cronbach's alpha = .703).

11. Presumably, mention of elections with no party names or recognizable political names is not stirring up participants' emotions.

12. Furthermore, responses to this question about the possibility of this technology did *not* correlate with responses to any statements about the consequences of this technology for free will or responsibility. It correlated with only one other statement: "If this technology existed, then people's reasons would have no effect on what they did" ($r = .196$, $p = .031$).

13. For what it is worth, we would respond that such technology is, in practice, impossible, because we think no technology will be able to both measure the incredibly complex activity of some neurobiological processes and simultaneously calculate the outcomes of such activity so as to predict *all* behavior with 100% accuracy. Assuming that conscious mental

processes supervene on neural processes, it is likely that some conscious deliberation processes cannot be predicted perfectly *prior* to their occurrence (see Nahmias, 2014, for discussion of how this point provides one response to the common claim that Libet-style results challenge free will). Of course, these points, like the ones raised by our participants, are consistent with the truth of naturalism, determinism, and the compatibility of free will with both.

14. Note, however, that the principle is not very informative, because (a) on its own, it tells us nothing about *when* people think an action is or is not produced by an agent and (b) it tells us nothing about the many circumstances in which people mitigate an agent's responsibility even though they also think she produced the behavior—for example, ignorance, coercion, compulsion, addiction. If one argues that these cases are best understood as cases where the agent does not really produce the behavior, then one seems to be adopting a compatibilist theory, such as the deep self view, which identifies the *responsible* agent with some subset of the agent's overall psychology.

15. This interpretation would be strengthened if the studies Knobe (this volume) describes included the contrastive description of decision making in Universe B, but we cannot tell whether he included the description of Universe B in these studies. CCP may also help to explain recent evidence that suggests that participants are less willing to hold an agent responsible for an action about which she is conflicted (Young, 2013). For example, an agent who wrinkles her face at her gay roommate having sex, even though she supports gay rights, is judged to be less responsible for wrinkling her face than an agent described as opposing or being indifferent towards gay rights. That is to say, participants judge those agents with psychological states that conflict with "endorsed" psychological states (reasons) to have less control of their resulting behavior compared to agents whose behavior does not conflict with endorsed psychological states. CCP explains the participants' reluctance to hold such agents responsible for their behavior: Their behavior is produced by states that conflict with their reasons.

16. Just as Copernicus provided good reasons to accept the heliocentric model, we have good reason to accept the naturalistic vision, but just as the Copernican model did not make sense of our experience of the earth being unmoving until Galileo's theory of inertia explained it, we lack a theory to help us understand how brain processes can explain our conscious experiences (for a valiant attempt, see Tononi, 2008).

17. For instance, see Doris (2002) and Nahmias (2007) for discussions of the ways that situationist social psychology raises challenges to our ordinary understanding of character traits, autonomy and moral responsibility.

References

Bering, J. (2006). The folk psychology of souls. *Behavioral and Brain Sciences, 29*, 453–462.

Björnsson, G., & Persson, K. (2012). A unified empirical account of responsibility judgments. *Philosophy and Phenomenological Research*. doi:10.1111/j.1933–1592.2012.00603.x

Bloom, P. (2004). *Descartes' baby: How the science of child development explains what makes us human*. New York, NY: Basic Books.

Buckwalter, W., & Phelan, M. (2013). Function and feeling machines: A defense of the philosophical conception of subjective experience. *Philosophical Studies, 166*, 349–361.

Cashmore, A. (2010). The Lucretian swerve: The biological basis of human behavior and the criminal justice system. *Proceedings of the National Academy of the Sciences, 107*, 4499–4504.

Coyne, J. (2012, January 1). Why you don't really have free will. *USA Today*. http://usatoday30.usa today.com/news/opinion/forum/story/2012-01-01/free-will-science-religion/52317624/1

Doris, J. (2002). *Lack of character: Personality and moral behavior*. New York, NY: Cambridge University Press.

Fischer, J.M., & Ravizza, M. (1998). *Responsibility and control: A theory of moral responsibility*. Cambridge, England: Cambridge University Press.

Frankfurt, H. (1988). *The importance of what we care about.* Cambridge, England: Cambridge University Press.

Greene, J., & Cohen J. (2004). For the law, neuroscience changes nothing and everything. *Philosophical Transactions of the Royal Society of London B, 359,* 1775–1778.

Harris, S. (2012). *Free will.* New York, NY: Free Press.

Hodge, K.M. (2008). Descartes' mistake: How afterlife beliefs challenge the assumption that humans are intuitive Cartesian substance dualists. *Cognition and Culture, 8,* 387–415.

Mele, A. (2012). Another scientific threat to free will? *The Monist, 95,* 422–440.

Monroe, A.E., Dillon, K.D., & Malle, B. F. (2013). *Bringing free will down to earth: People's psychological concept of free will and its role in moral judgment.* Manuscript in preparation.

Monroe, A.E., & Malle, B.F. (2010). From uncaused will to conscious choice: The need to study, not speculate about people's folk concept of free will. *Review of Philosophy and Psychology, 1,* 211–224.

Montague, R. (2008). Free will. *Current Biology, 18,* R584–585.

Murphy, N. (2006). *Bodies and souls, or spirited bodies?* New York, NY: Cambridge University Press.

Murray, D., & Nahmias, E. (2012). Explaining away incompatibilist intuitions. *Philosophy and Phenomenological Research.* doi:10.1111/j.1933–1592.2012.00609.x

Nadelhoffer, T., Shepard, J., Nahmias, E., Sripada, C., & Ross, L. T. (2013). *The free will inventory: Measuring beliefs about agency and responsibility.* Manuscript in preparation.

Nahmias, E. (2007). Autonomous agency and social psychology. In M. Marraffa, M. Caro, & F. Ferretti (Eds.), *Cartographies of the mind: Philosophy and psychology in intersection* (pp. 169–188). Dordrecht, the Netherlands: Springer.

Nahmias, E. (2014). Is free will an illusion? Confronting challenges from the modern mind sciences. In W. Sinnott-Armstrong (Ed.), *Moral psychology, vol. 4: Freedom and responsibility.* Cambridge, MA: MIT Press.

Nahmias, E., Coates, J., & Kvaran, T. (2007). Free will, moral responsibility, and mechanism: Experiments on folk intuitions. *Midwest Studies in Philosophy, 31,* 214–232.

Nahmias, E., Morris, S., Nadelhoffer, T., & Turner, J. (2006). Is incompatibilism intuitive? *Philosophy and Phenomenological Research, 73,* 28–53.

Nichols, S., & Knobe, J. (2007). Moral responsibility and determinism: The cognitive science of folk intuitions. *Noûs, 41,* 663–685.

Ryle, G. (1949). *The concept of mind.* London, England: Hutchinson's.

Sarkissian, H., Chatterjee, A., De Brigard, F., Knobe, J., Nichols, S., & Sirker, S. (2010). Is belief in free will a cultural universal? *Mind & Language, 25,* 346–358.

Sellars, W. (1956). Empiricism and the philosophy of mind. In H. Feigl & M. Scriven (Eds.), *Minnesota Studies in the Philosophy of Science,* vol. I (pp. 253–329). Minneapolis, MN: University of Minnesota Press.

Stoljar, D. (2009, Fall). Physicalism. *Stanford Encyclopedia of Philosophy.* http://plato.stanford.edu/archives/fall2009/entries/physicalism/

Tancredi, L. (2007). The neuroscience of "free will." *Behavioral Sciences and the Law, 25,* 295–308.

Tononi, G. (2008). Consciousness as integrated information: A provisional manifesto. *Biological Bulletin, 215,* 216–242.

Wolf, S. (1990). *Freedom within reason.* New York, NY: Oxford University Press.

Young, L. (2013). *The conflicted self does not cause its own actions.* Manuscript in preparation.

Part III Suggested Readings

Feltz, A., & Cokely, E. (2009). Do judgments about freedom and responsibility depend on who you are? Personality differences in intuitions about compatibilism and incompatibilism. *Consciousness and Cognition, 18*, 342–350.

Feltz and Cokely present some evidence that people's disposition to have compatibilist intuitions about free will and responsibility (i.e., to have the intuition that free will and responsibility are compatible with determinism) correlate with extraversion, one of the five personality dimensions.

Knobe, J. (2010). Person as scientist, person as moralist. *Behavioral and Brain Sciences, 33*, 315–329.

Knobe makes a case for the influence of moral considerations on judgment throughout cognition, including free will and responsibility.

Murray, D., & Nahmias, E. (in press). Explaining away incompatibilist intuitions. *Philosophy and Phenomenological Research*. doi:10.1111/j.1933–1592.2012.00609.x

This article argues that, when laypeople have incompatibilist intuitions about free will and responsibility (i.e., the intuition that free will and responsibility are incompatible with determinism), it is because they misunderstand determinism.

Nahmias, E., Coates, J., & Kvaran, T. (2007). Free will, moral responsibility, and mechanism: Experiments on folk intuitions. *Midwest Studies in Philosophy, 31*, 214–232.

This article examines whether describing determinism in psychological or neuroscientific terms has an influence on lay judgments about free will and responsibility.

Nahmias, E., Morris, S., Nadelhoffer, T., & Turner, J. (2006). Is incompatibilism intuitive? *Philosophy and Phenomenological Research, 73*, 28–53.

This groundbreaking article challenges the common view that laypeople are incompatibilist and suggests that people have compatibilist intuitions.

Nichols, S., & Knobe, J. (2007). Moral responsibility and determinism: The cognitive science of folk intuitions. *Noûs, 41*, 663–685.

Nichols and Knobe provide some evidence that judgments about free will and determinism vary depending on whether the judgments are about an emotion-eliciting situation.

Sarkissian, H., Chatterjee, A., De Brigard, F., Knobe, J., Nichols, S., & Sirker, S. (2010). Is belief in free will a cultural universal? *Mind & Language, 25*, 346–358.

This article provides evidence that some intuitions about free will and responsibility are found in many cultures.

Woolfolk, R.L., Doris, J.M., & Darley, J.M. (2006). Identification, situational constraint, and social cognition: Studies in the attribution of moral responsibility. *Cognition, 100,* 283–301.

Woolfolk and colleagues provide some evidence that judgments about responsibility are influenced by the extent to which an agent identifies with the action that he or she is doing, and that, as a result, people have compatibilist intuitions.

PART **IV**

Epistemology and the Reliability of Intuitions

CHAPTER 7

The Reliability of Epistemic Intuitions

KENNETH BOYD AND JENNIFER NAGEL

Abstract

This chapter argues that intuitions about particular instances of knowledge are generally a reliable guide to the nature of knowledge itself. We argue that there is antecedent reason to expect epistemic intuitions to be reliable due to their nature and function. We also argue that prominent challenges presented by experimental philosophers (e.g., that intuitions are susceptible to demographic and contextual variation) misrepresent available data and stem from debatable assumptions about the way people reason. Furthermore, we argue that disagreement about intuitions (both between "experts" and "laypeople" and among experts themselves) does not provide reason to think that epistemic intuitions are unreliable.

1. Introduction

You see Plato running right past you. Unfortunately, you mistake him for Socrates, and you form the confident belief that Socrates is running, based on what you have seen. As it happens, just at this very moment Socrates *is* running, in a distant city. Do you know that Socrates is running?

Trusting his audience to share his feeling that knowledge is absent here, the 14th-century philosopher Peter of Mantua used this example as ammunition against a theory according to which knowledge is just belief that is both confident and true (Boh, 1985). In doing so, he was engaging in a practice used by Eastern and Western philosophers from Plato's time to the present day: the practice of using epistemic intuitions—impressions about the presence or absence of knowledge and the like—as evidence in epistemology. Is this practice legitimate? Do these feelings about particular instances of knowledge generally serve as a reliable guide to the nature of knowledge itself? This chapter argues that they do and defends the practice of relying on intuitions against a variety of challenges.

The next section gives a brief overview of the nature of epistemic intuitions. Although people evaluate judgments along many dimensions of interest to epistemology, the main focus of this chapter is on propositional knowledge attributions, immediate judgments of the form "Jane knows that John is running." Section 3 lays out some of the main reasons why we might expect intuitions about the presence and absence of knowledge to be reliable. Section 4 examines the challenge of skepticism and discusses the difference between that challenge and the new challenge posed by non-skeptical experimentalists. Section 5 looks at evidence about variation in epistemic intuition across demographic factors such as ethnicity and gender. Section 6 looks at contextual variation in epistemic intuition, such as contrast effects. The final sections cover the impact of training in philosophy on epistemic intuitions and the problem of variation among philosophers in epistemic intuition.

2. The Nature of Epistemic Intuitions

We do not need to consult an explicit theory of knowledge in order to have the impression that someone knows something (or fails to know it). In describing epistemic intuitions as "immediate," we mean to contrast them with categorizations that require attention to a consciously available theory of the target concept. There are several signs that attention to an explicit theory of knowledge is not required when evaluating a case such as the one earlier. First, in evaluating such cases, we are not typically aware of any process of matching features of the case to features of a working theory of knowledge. It can sometimes be hard to say why one responded to a case as one did. Furthermore, it is possible for those who have a mistaken working theory of knowledge—such as Peter of Mantua's adversaries, perhaps—to find themselves responding intuitively to a novel case in a way that runs contrary to their working theory.

Intuitive judgments about knowledge and mere belief are not peculiar to philosophy. The words *know* and *think* are heavily used by ordinary people: They are the 8th and 12th most common verbs in English, and their counterparts are similarly common in other languages. All of the languages in the World Loanworld Database—a broad sampling of languages from every inhabited continent—report a word for *know* and *think*, both in the sense that embeds a propositional complement (Haspelmath & Tadmor, 2009). It is claimed that these verbs have the rare status of being "lexical universals," or terms with a precise (and typically one-word) translation in every natural language (Goddard, 2010). Children use both frequently, although *know* is acquired before *think* and is used more heavily (Bartsch & Wellman, 1995). The priority of knowledge attribution over belief attribution has been observed cross-culturally, in work on both the acquisition and use of the relevant verbs (e.g., Bassano, 1985; Tardif & Wellman, 2000) and in work on children's abilities to make sense of situations in which a person either has or lacks knowledge (e.g., Liu, Wellman, Tardif, & Sabbagh, 2008). From an early age, it is natural for human beings to make sense of others by thinking (and by talking) about what they know and about what they do not know. If—as seems to be the case—we generally do this without any explicit reflection on the concept of knowledge, then epistemic intuition is a feature of our everyday social navigation.

3. Why Expect Intuitions to Be Reliable?

The fact that people frequently make intuitive judgments about knowledge does not on its own establish that those judgments tend to be accurate. Some patterns of judgment are common and broadly shared but are systematically out of line with reality—for example, people show a tendency towards unrealistic optimism about themselves, their future, and their degree of personal control (Taylor & Brown, 1988). Such illusions are not pervasive, however: interestingly, they are suppressed when we deliberate, and surge when we must act (Taylor & Gollwitzer, 1995). Optimistic illusions are not helpful when we are figuring out what to do, but they serve a useful function in supporting confident action after a course of action has been decided. Those who are concerned about the reliability of epistemic intuition might wonder about the pressures toward accuracy or illusion shaping intuitive judgments about knowledge. Given that intuitive mechanisms are generally adaptive, a better understanding of the ordinary functions of epistemic intuition would help us answer this question.

Why do we have epistemic intuitions? The literature on mental state attribution identifies a variety of reasons why it is valuable for creatures like us to form rapid impressions about the presence or absence of knowledge. Animals living in social groups can better compete for resources (and keep control of them) when they are aware of whether their competitors do or do not know where the resources are located (Clayton, Dally, & Emery, 2007; Hare, Call, & Tomasello, 2001). More generally, the Machiavellian Intelligence Hypothesis (Whiten & Byrne, 1988) has stressed that animals in complex social groups gain competitive advantages from mindreading: Animals who are able to keep track of each others' underlying mental states do not simply expect the same surface patterns of behavior, but can more accurately anticipate changing behavior across changing circumstances. Specifically, competitive settings have worked to elicit impressive performance in mental state attribution from nonhuman primates and young children (Kaminski, Call, & Tomasello, 2008). In more cooperative settings—for example, in discriminating cues from "helpers," some of whom knew where food was located—nonhuman animals have performed poorly (Povinelli, Rulf, & Bierschwale, 1994). There is some evidence that nonhuman primates could sometimes gain advantages from recognizing each others' mental states in cooperative contexts (e.g., Russon, 1997), but the clearest evidence of cooperation eliciting mindreading comes from studies of humans. For example, 18-month-old toddlers seem to compensate for an adult's false belief in trying to help him (Buttelmann, Carpenter, & Tomasello, 2009).

Whether we are competing or cooperating, having accurate impressions of the epistemic states of others enables us to make better use of their expertise. If we can distinguish informants who are likely to know from those who are not, then the burden of gathering knowledge can be socially shared. In this vein, Sperber et al. (2010) have argued that mental state attribution plays a key role in "epistemic vigilance," or our capacity to monitor the quality of what others communicate to us. Developmental psychologists have shown that even very young children can apply their mindreading skills to distinguishing reliable from unreliable informants (e.g., Birch, Akmal, & Frampton, 2009). In this view, one reason why humans greatly outperform other animals in their recognition of states of knowledge and belief would be that communication is much richer in human than in nonhuman animals, warranting much more sensitive monitoring of its quality. The need for such monitoring constitutes one pressure toward accuracy in our intuitive attributions of knowledge.

Even experimentalists who challenge the reliability of epistemic intuitions sometimes explicitly grant that there could be a "common core" of shared and reliable intuitions (e.g., Starmans & Friedman, 2012; Weinberg, Nichols, & Stich, 2001). For example, their studies feature control condition cases whose subjects are consistently and unproblematically judged not to know, such as cases involving subjects who possess justified but false beliefs or unjustified but true beliefs. Strong agreement about simple cases arguably makes it more plausible that weaker agreement on more subtle cases arises from incidental features of the task of evaluating these cases, such as difficulty in following the narrative.

Whether agreement in the common core of intuition itself counts toward the evidential value of intuition in epistemology depends in part on the extent to which epistemology is guided by intuitions about these simple cases. One might argue that philosophical work on knowledge only concerns subtle cases that are not immediately decidable based on common and uncontroversially shared intuition. In subsequent sections, we take a closer look at the question of whether intuitions do reliably decide subtle cases, but however that issue is decided, it is plausible that at least some less subtle cases still matter to epistemology. For example, one place that core intuitions have had a significant impact is in the battle with skepticism: If most epistemologists are inclined to resist skepticism, this is perhaps in part because it seems intuitive that we do have knowledge in ordinary cases of clear perception and sound inference. Epistemological skepticism has, however, raised a deep challenge to the reliability of intuition even in these cases, a challenge that merits further examination.

4. The Challenge of Skepticism and the New Experimentalist Challenge

Skeptical philosophers typically acknowledge that we sometimes have the intuitive impression that someone has knowledge. Classical Pyrrhonian skeptics can be read as taking no position on the reliability of such impressions and as simply counseling that judgment be withheld on all matters. By contrast, the typical contemporary skeptic argues that positive impressions about knowledge are unreliable, at least if taken literally. According to this skeptic, human beings rarely if ever have knowledge of anything; although we often say such things as "he knows that it is raining out," such claims are almost always literally false.

On closer examination, the role assigned to epistemic intuitions within contemporary skepticism is somewhat tricky, and perhaps unstable. A useful illustration can be found in Peter Unger's (1971) early skepticism. Unger explains our intuitions about knowledge by means of a parallel with our intuitions about flatness, a concept he takes to have a similarly "absolute" structure. If we take even microscopic bumps into account, almost nothing is literally flat, but various surfaces (fields, roads, tables) may come closer than others to the condition of actual or absolute flatness. Conceding that our ordinary positive judgments about what is flat are not literally true, Unger leaves it open that these judgments reliably capture truths about what is flat enough for our purposes. In Unger's analogy, where flatness demands the absence of bumps, knowledge demands the absence of doubts. He contends that knowledge is absolute in the sense of requiring complete certainty, or the complete absence of doubt (apparently including even potential doubt). According to Unger, anyone who is more certain that $2 + 2 = 4$ than that $56 + 45 = 101$ cannot count as being fully certain or doubt-free in the latter judgment and, therefore, cannot count as knowing it. Read charitably, everyday attributions of knowledge to others amount to impressions that they have no actual or potential doubts that are relevant for our purposes, not that they have no actual or potential doubts whatsoever. Epistemic intuitions on this account do not track knowledge itself, but they do track some rough and purpose-relative approximation of knowledge and might still count as having some reliability in the sense of conveying useful information.

Interestingly enough, at a decisive point in his argument Unger himself relies on intuition: in defending the notion that complete certainty is indeed required for knowledge, Unger (1971) appeals to the intuitions we have when the key terms are emphasized. He observes that even if we initially find it acceptable to say that "he knows that it is raining, but he is not certain of it," we have a "feeling of contradiction" in response to "He really *knows* that it is raining, but he isn't actually *certain* of it" (Unger, 1971, p. 216). He concludes from this feeling that certainty is required for knowledge. How a skeptic can be so confident that such feelings are reliable is not obvious. Keith DeRose (1995) observes that there is an awkward asymmetry in the way the skeptic rejects all positive intuitions attributing knowledge while accepting negative intuitions about its absence.

Still, if the skeptic is right that there are ways of eliciting negative intuitions about ordinary mundane claims to knowledge—for example, by reflecting on problematic possibilities concerning brains in vats—then the epistemologist who trusts intuitions will have to come up with an explanation of those negative feelings and a story about how they fit with our more commonly positive feelings about the same judgments. One could follow DeRose (1995) himself in adopting contextualism, a view that takes the semantic content of the verb *know* to be variable, reflecting the concerns of the attributor of knowledge. On this view, intuitive claims about knowledge may be typically reliable, but their semantics is perhaps more complex than one might initially have imagined. It is also possible to advocate an error theory for the intuitions motivating skepticism, perhaps arguing that the skeptic's negative feelings arise from some psychological bias (Hawthorne, 2004; Nagel, 2010; Williamson, 2005b). Which approach is more satisfactory will presumably depend on factors going well beyond intuition itself, factors such as the internal coherence and empirical credentials of the relevant semantic, philosophical, or psychological theories.

The new experimentalist challenge to the reliability of epistemic intuitions is not a generic skeptical challenge: Experimental philosophers are not simply arguing that knowledge is impossible, nor are they arguing that intuitive capacities generally have unreliable or meaningless deliverances (Weinberg, 2007). Their claim instead is that we have empirical evidence for the unreliability of epistemic intuition. A review of this evidence is in order.

5. Demographic Variation

It has been claimed that epistemic intuitions vary according to ethnicity (Weinberg et al., 2001) and gender (Buckwalter & Stich, 2013). In their 2001 study, Weinberg et al. reported that participants of East Asian heritage were less likely to ascribe knowledge to the protagonist of a version of Lehrer's Truetemp case than were their Western counterparts and were much more likely to ascribe knowledge in Gettier cases, cases traditionally taken to show the difference between knowledge and justified true belief (Gettier, 1963). Meanwhile, Buckwalter and Stich reported significant differences in male and female intuitions about a wide range of philosophical topics, including Gettier cases, where one study found that female participants were much more likely to ascribe knowledge than were male participants. If people of differing ethnicity and gender disagree in their intuitions, then intuition-driven epistemology faces a problem. Jonathan Ichikawa (2014) calls the problem the "arbitrariness critique": Since my ethnic and sexual characteristics are purely arbitrary, so therefore are my epistemic intuitions. If my intuitions are arbitrary, then I should not consider them to be any special guide to the truth. Weinberg et al. put the question pointedly as follows: If my intuitions depend on whatever ethnic or sexual group I happen to be a part of, "why should we privilege our intuitions rather than the intuitions of some other group?" (2001, p. 45).

Many trusted sources of evidence have some arbitrary element: sensory perception, for example, typically has some margin of error, or some band within which judgments will vary arbitrarily. Experimentalists cannot criticize epistemic intuition simply on the grounds that not everyone reaches the same judgment at all times; a demand for perfect unanimity would be problematic for the sources of evidence that empirically motivated research programs need to take for granted. Systematic variation correlated with ethnicity or gender is also not in itself a reason to discount a source of information. For genetic reasons, women may have slightly better color vision, as a group, than men do; for reasons having to do with visual climate, some ethnic groups have slightly better eyesight than others. On certain subtle color discrimination tasks, there will be variation correlated with gender: A larger majority of women than men will get the right answer. However, such a finding should not incline either group to conclude that their color judgments lack evidential value. Demographically correlated variation in a capacity is consistent with its general reliability. We are forced to choose between our intuitions and those of some other group only if the relevant intuitions are deeply at odds with each other.

To date, there is no robust evidence that the epistemic intuitions of different demographic groups are deeply at odds with each other. Although the Weinberg et al. (2001) results have been heavily cited, it is doubtful that they are robust. The suggestion that South Asians tend not to feel Gettier case intuitions is especially puzzling; as early as the 8th century, South Asian philosophers developed cases very much like Gettier's—for example, cases in which someone infers a true conclusion from a false but reasonable belief—and reported that they took the subjects of such cases to lack knowledge (Matilal, 1986; Phillips, 2012; Stoltz, 2007). An effort to replicate the Weinberg et al. (2001) Gettier case results with multicultural North American participants failed to detect ethnically correlated differences in responding to Gettier cases (Nagel, San Juan, & Mar, 2013). A more thorough effort to replicate all the

Weinberg et al. (2001) epistemic case results with multicultural British participants also failed to turn up any ethnically correlated differences (Seyedsayamdost 2012, in press). John Turri (2013) also reports a lack of difference in evaluations of Gettier cases in tests of Western participants and participants from the Indian subcontinent, as well as between male and female participants.

It would, we think, be surprising if it turned out that the Weinberg et al. (2001) results were robust, given existing evidence of cross-cultural similarities in the ways states of knowledge and belief are attributed. It has been claimed, however, that there is independent contrary evidence that should lead us to expect cross-cultural disagreement about knowledge. Weinberg et al. (2001) cite as one main source of inspiration for their study, Nisbett, Peng, Choi, and Norenzayan's (2001) work on East–West differences in reasoning: The former group are said to favor more "holistic" reasoning, and the latter, a more "analytic" style. It's not obvious, however, how reasoning analytically rather than holistically would result in differences in epistemic intuitions, especially when facing Gettier cases, which are typically novel for study participants. Weinberg et al. (2001) mention that the Nisbett program has claimed that Westerners emphasize causation whereas Easterners emphasize similarity, and further observe that "in a large class of Gettier cases, the evidence that causes the target to form a belief turns out to be false" (pp. 442–443). However, it is not entirely obvious how knowledge attribution would differ as a function of increased attention to causation as opposed to similarity: Although it is true that there is something causally abnormal about these cases, given that most inferential knowledge is not derived from false beliefs, these Gettier cases show an equally conspicuous failure of similarity to ordinary cases of knowledge. In the absence of a clear story about the mechanism linking East–West differences to Gettier case responses, the Nisbett program does not give us clear reason to expect differences one way or the other.

Furthermore, the Nisbett program assumes that members of both cultures have both ways of thinking available to them; the difference is supposed to be one of prevalence and tendency rather than of capacity. Under conditions of similar motivation, and given similar prompts towards either analytic or holistic ways of thinking, members of either type of culture think in similar ways (Zhou, He, Yang, Lao, & Baumeister, 2012). The pressures involved in thinking carefully about philosophical cases would arguably be similar for Eastern and Western people, producing similar patterns of reasoning (which could be one reason why the Nagel et al. (2013), Seyedsayamdost (2012), and Turri (2013) results did not show culturally correlated divergence in epistemic intuition).

One could also challenge the empirical credentials of the Nisbett program itself: Some of its most epistemologically surprising claims, such as the claim that East Asians are tolerant of contradictions and weaker at rule-based reasoning, have not held up well under subsequent empirical testing or even in reanalysis of the original data (Friedman, Chen, & Vaid, 2006; Lee, Johson-Laird, & Sun, 2006; Unsworth & Medin, 2005). There is reason to suspect that at least some of the differences originally announced by the Nisbett program were overstated. Meanwhile, abundant cross-cultural similarities give us some reason to think that epistemic intuitions are more likely to be in agreement than disagreement with each other. For example, there are robust similarities across cultures in the development of mind reading, or "the capacity to interpret, predict, and explain the behavior of others in terms of their underlying mental states" (Scholl & Leslie, 1999, p. 132). Harris (1990) argues that available data "support the claim that the same theory of mind emerges universally in the young child with approximately the same time-table" (p. 222), and Segal (1996) argues that cross-cultural studies indicate that theory of mind development is "identical across the species" (p. 153). Similarly, Wellman, Cross, and Watson (2001) argue that performance on false-belief tasks "showed a consistent developmental pattern, even across various countries" (p. 655). Work on cross-cultural differences in mindreading tends to focus on disparities in performance, rather than underlying competence; indeed, it is stressed that the underlying competence is the same (e.g., Wu & Keysar, 2007). Empirical literature on cross-cultural variation in mindreading does not support the contention that the basic structural features of knowledge are seen to differ between cultures. At the structural level, commonalities are emphasized: "We can presume that people in all cultures operate on the same fundamental principles—we are all sentient, we all have knowledge, beliefs, desires and intentions, and these mental states interact in essentially similar ways" (Apperly, 2011, p. 165). Against this background, and without any clear story about why people from different cultures would disagree about the nature of knowledge, the burden of proof seems to lie on those who expect cross-cultural disagreement in epistemic intuition.

Similarly, although women and men differ in certain cognitive and non-cognitive tasks, it is again not obvious whether, if at all, such differences would affect epistemic intuitions. Beyond the age of 4, males and females in the non-clinical population do not seem to differ in the way they distinguish knowledge from ignorance and false belief (Charman, Ruffman, & Clements, 2002). To argue that men and women differ in their intuitions, Buckwalter and Stich (2013) actively solicited reports from experimental philosophers who had encountered significant gender differences in their experiments on intuitions. However, we should expect this method to turn up some significantly different results simply by chance: On the assumption that there is no significant relationship between gender and intuition, most studies will show men and women responding similarly, but some will show women outperforming men, and others will show men outperforming women. To establish that men and women really differ, one would need to disclose the total pool from which the disparities were drawn, to show the proportion of cases in which differences were found; Stich and Buckwalter have not done this.

The quality of the relevant studies also matters: much emphasis has been placed on a conference presentation presenting a gender difference in Gettier case recognition (Starmans & Friedman, 2009). Subsequent efforts to replicate that finding have failed (Seyedsayamdost, in press). Indeed, the authors of the 2009 presentation themselves regard their earlier finding as unrepresentative of male and female performance, and in a more recent and more detailed study they report no gender differences in epistemic intuitions (Starmans & Friedman, 2012).

Finding large gender differences on cognitive tasks is very unusual. After conducting a comprehensive review of 46 meta-analyses on gender differences, Janet Hyde (2005) summarized the available data as supporting the "gender similarities hypothesis," according to which "males and females are similar on most, but not all, psychological variables" (p. 581). The largest effect sizes in Hyde's meta-meta-analysis were found to be in motor performance and physical aggressiveness, that is, on noncognitive tasks (Hyde, 2005, p. 586). If males and females generally perform similarly on various cognitive tasks, we might expect them to have similar epistemic intuitions. Indeed, Banerjee, Huebner, and Hauser (2010) reported just such cross-gender similarity in intuitive moral judgments: They collected reports of intuitive moral judgments from over eight thousand subjects and found that while there was statistical significance in differences in the way that members of different genders responded in most scenarios, the overall effect size was "extremely small" (Banerjee et al., 2010, p. 270).

It is possible that there is some robust, large and yet-to-be-discovered demographic variation in epistemic intuitions, but the thought of this mere possibility does not constitute a positive empirical reason to consider epistemic intuitions unreliable.

6. Contextual Variation

In their 2008 study, Swain, Alexander, and Weinberg tested participants' intuitions about whether the main character of Lehrer's "Truetemp" case really knew what the temperature was or only believed it. The case concerns a man whose brain has received a prosthetic brain implant that gives him precise beliefs about the temperature: Unaware that his brain has been modified in this way, he finds himself reporting beliefs about the precise temperature, with no accompanying ideas about the credentials of these reports. The results of the study suggested that whether one reports the intuition that Truetemp has knowledge or only belief about the temperature correlates significantly with the order in which the case is presented. If the Truetemp case is presented immediately after a relatively clear case of ignorance—a case in which one claimed to know the result of a coin flip because of a "special feeling"—then subjects were much more likely to judge that Truetemp did, in fact, know what the temperature was. If, on the other hand, participants were first presented with a relatively clear case of knowledge—a case in which a chemist makes a well-informed judgment about the danger of mixing certain chemicals—they were less likely to judge that Truetemp had knowledge.

Interestingly, Swain et al. (2008) also tested the intuitions of participants about "Fake Barn" scenarios. This type of case can be described in a number of ways, but the classic example from Goldman (1976) concerns a man—call him Henry—who is driving through the country unaware that most of the things that look like barns are in fact mere facades. When Henry sees something that is in fact a barn and judges it to be one (but at such a distance, he would have been taken in by it, had it been one of the nearby facades), does he know that he is then looking at a barn? Swain et al. found the results for this case to be much less susceptible to contextual variation than the Truetemp cases (2008, p. 146). Notwithstanding this stability, Swain et al. consider their results to pose a twofold problem for those reliant on epistemic intuitions. First, that epistemic intuitions are susceptible to contextual variation suggests that such intuitions are "unstable" because they are "susceptible to manipulation" (Swain et al., 2008, p. 141). Of course, simply being susceptible to manipulation is not itself a reason to distrust intuition. Other faculties that we rely on are similarly susceptible but are nevertheless generally considered trustworthy; an obvious example is our reliance on perception. Indeed, as they note, Ernest Sosa (2007) anticipates the objection that manipulability is a reason to distrust a faculty:

> One would think that the ways of preserving the epistemic importance of perception in the face of such effects on perceptual judgments would be analogously available for the preservation of the epistemic importance of intuition in the face of such effects on intuitive judgments. The upshot is that we have to be *careful* in how we use intuition, not that intuition is useless. (p. 105)

However, Swain et al.'s second, and more significant, objection is that since certain intuitions seem to vary depending on context—for example, the Truetemp cases—and others do not—the Fake Barn cases—it's not clear which intuitions we can actually trust to remain stable and which we cannot. In relying on perception we are generally able to distinguish situations in which our perception is manipulated from those in which it is functioning properly— the philosopher's favorite "normal lighting conditions." Swain et al. argue that the case of perception and intuition are thus disanalogous: "[a]t this time, we don't know what is the parallel for intuition of making sure the light is on; that is, we do not know which are the circumstances that render intuition reliable or unreliable" (2008, p. 148). Of course, they do not deny that we might be able to find that something specific about the Truetemp cases makes them susceptible to contextual factors in a way that intuitions about other cases are not. However, if we are able to find out which intuitions are reliable and which are not, Swain et al. argue, it is not something that can be reasoned about a priori: Philosophers must get out of their armchairs to find the answers.

We take no issue with the suggestion that it would do philosophers some good to get out of their armchairs every once in a while. Once we are out of our seats, however, there is evidence that our intuitions may not be as unstable as Swain et al. (2008) make them out to be and that we do possess resources that allow us to know when the intuitive lighting conditions are normal. In her 2010 study, Wright similarly found contextual variation in responses to Truetemp cases and a lack of variation in responses to cases of "clear" knowledge or lack of knowledge (Swain et al.'s cases of testimonial inference and coin flips, respectively). The cases that elicited context-sensitive responses were dubbed "unstable," whereas those cases that did not elicit context-sensitive responses were dubbed "stable." Wright found, however, that participants reported "significantly more confidence when considering cases that elicited stable judgments than when considering cases that elicited unstable judgments, regardless of their order of presentation" (2010, p. 495) and had "significantly stronger beliefs (or, held their beliefs more strongly) about the stable cases than about the unstable cases" (2010, p. 500). Introspectively checking our confidence in an intuition that we possess might then be a good way of testing to see if the lighting conditions are normal. It is a general feature of intuitive judgment that more confident intuitive judgments are more likely to be stable within an individual and shared across populations (Koriat, 2012).

Wright (2010) cautions, however, that although laypeople's reported confidence and belief strength is lower in unstable cases than in stable ones, this is not necessarily the case for professional philosophers. A staunch defender of reliabilism might claim that they are very confident and believe very strongly that Truetemp has knowledge, whereas a critic might claim to have the same degree of confidence and belief strength in exactly the opposite position. What might explain the difference in confidence levels between trained and untrained philosophers? One obvious difference is the training itself: Wright suggests that trained philosophers might have more confidence in the "right" intuitions because they have a certain kind of expertise that the untrained do not. The next section takes a closer look at the idea that differences in intuition can be accounted for by differences in expertise.

7. Training in Philosophy

Is there evidence that laypeople's intuitions are systematically different from those of philosophers? Starmans and Friedman (2012) have claimed that laypeople differ from philosophers in their attributions of knowledge: Where trained philosophers recognize Gettier cases as involving justified true belief but a failure of knowledge, laypeople see only a special class of Gettier cases this way and, otherwise, equate knowledge with justified true belief. The special class of Gettier cases includes those about which an inference is made based on what they call "apparent evidence," where a subject infers something true from a false but reasonably held belief.

Starmans and Friedman (2012) posited expertise as one possible explanation for this discrepancy. For example, they considered the possibility that "philosophers might be very practiced in thinking about the myriad ways in which the truth of belief might rest on luck" (2012, p. 10). Starmans and Friedman did not find this explanation very plausible, however, since they claim that due to the quantity of questions and the way that the scenarios were set up, the luck element was "obvious" to participants (2012, p. 10). In a similar vein, Weinberg, Gonnerman, Buckner, and Alexander (2010) argued that there is a problem with favoring philosophers' intuitions on the grounds of their expertise, where expertise is being "able to efficiently pick out just the epistemologically-relevant features of hypothetical cases" (p. 338). This characterization is so nondescript, they caution, that it will be hard to know whether one actually possesses expertise, or if it really makes any difference. According to Weinberg et al., the "explicitness and clarity" of other philosophical distinctions (e.g., the use/mention, epistemological/metaphysical, and semantic/pragmatic distinctions) "stands in very sharp contrast to the complete inarticulateness of the . . . well, *whatever* it would be, that is supposed to help trained philosophers to categorize Gettier cases as non-knowledge" (2010, p. 342, ellipsis in original). Weinberg et al. do not argue that philosophers are wholly lacking in specialized professional expertise; for example, they explicitly grant that philosophers may have special skills in "the close analysis of texts" (2010, p. 335). There may be some room for the defender of epistemic intuition here. Although it is true that we do not have a full theory of whatever it is that enables us to recognize Gettier cases, one might wonder whether the skill and motivation needed to attend to and analyze a difficult text could itself be part of what is involved in the ability "to efficiently pick out just the epistemologically relevant features of hypothetical cases" (cf. Williamson, 2011).

Furthermore, it is an open question just how much disagreement there is between professional philosophers and laypeople. For example, if we look more closely at the scenarios Starmans and Friedman (2012) presented to their participants, we will find that they do not provide a strong case for the view that philosophers are unusual in their intuitions. Both of Gettier's original cases are clearly cases of inferring a true conclusion from a justified false belief (or "apparent evidence" cases, in Starmans and Friedman's, 2012, terminology). For epistemologists who rely on intuitions to guide and support their theories of knowledge, it would be heartening to read that the majority of lay participants are expected to agree with the standard verdict on the original Gettier cases. Starmans and Friedman cite Williamson (2005a) as evidence that philosophers "with near unanimity" believe that subjects in Gettier cases do not have knowledge (p. 9); however, Williamson is referring specifically to the response of philosophers to Gettier's original cases, a response which would be *supported* by Starmans and Friedman's (2012) results.

Starmans and Friedman (2012) did not actually test philosophers on the problematic cases in which laypeople unexpectedly attributed knowledge; instead, they support their contention that laypeople and philosophers would differ on these cases by noting structural similarities between these cases and some existing Gettier cases in the philosophical literature. One particular worry about the cases for which Starmans and Friedman found anomalous results is that they involved strange narratives in which an item is replaced with an identical duplicate behind a subject's back, and in at least some cases, it is somewhat unclear whether the replacement might have been managed precisely to ensure that the state of the world after the substitution matches the subject's original state of mind. It is not obvious that these really are Gettier cases, or that philosophers would respond to them differently than the laypeople, or that any discrepancies in lay responses to these cases arise from a different lay grasp of knowledge as opposed to differences in how attentively laypeople and philosophers are construing these hard-to-follow cases. Further research may help us understand whether philosophers really are different in their intuitive responses for these cases and, if so, why.

Some philosophers have suggested that philosophers' intuitive responses may be shaped by their intellectual climate (e.g., Gendler & Hawthorne, 2005). It is not clear, as a matter of empirical fact, whether this is true: They suggest that negative intuitions about Fake Barn cases may be traceable to some peculiarly philosophical pressures, but these intuitions have also been found in laypeople (Nagel et al., 2013; Wright, 2010). If philosophical climates do shape epistemic intuitions, this may or may not be a good thing. Perhaps the competition among theories of knowledge leads to a sharpening of the relevant intuitive capacities. If on the other hand the dominance of influential theories is driven primarily by factors unrelated to the truth of the claims they make, then perhaps any influence of philosophical climate on intuitions would diminish their reliability. However, there is no obvious reason to suppose that philosophical theories, unlike theories in other disciplines, tend to thrive for reasons completely unrelated to their truth. In any event, it is not clear to what extent theoretical commitments alter one's epistemic intuitions. It is certainly possible to have intuitions that go against one's own working theory of knowledge; for example, Alvin Goldman shifted from his early causal theory of knowledge (1967) to his later reliabilist theory (1976) in part because he came up with certain examples that did not intuitively seem to be examples of knowledge, notwithstanding their conformity to his earlier theory. As far as we now know, it may even be that one's epistemic intuitions are wholly insulated from theoretical commitments in epistemology, as judgments in syntax appear to be insulated from theoretical commitments in syntactic theory (Sprouse & Almeida, 2012; Sprouse, Schutze, & Almeida, 2013). Further research could improve our understanding of the relationship between epistemological theory and epistemic intuition; meanwhile, the hypothetical possibility that intuitions could be shifted by theory is not in itself a reason to doubt the reliability of epistemic intuition.

8. Disagreement Among Philosophers

Philosophers sometimes report disagreement about particular cases. In epistemology, there has been particular controversy over whether subjects in Fake Barn–type cases lack knowledge (Millikan, 1984; Turri, 2011). Many, but not all, philosophers have reported the intuition that the subject does not have knowledge in these cases and have diagnosed this verdict as arising from an implicit recognition that knowledge requires reliability, or more specifically safety from error: If a person knows, he or she could not easily have gone wrong in a similar case.

A split in intuitive reactions to this case might be taken as a sign that some people but not others operate with an implicit theory of knowledge according to which knowledge requires safety, and that common epistemic intuition is therefore powerless to decide the question. However, it is conceivable that discord is arising from incidental features of the case, rather than variation in implicit understandings of knowledge itself. The original story is arguably ambiguous about whether Henry's judgment is safe. The standard description of the case leaves it quite open exactly what risk Henry is exposed to, in part because it does not specify what kind of inquiry Henry is engaging in as he drives along, whether he is trying to make his mind up about everything he sees and whether there is a serious chance of his looking at a fake barn at the moment he sees the real one. In support of such a line of thought, Keith DeRose (2009) observes that intuitions about this case are very sensitive to details about how it is fleshed out. For example, if we describe Henry as making a string of false "barn" judgments about a series of facades before he encounters the one real barn, it is easier to see that latter judgment as failing to exemplify knowledge (DeRose, 2009, p. 49).

Cases will not be informative if they simply stipulate their verdicts, but they must say enough to trigger an implicit classification of the judgment one way or the other. Because various details are inevitably left to the reader's imagination, many controversial cases lend themselves to a variety of different construals, and in some cases, these differences can be epistemologically significant. For example, Jennifer Nagel (in press) has argued that many of the cases involved in the clash between internalism and externalism—including the Truetemp case—are open to being read either as examples of knowledge or ignorance, depending on whether we represent the subject of the case as being self-conscious about the peculiarity of his or her belief formation; if internalists are inclined to read the case one way, and externalists another, they may not be giving different answers to the same question. If this approach is right, then greater care in our stipulations can produce greater uniformity in our subsequent epistemic intuitions. One of the difficulties involved in setting up a case is to say enough about the situation to ensure that one's reader will share one's understanding of its underlying facts; given that we do not yet fully understand the nature of knowledge, there is no quick formula to check that any given scenario has specified all the relevant facts in sufficient detail.

Even with all the relevant facts made clear, if epistemic intuitions still vary among individuals on certain cases, this is not necessarily a sign that intuition is generally unreliable. If some individuals have a form of color-blindness to certain types of problem, it would be hasty to conclude that intuitions should be seen as unreliable across the board. Contemporary epistemologists have conflicting rival theories but share a considerable band of common intuitions about philosophically interesting cases. In cases where intuition is divided, intuition can be retested on clearer and less ambiguous cases; intuition can also be corroborated or corrected by theoretical and empirical work in logic, psychology, semantics, and philosophy itself. Epistemic intuition is not infallible, but at present it looks reliable enough to continuing serving its traditional function of supplying us with valuable evidence about the nature of knowledge.

References

Apperly, I. (2011). *Mindreaders: The cognitive basis of "theory of mind."* Hove, England, and New York, NY: Psychology Press.

Banerjee, K., Huebner, B., & Hauser, M. (2010). Intuitive moral judgments are robust across variation in gender, education, politics and religion: A large-scale web-based study. *Journal of Cognition and Culture, 10,* 253–281.

Bartsch, K., & Wellman, H. (1995). *Children talk about the mind.* New York, NY: Oxford University Press.

Bassano, D. (1985). Five-year-olds' understanding of "savoir" and "croire." *Journal of Child Language, 12,* 417–432.

Birch, S.A.J., Akmal, N., & Frampton, K.L. (2009). Two-year-olds are vigilant of others' nonverbal cues to credibility. *Developmental Science, 13,* 363–369.

Boh, I. (1985). Belief, justification and knowledge—Some late medieval epistemic concerns. *Journal of the Rocky Mountain Medieval and Renaissance Association, 6*, 87–103.

Buckwalter, W. & Stich, S. (2013). Gender and philosophical intuition. In J. Knobe & S. Nichols (Eds.), *Experimental philosophy, volume II*. New York, NY: Oxford University Press.

Buttelmann, D., Carpenter, M., & Tomasello, M. (2009). Eighteen-month-old infants show false belief understanding in an active helping paradigm. *Cognition, 112*, 337–342.

Charman, T., Ruffman, T., & Clements, W. (2002). Is there a gender difference in false belief development? *Social Development, 11*, 1–10.

Clayton, N. S., Dally, J. M., & Emery, N. J. (2007). Social cognition by food-caching corvids: The western scrub-jay as a natural psychologist. *Philosophical Transactions of the Royal Society B: Biological Sciences, 362*, 507–522.

DeRose, K. (1995). Solving the skeptical problem. *Philosophical Review, 104*, 1–52.

DeRose, K. (2009). *The case for contextualism: Knowledge, skepticism, and context, volume 1*. New York, NY: Oxford University Press.

Friedman, M., Chen, H. C., & Vaid, J. (2006). Proverb preferences across cultures: Dialecticality or poeticality? *Psychonomic Bulletin & Review, 13*, 353–359.

Gendler, T. S., & Hawthorne, J. (2005). The real guide to fake barns: A catalogue of gifts for your epistemic enemies. *Philosophical Studies, 124*, 331–352.

Gettier, E. (1963). Is justified true belief knowledge? *Analysis, 23*, 121–123.

Goddard, C. (2010). Universals and variation in the lexicon of mental state concepts. In B. Malt & P. Wolff (Eds.), *Words and the mind* (pp. 72–93). New York, NY: Oxford University Press.

Goldman, A. (1967). A causal theory of knowing. *The Journal of Philosophy, 64*, 357–372.

Goldman, A. (1976). Discrimination and perceptual knowledge. *The Journal of Philosophy, 73*, 771–791.

Hare, B., Call, J., & Tomasello, M. (2001). Do chimpanzees know what conspecifics know? *Animal Behaviour, 61*, 139–151.

Harris, P. (1990). The child's theory of mind and its cultural context. In G. Butterworth & P. Bryant (Eds.), *Causes of development: Interdisciplinary perspectives* (pp. 215–237). Hillsdate, NJ: Erlbaum.

Haspelmath, M., & Tadmor, U. (2009). *World Loanword Database*. Retrieved from http://wold.livingsources.org/

Hawthorne, J. (2004). *Knowledge and lotteries*. New York, NY: Oxford University Press.

Hyde, J. S. (2005). The gender similarities hypothesis. *American Psychologist, 60*, 581–592.

Ichikawa, J. (2014). Who needs intuitions? Two experimentalist critiques. In A. Booth & D. Rowbottom (Eds.), *Intuitions*. Oxford, England: Oxford University Press.

Kaminski, J., Call, J., & Tomasello, M. (2008). Chimpanzees know what others know, but not what they believe. *Cognition, 109*, 224–234.

Koriat, A. (2012). The self-consistency model of subjective confidence. *Psychological Review, 119*, 80–113.

Lee, N. Y. L., Johnson-Laird, P., & Sun, R. (2006). Are there cross-cultural differences in reasoning? In R. Sun (Ed.), *Proceedings of the 28th Annual Meeting of the Cognitive Science Society* (pp. 459–464). Mahwah, NJ: Erlbaum.

Liu, D., Wellman, H. M., Tardif, T., & Sabbagh, M. A. (2008). Theory of mind development in Chinese children: A meta-analysis of false-belief understanding across cultures and languages. *Developmental Psychology, 44*, 523.

Matilal, B. K. (1986). *Perception: An essay on classical Indian theories of knowledge*. Oxford, England: Oxford University Press.

Millikan, R. (1984). Naturalist reflections on knowledge. *Pacific Philosophical Quarterly, 65*, 315–334.

Nagel, J. (2010). Knowledge ascriptions and the psychological consequences of thinking about error. *Philosophical Quarterly, 60*, 286–306.

Nagel, J. (in press). Knowledge and reliability. In H. Kornblith & B. McLaughlin (Eds.), *Goldman and his critics*. Oxford, England: Blackwell.

Nagel, J., San Juan, V., & Mar, R. (2013). Lay denial of knowledge for justified true beliefs. *Cognition, 129*, 652–661.

Nisbett, R., Peng, K., Choi, I., & Norenzayan, A. (2001). Culture and systems of thought: Holistic versus analytic cognition. *Psychological Review, 108*, 291–310.

Phillips, S. H. (2012). *Epistemology in Classical India: The knowledge sources of the Nyaya School.* New York, NY: Routledge.

Povinelli, D. J., Rulf, A. B., & Bierschwale, D. T. (1994). Absence of knowledge attribution and self-recognition in young chimpanzees (Pan troglodytes). *Journal of Comparative Psychology, 108*, 74–80.

Russon, A. E. (1997). Exploiting the expertise of others. In R. W. Byrne & A. Whiten (Eds.), *Machiavellian intelligence II: Extensions and evaluations* (pp. 174–206). New York, NY: Oxford University Press.

Scholl, B. J., & Leslie, A. M. (1999). Modularity, development and "theory of mind." *Mind & Language, 14*, 131–153.

Segal, G. (1996). The modularity of theory of mind. In P. Carruthers & P. K. Smith (Eds.), *Theories of theories of mind* (pp. 141–157). Cambridge, England: Cambridge University Press.

Seyedsayamdost, H. (in press). On gender and philosophical intuition: Failure of replication and other negative results. *Philosophical Psychology.*

Seyedsayamdost, H. (2012). On normativity and epistemic intuitions: Failure of replication. Manuscript in preparation.

Sosa, E. (2007). Experimental philosophy and philosophical intuition. *Philosophical Studies, 132*, 99–107.

Sperber, D., Clement, F., Heintz, C., Mascaro, O., Mercier, H., Origgi, G., & Wilson, D. (2010). Epistemic vigilance. *Mind & Language, 25*, 359–393.

Sprouse, J., & Almeida, D. (2012). Assessing the reliability of textbook data in syntax: Adger's core syntax. *Journal of Linguistics, 48*, 609–652.

Sprouse, J., Schutze, C., & Almeida, D. (2013). A comparison of informal and formal acceptability judgments using a random sample from *Linguistic Inquiry* 2001–2010. *Lingua, 134*, 219–248.

Starmans, C., & Friedman, O. (2009, October). *Is knowledge subjective? A sex difference in adults.* Paper presented at the 6th Biennial Meeting of the Cognitive Development Society, San Antonio, Texas.

Starmans, C., & Friedman, O. (2012). The folk conception of knowledge. *Cognition, 124*, 272–283.

Stoltz, J. (2007). Gettier and factivity in Indo-Tibetan epistemology. *The Philosophical Quarterly, 57*, 394–415.

Swain, S., Alexander, J., & Weinberg, J. M. (2008). The instability of philosophical intuitions: Running hot and cold on Truetemp. *Philosophy and Phenomenological Research, 76*, 138–155.

Tardif, T., & Wellman, H. M. (2000). Acquisition of mental state language in Mandarin- and Cantonese-speaking children. *Developmental Psychology, 36*, 25–43.

Taylor, S., & Gollwitzer, P. (1995). Effects of mindset on positive illusions. *Journal of Personality and Social Psychology, 69*, 213–226.

Taylor, S. E., & Brown, J. D. (1988). Illusion and well-being: A social psychological perspective on mental health. *Psychological Bulletin, 103*, 193–210.

Turri, J. (2011). Manifest failure: The Gettier problem solved. *Philosophers' Imprint, 11*, 1–11.

Turri, J. (2013). A conspicuous art: Putting Gettier to the test. *Philosophers' Imprint, 13*, 1–16.

Unger, P. (1971). A defense of skepticism. *The Philosophical Review, 80*, 198–219.

Unsworth, S. J., & Medin, D. L. (2005). Cultural differences in belief bias associated with deductive reasoning? *Cognitive Science, 29*, 525–529.

Weinberg, J. M. (2007). How to challenge intuitions empirically without risking skepticism. *Midwest Studies in Philosophy, 31*, 318–343.

Weinberg, J. M., Gonnerman, C., Buckner, C., & Alexander, J. (2010). Are philosophers expert intuiters? *Philosophical Psychology, 23*, 331–355.

Weinberg, J. S., Nichols, S., & Stich, S. (2001). Normativity and epistemic intuitions. *Philosophical Topics, 29,* 429–460.

Wellman, H., Cross, D., & Watson, J. (2001). Meta-analysis of theory of mind development: The truth about false belief. *Child Development, 72,* 655–684.

Whiten, A., & Byrne, R. W. (Eds.). (1988). *Machiavellian intelligence: Social expertise and the evolution of intelligence in monkeys, apes and humans.* Oxford, England: Clarendon Press.

Williamson, T. (2005a). "Armchair" philosophy, metaphysical modality and counterfactual thinking. *Proceedings of the Aristotelian Society, 105,* 1–23.

Williamson, T. (2005b). Contextualism, subject-sensitive invariantism and knowledge of knowledge. *The Philosophical Quarterly, 55,* 213–235.

Williamson, T. (2011). Philosophical expertise and the burden of proof. *Metaphilosophy, 42,* 215–229.

Wright, J. C. (2010). On intuitional stability: The clear, the strong, and the paradigmatic. *Cognition, 115,* 491–503.

Wu, S., & Keysar, B. (2007). The effect of culture on perspective taking. *Psychological Science, 18,* 600–606.

Zhou, X., He, L., Yang, Q., Lao, J., & Baumeister, R. F. (2012). Control deprivation and styles of thinking. *Journal of Personality and Social Psychology, 102,* 460–478.

CHAPTER 8

The "Unreliability" of Epistemic Intuitions

JOSHUA ALEXANDER AND JONATHAN M. WEINBERG[1]

Abstract

Debate over the status of intuitions in philosophical practice is marred by an ambiguity about "unreliability." Many authors, including Boyd and Nagel in this volume, have defended the reliability of intuitions in the baseline accuracy sense of "on balance, right more often than wrong." We agree that intuitions should likely be considered reliable in that sense. But that is not the sense in which their reliability has been under attack. Rather, the sense of reliability most relevant for understanding experimentalist critiques of intuitions is trustworthiness, for which baseline accuracy is perhaps a necessary, but by no means sufficient condition.

1. Introduction

According to a rather common way of thinking about philosophical methodology, philosophical intuitions play a significant role in contemporary philosophy.[2] On this view, they are an essential part of our "standard justificatory procedure" (Bealer, 1998) or the "method of standard philosophical analysis" (Pust, 2000) and are part of what makes philosophical methodology unique (Goldman, 2007; Levin, 2004). We advance philosophical theories on the basis of their ability to explain our philosophical intuitions, and appeal to them as evidence that these theories are true and as reasons for believing as such. Although examples of this way of thinking about philosophical methodology abound, the example most frequently discussed by Kenneth Boyd and Jennifer

Nagel (and passim in the literature) comes from Gettier (1963), which aims to show that knowledge is not simply justified true belief. Gettier's paper included two hypothetical cases involving a person who has deduced a true belief on the basis of a justified false belief and, on that basis, formed a justified true belief that doesn't *seem* to count as knowledge. We are supposed to just see this, and this philosophical intuition is in turn supposed to count as sufficient evidence against the claim that a person knows that p just in case that person's true belief that p is justified.

Whether these authors have characterized this practice in exactly the right way, we take there to be a broad consensus that these characterizations are at least in the right neighborhood, and something roughly like this methodological practice is operative with some substantial currency in analytic epistemology today, and for at least the last few decades.[3] Over the last several years, this way of thinking about philosophy has been repeatedly challenged on the basis of both general epistemological reasons (Cummins, 1998; Kornblith, 2002; Stich, 1988) and more specific methodological concerns (Alexander, 2012; Alexander & Weinberg, 2007; Weinberg, 2007). These methodological challenges have focused not on whether philosophical intuitions *could* be a good source of evidence of some sort but rather on whether such intuitions are to be trusted in the ways that they are currently used in actual philosophical practice, given how little we know about them, and given some of the dangerous bits of information that we have about them. Although it has become somewhat standard to frame these methodological concerns in terms of the *reliability* of philosophical intuitions, we want to resist this move, arguing instead that the central methodological concern is about intuitional *sensitivity*.

Like Boyd and Nagel, we focus on *epistemic* intuitions and argue that recent concerns about the evidential status of epistemic intuitions can unproblematically acknowledge their overall reliability, at least as "reliability" is standardly used in epistemology today. If the evidential status of such intuitions in epistemology is going to be defended from this challenge, then it will just not help much to argue that they are on average true more often than false. As we argue, any attempts to defend current epistemological practice would require work of a different sort, targeting not baseline accuracy, but rather inappropriate sensitivity.

2. Two Senses of Reliability

Let's distinguish two meanings of *reliability*, because we want to dispute whether epistemic intuitions are currently reliable in one sense, while stipulating to their reliability in another sense. In ordinary usage, *reliable* is basically a synonym either for *trustworthy* or *highly predictable*. It applies not only in epistemic contexts, where we talk about things like reliable eyewitnesses, but beyond such contexts as well. We talk, for example, about someone's being a reliable friend or a reliably good guest at a dinner party. Someone who is reliable at x is someone can be expected to hit a high x-value some suitably large proportion of the time, where what counts as a suitably large proportion will be domain relative. Reliably safe drivers had better get into a wreck no more than a vanishingly small percentage of the times they get behind the wheel, whereas someone who gets onto base "only" 40% of the time is a fabulously reliable batter. There are perhaps pejorative applications of the ordinary "reliably" as well; for example, someone who is reliably late for dinner is someone who is tardy to the table more often than is ideal. Nonetheless, we name this the *trustworthiness* sense of reliability. Compare this with epistemological use of this term, where *reliable* is defined strictly in terms of the propensity of true deliverances of some source of evidence or belief-forming process, and where something's reliability is measured on a somewhat standard scale with a floor somewhere significantly about 50% and a threshold probably not greater than 95% and certainly not as high as 100%—reliability need not require infallibility. We will call this the *baseline accuracy* sense of "reliability," and have in mind something quite like what Goldman (1979) is talking about when he says, "(as a first approximation) *reliability* consists in the tendency of a process to produce beliefs that are true rather than false" (p. 10, italics original).

The baseline accuracy sense of reliability plays an obvious role in epistemology, where philosophers have used this notion of reliability to build theories of knowledge and justification, but many other debates in philosophy can also be appropriately framed in terms of baseline accuracy. The "rationality wars," for example, may well be fought over whether or not our ordinary inferential capacities are baseline accurate. And even debates about eliminativism about propositional attitudes can perhaps be understood in terms of whether our descriptive and predictive folk-psychological practices are more or less accurate or are wholesale mistaken. It is important to note that baseline accuracy is a fairly coarse-grained concept, but these are debates that can operate at a fairly coarse grain. Even champions of propositional attitudes such as Fodor would be happy to grant that we can be wrong fairly often in our attributions of beliefs and desires, arguing that these mistakes, as common as they may be, need to be viewed against a background of a pretty high level of success.

Although they do not always explicitly state it in such terms, the nature of their arguments throughout indicates that Boyd and Nagel are clearly interested in a project of defending the overall baseline accuracy of our folk epistemic intuitions, and we have no objections to this kind of project.[4] We think that it is a perfectly respectable project for philosophers to pursue, and for experimental philosophers to pursue in particular, and we are broadly inclined to agree with their assessment that our folk epistemic intuitions are generally, and on the whole, reliable. Let's call this the *general reliability thesis* (GRT). It is not unheard of for debates about the evidential status of philosophical intuitions to be framed in terms of GRT. Goldman (2007) defends the use of philosophical intuitions on explicitly reliabilist grounds, as does Bealer (1998) in terms of a modally strong form of reliability, and even some critics have framed their arguments in terms of a deficit of reliability (for example, Machery, 2011). Nonetheless, reliability is not the only epistemological machinery that has been used to frame these kinds of debates. Stich (1988), one of the urtexts in recent debates about philosophical methodology, raises worries about how we would justify picking between systematically different, but locally coherent sets of philosophical intuitions.[5] Cummins (1998) raises worries about our inability to independently calibrate philosophical intuitions in situations in which we are worried that they may have gone awry. More recently, Weinberg (2007) stipulates to the baseline accuracy of intuitions, but goes on to allege that a paucity of resources for error detection and error correction renders much current philosophical practice with intuitions "hopeless."

Those challenges do not require anything like the denial of GRT, and we are inclined to think that any successful attempt to challenge the evidential status of epistemic intuitions on the basis of the kind of work being done in experimental philosophy has to follow suit. Here is why. GRT is a thesis about an overall propensity for correctness—that is, for the proportion of verdicts that are true out of the total set of verdicts. The kind of work being done in experimental philosophy raises worries about our intuitions about specific hypothetical cases or families of cases. This kind of work does not show anything about what proportion of the total set of relevant cases these specific hypothetical cases compose, and it is hard to see how it possibly could. Even if there were dozens of such cases—and there are only a handful at this time—that would not go very far at all toward establishing the negation of GRT unless we had good reason to think that the total reference class of cases has a cardinality similarly in the dozens, which does not strike us as antecedently plausible. Moreover, any argument against the GRT needs to make serious estimates of the ratio of bad apples to the total volume of the barrel, and no one has to our knowledge even attempted to make such estimates.[6] We also wholeheartedly agree with those who, in trying to defend epistemic intuitions, have pointed out that if our intuitive capacities on the whole were unreliable in the baseline accuracy sense, that would be tantamount to an unpalatably strong form of skepticism. That is not a consideration that can preempt any serious empirical attempt to falsify GRT, but, as far as we are concerned, it is a reason to want to find a way to raise concerns about the evidential status of epistemic intuitions that is consistent with a broad endorsement of GRT. Put another way, any successful challenge to the evidential status of epistemic intuitions needs to focus on whether they are trustworthy, while respecting the fact that they are reliable in the baseline accuracy sense of reliability at stake in GRT.

3. The Restrictionist Challenge and the Threat of Inappropriate Intuitional Sensitivity

Intuitional diversity has gotten perhaps the most attention, critical and otherwise. It is easy to see why, because part of what underwrites the practice of pursuing epistemological questions through the lens of our epistemic intuitions is the (often unarticulated) presupposition that these intuitions are more or less universally shared.[7] Moreover, standard machinery from the epistemology of disagreement might make it seem relatively easy to move from intuitional diversity to worries about the reliability of intuitional evidence; after all, evidence of disagreement is prima facie reason to worry about evidence.[8] So we understand why so many authors engaging with this topic, including Boyd and Nagel, have focused so much of their attention on the diversity results. There is something odd about what they have to say about intuitional diversity, however. They suggest that intuitional diversity is a problem only in contexts where the relevant intuitions are "deeply at odds with one another," going on to argue that there is currently "no robust evidence that the epistemic intuitions of different demographic groups are deeply at odds with each other" (Boyd & Nagel, this volume, p. 115). But this is a mistake. All that is needed in order for intuitional diversity to be a problem is that the diversity reflects different "epistemic vectors" of the sort that would become encoded in similarly divergent epistemological theories (see Weinberg, Nichols, & Stich, 2001). If different groups of people have intuitions that are subtly sensitive to different sorts of factors (and if we are going to avoid epistemic relativism), then someone's intuitions have to turn out to be sensitive to the wrong things.[9]

There is also danger here in focusing too tightly on questions of diversity. So far as the larger debate about philosophical methodology is concerned, intuitional diversity is really just a species of a more general category of problematic intuitional *sensitivity*. We want our sources of evidence to be sensitive, of course, but we want them to be sensitive to all and only the right kinds of things; that is, whatever is relevant to the truth or falsity of the relevant set of claims. It turns out that at least some epistemic intuitions are sensitive to more than just these kinds of things; they are sensitive to aspects of who we are, what we are being asked to do, and how we are being asked to do it. There is a large range of well-motivated and prima facie–substantiated hypotheses about such sources of noise in various sorts of philosophical intuitions, far more than just ethnicity, gender, and order effects, including such demographic dimensions as personality (Feltz & Cokely, 2009) and such seemingly philosophically irrelevant differences as whether people are asked to imagine themselves thinking about the case "in a few days" versus "in a few years" (Weigel, 2011), or even what font the case is presented in (Weinberg, Alexander, Gonnerman, & Reuter, 2012). Some of these have been observed specifically in knowledge attribution tasks, too, such as an apparent effect of age on fake barn intuitions (Colaço, Buckwalter, Stich, & Machery, in press), and the influence of the moral valence of a proposition on whether or not an agent counts as knowing it (Beebe & Buckwalter, 2010)—an effect apparently capable of leading subjects to attribute knowledge in what otherwise should be Gettier (1963) cases. These kinds of intuitional sensitivity are both *unwelcome* and *unexpected*, and the very live empirical hypotheses of their existence create a specific kind of methodological challenge to armchair intuitional practices in philosophy, which we have called the *restrictionist challenge* (Alexander & Weinberg, 2007).

The restrictionist challenge starts by raising an empirically plausible concern that such sensitivity may very well be found in intuitions of the sorts commonly found in contemporary philosophical practice, and as used in that practice. Given that concern, restrictionists suggest that we must pursue both local methodological restrictions on our uses of intuitional evidence at the practical level and a global shift in how we think about intuitional evidence and the business of doing philosophy. To understand what this means, think about the frequent comparison between intuitional evidence and perceptual evidence, a comparison endorsed by Boyd and Nagel (this volume). Ernest Sosa (2007) argues that, although we know that perceptual evidence displays patterns of unwelcome sensitivity, this simply causes us to be more careful about what perceptual evidence we use and when we use it. But it pays to be careful only when we know what it means to be careful, and here is where the comparison between intuitional evidence and perceptual evidence breaks down. We have a pretty good understanding of when sense perception goes wrong, something reflected in our perceptual practices and reinforced by a communal scientific understanding of the mechanisms responsible for our perceptual judgments. This prevents worries about unwelcome perceptual sensitivity from giving rise to global concerns about the epistemic standing of perceptual evidence. The problem is that we are not in the same position with respect to intuitional evidence. Our comparatively scarce resources for predicting unwelcome intuitional sensitivity put us in a different epistemic position with respect to intuitional evidence than we are in with respect to perceptual evidence.[10] In a sense, we have not learned yet what it would mean to be careful. Learning how to be careful will require developing a better understanding of how epistemic intuitions work. If we are going to learn what intuitional evidence can be used and when intuitional evidence can be used, we need to know more about where epistemic intuitions come from, what mechanisms are responsible for producing them, and what factors influence them, and this will require looking to the relevant psychology, cognitive science, and empirically informed philosophy of mind. It is important to be clear that the restrictionist challenge nowhere involves the argument that philosophical intuitions are evidentially bankrupt, in their entirety and once and for all time.[11] Rather, what is being urged is that the proper evidential role for philosophical intuitions is one that can only be viewed clearly from outside the armchair, and both bounded by and grounded in a scientific understanding of them.

For present purposes, it is particularly important to see that the restrictionist challenge does not take a stand on the overall reliability of epistemic intuitions on the whole; the central methodological problem is that we know that at least some intuitional evidence is problematically sensitive without being able to predict what intuitional evidence is problematically sensitive, and this is a problem regardless of the overall reliability of our epistemic intuitions. Our limited ability to predict when and where a problem will arise can be dangerous, even if we were to have reason to think that the problem will arise only rarely. This is especially true when the stakes are high, for example, in situations in which a small number of cases are granted large amounts of power in theory selection.[12] Here, the Gettier (1963) cases are again illustrative. Our (allegedly) shared epistemic intuitions about these cases are supposed to count as sufficient evidence that a person's justified true belief need not count as knowledge. This is only one (rather famous) example in which our shared epistemic intuitions have been allowed to trump theory, but there are many others, and when the stakes are this high, understanding how and when things go wrong becomes more important than knowing that they *usually* go right. This example also provides us with a different way of understanding why GRT does not matter all that much in this kind of debate about philosophical methodology. It is a basic constraint in contemporary epistemology that any reasonable theory of knowledge needs to deny that Gettier cases involve knowledge. If epistemologists were wrong about these cases, then pretty much every mainstream theory of knowledge would turn out to be incorrect. Still, Gettier cases compose a miniscule fraction of potential cases involving knowledge attribution. So even if epistemologists were wrong *only* about Gettier cases, although the overall reliability of our epistemic intuitions would be enormously high, we would still be in a state of complete epistemological disaster.

Setting even these kinds of worries aside, another reason to worry is that there is an important mismatch between the kind of reliability thesis that Boyd and Nagel defend in their chapter and the one that is actually at stake in recent debates about philosophical methodology. Remember that trustworthiness is relative to domains, and also to purposes. The restrictionist challenge aims at a practice whose scope and goals may diverge substantially from those of our folk epistemic practices, even despite a fair amount of similarity and overlap between the practices of analytic epistemology and our epistemic folkways. Here, we focus on three kinds of divergence and point out that each further undercuts the relevance of the baseline accuracy of our folk epistemic attributions to the methodological debate at hand.

First, epistemologists are very often interested in cases that involve extensive details that we suspect are not ecologically valid. Very often, these cases include highly specific information about an agent's mental states and processes, together with some story about how these states and processes connect with other features of the fictional vignette, where this information may not be available to the agent and is of a sort almost never available in the real world. Gettier (1963) cases are again good examples of this, and it is important to keep this feature of these cases in mind regardless of whether non-hypothetical analogs can be constructed for many hypothetical thought-experiments (Williamson, 2007).[13] Our folk capacity to think about epistemological issues has likely been shaped to evaluate situations where we typically have rather sparser, noisier access to what might be going on in someone's head. This mismatch between philosophical thought experiments and the proper domain of our folk epistemic capacities will weaken an attempted inference from accuracy on the latter to our trustworthiness in using the former.[14]

Second, epistemologists want to do something with knowledge attributions that the folk are not typically interested in doing, namely, using them to argue for their preferred epistemological theories. Although Gettier (1963) cases are perhaps the most famous paradigm of high-stakes cases in epistemology, they are not the only members of that set. The literature is full of important cases, and our intuitions about such cases are often meant to place substantial constraints on our epistemological theorizing: to comply with their verdicts or face a nontrivial burden of otherwise accommodating them when we wish to dissent from them. Some of these cases are fairly ordinary, such as the intuition that one typically does not know in advance that one has lost a lottery simply in virtue of knowing that the odds of one's having won are miniscule. But very often they are more high-flying or esoteric, such as those involving evil demons (old and new), or clairvoyants, or bizarre brain lesions with weird effects not to be found even in the works of Oliver Sacks. There's a good methodological reason that such funky cases are both common and important in analytic epistemology: We are often trying to get some evidential traction in the slippery effort of rationally preferring one very good epistemological theory over rival, very good epistemological theories. This helps show how Boyd and Nagel get matters somewhat the wrong way around in their discussion of ordinary versus subtle cases; it does not really matter much whether epistemologists sometimes, or even very often, deploy ordinary cases, so long as they also rely crucially on more esoteric cases. Yet the very factors that make intuitions about unusual cases methodologically crucial also lead us to expect them generally to be more error prone. They will be more susceptible to subtle effects of context, for example, because they will often involve splitting apart distinct features that commonly go together in knowledge attribution and using them against one another, such as the baseline accuracy of a piece of cognition and the availability of at least some considerations that speak in favor of that accuracy. Different contexts may cue up different weightings of such features in our unconscious categorizing systems and, thus, have an increased potential to produce different attributions.

As for group differences in cognition, that stands as a vibrant and hotly debated topic in psychology these days, and, we think, a rather more open question than Boyd and Nagel take it to be. But we do not need to take sides in that ongoing debate here. For our purposes, it is enough to note that in order to raise worries about the relevant philosophical practices, one need not go as far as Nisbett, Peng, Choi, and Norenzayan (2001) or Henrich, Heine, and Norenzayan (2010), and claim strong and pervasive differences between "WEIRD" Westerners and the rest of the world. For example, although he is a prominent critic of those authors and their claims of deep group differences in cognition, even Mercier (2011) suggests that we should still expect to find fine-grained cultural differences in knowledge attributions, even against a widely shared background of cognitive convergence. We conjecture that these more subtle differences in folk epistemologies will be more likely to manifest in the unusual and marginal sorts of cases that are popular with epistemologists, than in ones that are evaluated and discussed in some frequency in civilian life. It is thus consistent with high baseline accuracy for epistemic intuitions in general that the sorts of intuitions that are important in analytic epistemology may suffer more from unwanted and unanticipated sensitivities.[15]

Third, a key feature of analytic epistemology involves the kinds of inferences in which our epistemic intuitions play a role.[16] Boyd and Nagel conclude with the claim that epistemic intuition is "reliable enough." But one question that must be asked here is, Reliable enough *for what cognitive purposes*? For most of the purposes involved in everyday cognition, we are inclined to agree with Boyd and Nagel that epistemic intuitions are probably trustworthy enough to guide us in our quotidian transactions with the world. But our philosophical purposes are far more exacting, and one clear way to see this is in the kinds of inferential uses to which epistemic intuitions are put in epistemology, but not in ordinary life. It is not an exaggeration to think that *every* epistemological theory that is based at all on our epistemic intuitions is based on sophisticated inferences driven substantially by those intuitions—no one thinks that they can just read the correct epistemological theory directly off of the cases, non-inferentially. As such, to the extent that we are interested in questions about baseline accuracy here, it seems that we should not particularly care about the baseline accuracy of the epistemic intuitions themselves but rather about the inferences that will be based on those intuitions. We do not just want our theories to be based on premises that are mostly true; we also want our theories themselves to be mostly true. What is at issue is not the obvious point that inferences should be conditionally reliable, but whether conditional reliability is enough, and there is reason to worry that it is not, and that some additional dimension of epistemic evaluation is needed.

To see why, consider two inference rules that are equally reliable on all true inputs but whose reliability diverges sharply as soon as the quality of the inputs begins to degrade: one inference rule that takes 10 propositions as inputs and outputs their 10-way conjunction and another inference rule that takes the same 10 propositions as inputs and outputs their 10-way disjunction. These two rules are maximally conditionally reliable; when all of the inputs are true, both will produce true outputs. Yet when the quality of the inputs degrades, so does their reliability—but not in the same way, and that is where this other dimension of evaluation can be seen. For the 10-way conjunction rule becomes maximally conditionally *un*reliable as soon as any of its inputs deviate from the truth, whereas the 10-way disjunction remains maximally conditionally reliable so long as at least one of its inputs is true. This dimension of the evaluation of rules of inference closely resembles a related issue in the evaluation of models, in which we evaluate them in terms of *robustness*, or how well they withstand alterations to their basic assumptions and parameter settings. So, let us call this dimension of inference evaluation *error robustness*. Here we want to suggest that part of determining whether our epistemic intuitions are trustworthy involves determining how error robust are the epistemological inferential practices that take epistemic intuitions as inputs. The more error-fragile one's inference rules are, the less tolerant of unwanted sensitivities one can afford to be in one's premises.[17]

And there is good reason to worry that the inferential practices of analytic epistemology are highly error fragile. Remember that we are talking about a practice whose operating norms allow counterexamples to trump theory. Weatherson (2003) provides a nice description of this feature of analytic epistemology (and other areas of analytic philosophy):

> In epistemology, particularly in the theory of knowledge, and in parts of metaphysics, particularly in the theory of causation, it is almost universally assumed that intuition trumps theory. Shope's *The Analysis of Knowledge* contains literally dozens of cases where an interesting account of knowledge was jettisoned because it clashed with intuition about a particular case. In the literature on knowledge and lotteries it is not as widely assumed that intuitions about cases are inevitably correct, but this still seems to be the working hypothesis. (p. 1)

Weatherson immediately goes on to claim that epistemologists (and other philosophers) are wrong to let counterexamples trump theory, and indeed to argue very cleverly for this claim over the course of his paper.[18] But to the extent that his description of the inferential practices of analytic epistemology is correct, and we think he is largely on target here, this suggests that the inferential practices of analytic epistemology will be highly error fragile.[19] This means that very little threat of error is needed in order to generate the kinds of methodological concerns that drive debates about the evidential status of epistemic intuitions.

4. Defending the Evidential Status of Epistemic Intuitions: Is There Life Beyond the Armchair?

Because the restrictionist challenge does not take a stand on the overall reliability of our epistemic intuitions, it makes little difference whether the overall baseline accuracy of our epistemic intuitions turns out to follow from some widely shared, ordinary folk capacity to think about epistemic issues. This suggests that a different kind of defense of the evidential status of epistemic intuitions in philosophical practice is needed, one that goes beyond merely affirming the baseline accuracy of folk epistemic intuitions, and is instead pitched more directly both at the specific sorts of intuitional sensitivity that experimental philosophers are warning about, and at the specific contours of analytic epistemology. But what could that defense look like? There seem to be at least two options. One option involves taking the second part of the restrictionist challenge seriously by engaging in the kind of careful empirical work needed to understand where epistemic intuitions come from, what mechanisms are responsible for producing them, and what factors influence them. This means *more* empirical work for philosophers, not less. It also means that philosophers need to continue to improve the methods used to study philosophical cognition, combining survey methods with more advanced statistical methods and analyses, and supplementing survey methods with a wider variety of methods from the social and cognitive sciences (Alexander, 2010, 2012; Scholl, 2007; Weinberg, in press). Perhaps most important, it means that philosophers have to resist the temptation to jump too quickly to broad philosophical conclusions based on what individual studies seem to show. Science is slow business, and we need to resist the urge to make it go faster simply because that would better suit our philosophical goals.

Now, Boyd and Nagel are at least somewhat on the same page here, in that they happily acknowledge the importance and relevance of experimental work. And some of Nagel's own scientific work represents a high-water mark in exactly the kind of careful investigation of epistemic intuitions that we are advocating here. Where we sharply diverge from their take on the current state of play, however, is on the *necessity* of such work. Because they only consider the question of baseline accuracy of epistemic intuitions, primarily with a focus on the question of "deep" intergroup differences, they are comfortable taking current philosophical practice to be more or less in good order as it stands. Although these practices can be usefully supplemented by experimental work, on their view, such work would basically be methodologically supererogatory. Intuitions are already, they say, "reliable enough." However, once we recognize that baseline accuracy is insufficient for methodological trustworthiness, it should also become clear that current intuitional practice cannot be adequately defended on the terms that Boyd and Nagel offer. There is too much threat of error from too many possible sources of sensitivity, and we are still at such an early stage of these investigations that mostly what we are learning is how much we yet have to learn, with strange new candidates for unwanted effects popping up every year. (For example, Nagel, San Juan, and Mar (2013) can be viewed as identifying a surprising new pattern of intuitional sensitivity in terms of empathy.) Given the nature of the restrictionist challenge, then, defending the reliability-as-trustworthiness-for-epistemological-purposes of intuitions will *require* the sorts of work we are advocating, and on a fairly expansive scale.

The understandable desire to avoid needing to shoulder such a burden may explain the popularity of another family of defenses: arguing that experimental philosophers have not actually been studying the right *kind* of thing. These kinds of defenses look to preempt the restrictionist challenge before it can even get off the ground: If there are no appropriate studies that have yet been performed, then our armchair methods are not (yet) in a state of challenge. As Boyd and Nagel note, one particularly popular version of this kind of response, which we have called the *expertise defense*, involves arguing that philosophers are interested in expert philosophical intuitions rather than folk philosophical intuitions (Hales, 2006; Ludwig, 2007; Williamson, 2007). But who has expertise about what and under what circumstances turns out to be a rather complicated empirical question. It seems that only certain kinds of training help improve task performance and, even then, only for certain kinds of tasks, and there is reason to worry that philosophical training is not the right kind of training and that philosophical thought experimenting is not the right kind of task (Alexander, 2012; Weinberg, Gonnerman, Buckner, & Alexander, 2010). What is more is that what empirical work has been done on expert philosophical intuitions does not look particularly promising for proponents of the expertise defense. These studies seem to suggest that expert intuitions display much of the same kind of intuitional sensitivity that folk intuitions display (Knobe & Samuels, 2013; Machery, 2012; Schultz, Cokely, & Feltz, 2011; Schwitzgebel & Cushman, 2011; Tobia, Buckwalter, & Stich, 2013). There is plenty of room for further empirical investigation here, and we would expect that philosophical training (or selection) will ward off at least *some* of the unwanted effects that may afflict folk epistemic intuitions. But we can see no intellectually respectable way at this time, given the current state of the literature, to hold to the expertise defense without any such further results in hand.

There is an illuminating comparison here to linguistics, especially if we connect the expertise question up with the issue of error fragility discussed earlier. Boyd and Nagel cite some interesting recent work that suggests that syntactic intuitions of professional linguists are *generally* well-shielded from unwanted influence of the theoretical background of the intuiting linguists. But the sorts of inferences that linguists make are so error fragile that even the fairly small remaining degree of intuitional error on the part of linguists poses a dire methodological threat. For example, Gibson, Piantadosi, and Fedorenko (2013) point out that even the low intuitional error rate of 2% to 5%, as estimated by the authors cited by Boyd and Nagel, means that once you have more than about a half dozen to a dozen data points that are crucial to your linguistic inference, the odds of such an inference being correct start to drop rapidly below any minimally acceptable threshold of inferential accuracy. The problem becomes compounded when, of course, we lack useful ways of determining which few of some large set of intuitions are going awry—in a nice convergence with the arguments of the restrictionists in experimental philosophy, Gibson et al. also emphasize the importance of experimental methods in recognizing and correcting errors in linguists' own intuitions. Expertise can at best only improve our intuitions so far, and the greater the error fragility of our inferences, the smaller the consolation that can be provided by even a generous stretch of expert improvement.

A different way of trying to reduce the significance of experimental philosophy has been to shift attention from *whose* philosophical intuitions are relevant to *what* philosophical intuitions are relevant, a move that we have called the *thickness defense* because it typically involves adopting a "thick" conception of philosophical intuition; that is, a conception that includes specific semantic, phenomenological, etiological, or methodological conditions on what counts as a genuine philosophical intuition (Weinberg & Alexander, in press). The basic idea is both simple and attractive. If only certain kinds of mental states count as genuine epistemic intuitions, and these are not the kinds of things that have been studied by experimental philosophers, then the kinds of methodological worries that have been raised are not worries about the actual methods used in philosophical practice (Bengson, 2012; Cullen, 2010; Kauppinen, 2007; Ludwig, 2007). In our forthcoming paper, we argue that this strategy works only if certain conditions are met, conditions having to do with the propensity of "genuine" philosophical intuitions to avoid error and with our ability to successfully identify in practice which mental states count as genuine philosophical intuitions. If it turned out that philosophical intuitions were no more likely to track philosophical truth than the kinds of mental states studied by experimental philosophers or that they were prone to other sorts of errors, then there would be little comfort in finding out that experimental philosophers have not been studying genuine philosophical intuitions all along. Likewise, there would be little comfort in knowing that experimental philosophers have not been studying the right kind of mental states unless we already have ready at hand the resources needed to pick out those right kinds of mental states. We argue that no version of the thickness defense currently on offer comes close to meeting all of these conditions: Some versions treat philosophical intuitions in such a way that we either have good reason to worry that they will not track philosophical truth or else lack the means to distinguish them from other kinds of mental states, whereas other versions simply leave it an empirically open question whether the conditions have been met, which again means more experimental work, not less, will be needed. As a conjectural road map to future research in experimental philosophy, some versions of the thickness defense may be promising, but as a means to avoid the challenge raised by experimental philosophy, they have thus far proved inadequate.

These conditions are almost certainly not exhaustive, but they do provide a place to start. For present purposes, what is important is that these conditions provide a framework for understanding what a successful defense of the evidential status of epistemic intuitions must look like. They also serve to remind us how important it is to understand what is at stake in this debate and help us move beyond the tendency to measure success in the tedious terms of shifting burdens. When both sides start out with a clear sense of what moves (and countermoves) are available, we hope that the debate can begin to bring more light and less heat. We do think that one result is coming clearly into view at this point, however: There are vanishingly few moves left available to those who wish to defend the armchair while remaining in it. Too many questions pertinent to evaluating the trustworthiness of epistemic intuitions can only be addressed properly with some substantial reliance on scientific methods.

5. Conclusion

In the end we suspect that some ambiguity in the term *reliability* has muddied the debates about how these kinds of methodological debates should be framed, and consequently how we should score specific moves in these debates. Boyd and Nagel frame concerns about the evidential status of epistemic intuitions in terms of the overall baseline accuracy of our epistemic intuitions. Given this way of framing things, it makes perfect sense to argue in defense of GRT, and to do so in a largely defensive manner by pointing out that experimental philosophers have not done enough to show that GRT is false. We hope to have shown that this is all rather beside the point, that the restrictionist challenge should not be framed in terms of anything as strong as

GRT, and, moreover, that the relevant experimental philosophy papers should not be read as trying to pursue such a target. Given the purposes and needs of analytic epistemology, all that is needed in order to establish the "unreliability" of epistemic intuitions—not once and for all, but only under our current state of substantial ignorance about them—is something much weaker. All that is needed to raise the restrictionist challenge is the existence of an empirically plausible threat of unwelcome and unexpected intuitional sensitivity. Boyd and Nagel successfully argue that the very high bar of falsifying the GRT would be a perilously difficult leap to attempt. Thankfully, restrictionists can safely operate at altitudes much closer to the ground, and still make plenty of trouble for current philosophical practices with epistemic intuitions.

Notes

1. Authorship is equal.
2. Here, and in what follows, we remain neutral on the precise psychological nature of philosophical intuitions and whether treating philosophical intuitions as evidence involves treating psychological states (or propositions about psychological states) as evidence or treating the *contents* of those psychological states as evidence.
3. Williamson (2007) suggests that it is misleading to talk of "intuitions" here; however, he basically endorses the methodological picture otherwise. We take our discussion in this paper to apply to philosophical practices as he understands them, needing only suitable terminological tweaks. More radical critics of the descriptive adequacy of this picture include Deutsch (2011) and Cappelen (2012), but we find these philosophers' accounts themselves inadequate to capture and explicate the argumentative strategies in the relevant portions of philosophy, and although this question is worthy of debate, we do not pursue it here. For additional discussion, see Alexander (2010, 2012) and Weinberg and Alexander (forthcoming).
4. For example, Boyd and Nagel gloss reliability in terms of whether a class of judgments "tend to be accurate" at the start of their Section 2 (p. 111).
5. Boyd and Nagel seem, by our lights, to have misconstrued Stich's argument as one that is concerned with baseline accuracy, which leads them to the mistaken view that the argument requires such variation to reflect profound differences between the groups. See the following for further discussion of this question of how "deeply at odds" a set of groups need to be in order for methodological worries to arise.
6. It is possible to draw inferences about proportions without knowing the total size of the reference class, if we have good reason to think that our sample is both large enough and sufficiently representative of the whole class. But the particular set of cases used in experimental philosophy studies are most definitely not a representative sample of the class of epistemic intuitions on the whole. Rather, they have started with the already rather contrived set of cases that are the stock-in-trade of analytic epistemology (see the following for some discussion of how we should expect such cases to be more prone to trouble than more ordinary cases). And from that already funky set, the experimentalists will select for study the ones that they particularly think will be most likely to display the desired effects. So this inferential route from experimental philosophy results to a possible attack on GRT is also closed.
7. Some philosophers have argued that intuitional diversity is *not* a problem. Goldman (2007) argues that intuitional diversity reflects conceptual diversity, and that not all forms of conceptual diversity are necessarily problematic; Sosa (2009) suggests that intuitional disagreement might only be superficial; and Zamzow and Nichols (2009) argue that lessons from the history of science, together with work from the social and cognitive sciences, such as Page (2008),

suggest that evidential diversity is actually an epistemic good that helps us to overcome several kinds of well-known cognitive biases. For discussion, see Alexander and Weinberg (2007) and Alexander (2012).

8. Although it is important to say again that if intuitional diversity is going to threaten GRT then there needs to be a reference class against which the proportion of disagreement to agreement can be measured, which is something we just don't have.

9. Boyd and Nagel's misplaced emphasis on "deeply at odds" differences may also explain why they consider only the Gettier case preliminarily reported in Weinberg et al. (2001), and not the several other group differences that are discussed, for example, on a range of varying Truetemp-style cases, which are subtler in effect size but may be particularly salient here as prima facie evidence of such differences in epistemic vectors across those groups.

10. That this important epistemic disanalogy blocks any slide into skepticism is one of the key points of Weinberg (2007).

11. Restrictionists have been making this point for some time. See, for example, Alexander & Weinberg (2007, p. 71); Swain, Alexander, and Weinberg (2008, p. 153); and Weinberg (2007, passim).

12. We suggest later that this is, in fact, a fairly common situation, given current epistemological practice.

13. Although we do not want to press this concern here, we seriously doubt that ordinary folks perform knowledge attributions about real-world analogs in anything like their full Gettierized complexity.

14. See Machery (2011, pp. 201–205) for a similar line of argument.

15. It is important to note that these concerns do not apply back to the more ordinary sorts of cases. This is one reason why an "Austinian" version of restrictionism, in which the restriction in question is to cases that are well-attested in everyday discourse, may be well worth considering. However, although we think that such a restriction would be a good option to consider, it is neither necessary nor sufficient as a response to the restrictionist challenge. It is not sufficient because there is still likely *some* effect of context, demographic variation, etc. on at least some ordinary cases. And it is also not necessary, so long as one undertakes the restrictionist challenge's methodological recommendations, and explores more closely just where these effects do—and do *not*—apply. That is, we may learn that certain sorts of weird cases are not susceptible to any of these effects, and could thus be appealed to in greater confidence. The main point of the restrictionist challenge in all of this is simply that, even if that turns out to be true, then it is a fact that needs to be *learned*, and not something we can yet count on.

16. Even if—as is surely the case—epistemological theorizing encompasses substantial resources beyond such intuitions, that does not blunt the worry here that very often the case verdicts play a real and substantial role as premises in epistemological arguments. It goes no distance to avoid the restrictionist challenge to point out the existence of such resources; rather, one would need to show that such resources render the case verdicts evidentially inert.

17. For further discussion of error robustness, particularly in the context of Goldman's epistemology, see Gonnerman and Weinberg (in press).

18. Weatherson does also claim that, consistent with his arguments there, nonetheless epistemological practice can continue on *largely* as it has, and we think he is perhaps too optimistic about this (see Weinberg & Crowley, 2010).

19. Of course, other forms of inference used by epistemologists may be less error fragile. We are, again, only targeting current sorts of intuition-driven methods in epistemology.

References

Alexander, J. (2010). Is experimental philosophy philosophically significant? *Philosophical Psychology, 23*, 377–389.

Alexander, J. (2012). *Experimental philosophy: An introduction.* Cambridge, England: Polity Press.

Alexander, J., & Weinberg, J. (2007). Analytic epistemology and experimental philosophy. *Philosophy Compass, 2*, 56–80.

Bealer, G. (1998). Intuition and the autonomy of philosophy. In M. DePaul & W. Ramsey (Eds.), *Rethinking intuition* (pp. 201–240). Lanham, MD: Rowman and Littlefield.

Beebe, J., & Buckwalter, W. (2010). The epistemic side-effect effect. *Mind & Language, 25*, 474–498.

Bengson, J. (2012). Experimental attacks on intuitions and answers. *Philosophy and Phenomenological Research, 86*, 495–532.

Cappelen, H. (2012). *Philosophy without intuitions.* Oxford, England: Oxford University Press.

Colaço, D., Buckwalter, W., Stich, S. P, & Machery, E. (in press). Epistemic intuitions in fake-barn thought experiments. *Episteme.*

Cullen, S. (2010). Survey-driven romanticism. *Review of Philosophy and Psychology, 1*, 275–296.

Cummins, R. (1998). Reflections on reflective equilibrium. In M. DePaul and W. Ramsey (Eds.), *Rethinking intuition* (pp. 113–128). Lanham, MD: Rowman and Littlefield.

Deutsch, M. (2011) Intuitions, counter-examples, and experimental philosophy. *Review of Philosophy and Psychology, 1*, 447–460.

Feltz, A., & Cokely, E. (2009). Do judgments about freedom and responsibility depend on who you are? Personality differences in intuitions about compatibilism and incompatibilism. *Consciousness and Cognition, 18*, 342–350.

Gettier, E. (1963). Is justified true belief knowledge? *Analysis, 23*, 121–123.

Gibson, E., Piantadosi, S., & Fedorenko, E. (2013), Quantitative methods in syntax/semantics research: A response to Sprouse and Almeida. *Language and Cognitive Processes, 28*, 88–124.

Goldman, A. (1979). What is justified true belief? In G. Pappas (Ed.), *Justification and knowledge* (pp. 1–23). Dordrecht, the Netherlands: D. Reidel.

Goldman, A. (2007). Philosophical intuitions: Their target, their source, and their epistemic status. *Grazer Philosophische Studien, 74*, 1–26.

Gonnerman, C., & Weinberg, J. (in press). Why messy minds make for messier armchairs: Goldman and the epistemology of categorizer pluralism. In H. Kornblith and B. McLaughlin (Eds.), *Goldman and his critics.* Malden, MA: Wiley-Blackwell.

Hales, S. (2006) *Relativism and the foundations of philosophy.* Cambridge, MA: MIT Press.

Henrich, J., Heine, S., & Norenzayan, A. (2010). The weirdest people in the world? *Behavioral and Brain Sciences, 33*, 1–75.

Kauppinen, A. (2007). The rise and fall of experimental philosophy. *Philosophical Explorations, 10*, 95–118.

Knobe, J., & Samuels, R. (2013). Thinking like a scientist: Innateness as a case study. *Cognition, 126*, 72–86.

Kornblith, H. (2002). *Knowledge and its place in nature.* Oxford, England: Oxford University Press.

Levin, J. (2004). The evidential status of philosophical intuition. *Philosophical Studies, 121*, 193–224.

Ludwig, K. (2007). The epistemology of thought experiments: First person versus third person approaches. *Midwest Studies in Philosophy, 31*, 128–159.

Machery, E. (2011). Thought experiments and philosophical knowledge. *Metaphilosophy, 42*, 191–214.

Machery, E. (2012). Expertise and intuitions about reference. *Theoria, 27*, 37–54.

Mercier, H. (2011). On the universality of argumentative reasoning. *Journal of Cognition and Culture, 11*, 85–113.

Nagel, J., San Juan, V., & Mar, R. (2013). Lay denial of knowledge for justified true beliefs. *Cognition, 129*, 652–661.

Nisbett, R., Peng, K., Choi, I., & Norenzayan, A. (2001). Culture and systems of thought: Holistic versus analytic cognition. *Psychological Review, 108*, 291–310.

Page, S. (2008) *The difference.* Princeton, NJ: Princeton University Press.

Pust, J. (2000). *Intuitions as evidence*. New York, NY: Routledge.

Scholl, B. (2007). Object persistence in philosophy and psychology. *Mind & Language, 22*, 563–591.

Schultz, E., Cokely, E., & Feltz, A. (2011). Persistent bias in expert judgments about free will and moral responsibility: A test of the expertise defense. *Consciousness and Cognition, 20*, 1722–1731.

Schwitzgebel, E., & Cushman, F. (2012). Expertise in moral reasoning? Order effects on moral judgment in professional philosophers and non-philosophers. *Mind & Language, 27*, 135–153.

Sosa, E. (2007). Experimental philosophy and philosophical intuition. *Philosophical Studies, 132*, 99–107.

Sosa, E. (2009). A defense of the use of intuitions in philosophy. In M. Bishop & D. Murphy (Eds.), *Stich and his critics* (pp. 101–112). Malden, MA: Wiley-Blackwell.

Stich, S. (1988). Reflective equilibrium, analytic epistemology, and the problem of cognitive diversity. *Synthese, 74*, 391–413.

Swain, S., Alexander, J., & Weinberg, J. (2008). The instability of philosophical intuitions: Running hot and cold on Truetemp. *Philosophical and Phenomenological Research, 76*, 138–155.

Tobia, K., Buckwalter, W., & Stich, S. (2013). Moral intuitions: Are philosophers experts? *Philosophical Psychology, 26*, 629–638.

Weatherson, B. (2003). What good are counterexamples? *Philosophical Studies, 115*, 1–31.

Weigel, C. (2011). Distance, anger, freedom: An account of the role of abstraction in compatibilist and incompatibilist intuitions. *Philosophical Psychology, 24*, 803–823.

Weinberg, J. (2007). How to challenge intuitions empirically without risking skepticism. *Midwest Studies in Philosophy, 31*, 318–343.

Weinberg, J. (in press). The promise of experimental philosophy and the inference to signal. In J. Beebe (Ed.), *Advances in experimental epistemology*. London, England: Bloomsbury Academic.

Weinberg, J., & Alexander, J. (in press). The challenge of sticking with intuitions through thick and thin. In A. Booth and D. Rowbottom (Eds.), *Intuition*. Oxford, England: Oxford University Press.

Weinberg, J. M., Alexander, J., Gonnerman, C., & Reuter, S. (2012). Restrictionism and reflection. *The Monist, 95*, 200–222.

Weinberg, J., & Crowley, S. (2010). Loose constitutivity and armchair philosophy. *Studia Philosophica Estonica, 2*, 177–195.

Weinberg, J., Gonnerman, C., Buckner, C., & Alexander, J. (2010). Are philosophers expert intuiters? *Philosophical Psychology, 23*, 331–355.

Weinberg, J., Nichols, S., & Stich, S. (2001). Normativity and epistemic intuitions. *Philosophical Topics, 29*, 429–460.

Williamson, T. (2007). *The philosophy of philosophy*. Oxford, England: Blackwell Publishing.

Zamzow, J., & Nichols, S. (2009). Variations in ethical intuitions. *Philosophical Issues, 19*, 368–388.

Part IV Suggested Readings

Alexander, J., & Weinberg, J. (2007). Analytic epistemology and experimental philosophy. *Philosophy Compass, 2*, 56–80.
This article reviews the early research in experimental epistemology.
Beebe, J.R., & Buckwalter, W. (2010). The epistemic side-effect effect. *Mind & Language, 25*, 474–498.
This article provides evidence that moral considerations have an influence on our disposition to ascribe knowledge to others.
Buckwalter, W. (2012). Non-traditional factors in judgments about knowledge. *Philosophy Compass, 7*, 278–289.
Buckwalter reviews the variety of cues that influence knowledge ascriptions.
Colaço, D., Buckwalter, W., Stich, S. P, & Machery, E. (in press). Epistemic intuitions in fake-barn thought experiments. *Episteme.*
Colaço and colleagues provide evidence that age influences knowledge attribution in fake-barn cases.
Goldman, A. (2007). Philosophical intuitions: Their target, their source, and their epistemic status. *Grazer Philosophische Studien, 74*, 1–26.
Goldman provides an account of intuitions that justifies their evidential status for the study of philosophical concepts.
Livengood, J., Sytsma, J. M., Feltz, A., Scheines, R., & Machery, E. (2010). Philosophical temperament. *Philosophical Psychology, 23*, 313–330.
This article provides evidence that philosophers are particularly reflective: They are more likely to challenge their gut intuitions and to submit them to criticism.
Ludwig, K. (2007). The epistemology of thought experiments: First person versus third person approaches. *Midwest Studies in Philosophy, 31*, 128–159.
This article is an early, influential criticism of experimental philosophy, particularly experimental epistemology. Weinberg et al. (2001) is discussed at length.
Machery, E. (2011). Thought experiments and philosophical knowledge. *Metaphilosophy, 42*, 191–214.
This article examines whether judgments elicited by thought experiments can be a source of evidence in philosophy.

Machery, E. (2012). Expertise and intuitions about reference. *Theoria, 27*, 37–54.
This article provides evidence that the disciplinary background of linguists and philosophers of language biases their judgments about the reference of proper names.

Nagel, J. (2007). Epistemic intuitions. *Philosophy Compass, 2*, 792–819.
This article reviews some research in experimental epistemology.

Nagel, J. (2012). Intuitions and experiments: A defense of the case method in epistemology. *Philosophy and Phenomenological Research, 85*, 495–527.
This article argues that the research in experimental philosophy has not successfully challenged the use of intuitions as a source of evidence.

Nagel, J. (2013). Defending the evidential value of epistemic intuitions: A reply to Stich. *Philosophy and Phenomenological Research, 87*, 179–199.
This article responds to Stich (2013).

Nagel, J., San Juan, V., & Mar, R. (2013). Lay denial of knowledge for justified true beliefs. *Cognition, 129*, 652–661.
Nagel and colleagues argue that lay people share philosophers' intuition that knowledge differs from simply true justified belief.

Pinillos, N. Á. (2011). Some recent work in experimental epistemology. *Philosophy Compass, 6*, 675–688.
Pinillos reviews some work in experimental epistemology.

Schultz, E., Cokely, E., & Feltz, A. (2011). Persistent bias in expert judgments about free will and moral responsibility: A test of the expertise defense. *Consciousness and Cognition, 20*, 1722–1731.
Schultz and colleagues argue that, just like lay judgments, expert judgments about free will and responsibility correlate with personality.

Schwitzgebel, E., & Cushman, F. (2012). Expertise in moral reasoning? Order effects on moral judgment in professional philosophers and non-philosophers. *Mind & Language, 27*, 135–153.
This article shows that philosophers' judgments about moral cases are biased by the order in which cases are presented.

Sosa, E. (2007). Experimental philosophy and philosophical intuition. *Philosophical Studies, 132*, 99–107.
This article examines the implications of experimental philosophy for the use of intuitions in philosophy.

Starmans, C., & Friedman, O. (2012). The folk conception of knowledge. *Cognition, 124*, 272–283.
Starmans and Friedman examine in detail how laypeople conceive of knowledge.

Stich, S. P. (2013). Do different groups have different epistemic intuitions? A reply to Jennifer Nagel. *Philosophy and Phenomenological Research, 87*, 151–178.
This article responds to Nagel (2012).

Swain, S., Alexander, J., & Weinberg, J. (2008). The instability of philosophical intuitions: Running hot and cold on Truetemp. *Philosophical and Phenomenological Research, 76*, 138–155.
This article shows that laypeople's judgments about knowledge can be influenced by the order in which cases are presented.

Tobia, K., Buckwalter, W., & Stich, S. (2013). Moral intuitions: Are philosophers experts? *Philosophical Psychology, 26*, 629–638.
This article presents evidence that philosophers' intuitions suffer from the actor/observer bias: Their moral judgments vary depending on whether they are about themselves or others.

Turri, J. (2013). A conspicuous art: Putting Gettier to the test. *Philosophers' Imprint, 13*, 1–16.
This article presents evidence that, when experiments are done with sufficient care, laypeople share philosophers' epistemological judgments about Gettier cases.

Weatherson, B. (2003). What good are counterexamples? *Philosophical Studies, 115*, 1–31.
Weatherson examines the practice of giving counterexamples in philosophy.

Weinberg, J. (2007). How to challenge intuitions empirically without risking skepticism. *Midwest Studies in Philosophy, 31*, 318–343.
Weinberg argues that philosophical intuitions fail to provide evidence because they are not "hopeful."

Weinberg, J., Gonnerman, C., Buckner, C., & Alexander, J. (2010). Are philosophers expert intuiters? *Philosophical Psychology, 23,* 331–355.

This article argues that philosophers are unlikely to have expert intuitions because the conditions that lead to the development of expertise are not met in philosophy.

Weinberg, J., Nichols, S., & Stich, S. (2001). Normativity and epistemic intuitions. *Philosophical Topics, 29,* 429–460.

This groundbreaking article provides evidence that epistemological intuitions may vary across cultures.

Williamson, T. (2007). *The philosophy of philosophy.* Oxford, England: Blackwell Publishing.

This book provides an influential theory about the nature of philosophy.

Wright, J.C. (2010). On intuitional stability: The clear, the strong, and the paradigmatic. *Cognition, 115,* 491–503.

Wright provides evidence that people have a sense of whether their epistemic intuitions are likely to be unstable.

Supplemental Guide to Further Controversies

The preceding sections in this volume present four central controversies in experimental philosophy. The following three additional controversies have also been important. For each of these controversies, we list the essential readings.

Experimental Epistemology: Assessing the Influence of Context and Stakes on Knowledge Ascription

Brown, J. (2013). Experimental philosophy, contextualism and SSI. *Philosophy and Phenomenological Research, 86,* 233–261.

Buckwalter, W. (2010). Knowledge isn't closed on Saturday: A study in ordinary language. *Review of Philosophy and Psychology, 1,* 395–406.

Buckwalter, W. (2012). Non-traditional factors in judgments about knowledge. *Philosophy Compass, 7,* 278–289.

Buckwalter, W., & Schaffer, J. (in press). Knowledge, stakes, and mistakes. *Noûs.*

DeRose, K. (2011). Contextualism, contrastivism, and X-Phi surveys. *Philosophical Studies, 156,* 81–110.

Hansen, N., & Chemla, E. (2013). Experimenting on contextualism. *Mind & Language, 28,* 286–321.

May, J., Sinnott-Armstrong, W., Hull, J. G., & Zimmerman, A. (2010). Practical interests, relevant alternatives, and knowledge attributions: An empirical study. *Review of Philosophy and Psychology, 1,* 265–273.

Pinillos, N. Á. (2011). Some recent work in experimental epistemology. *Philosophy Compass, 6,* 675–688.

Pinillos, N. Á. (2012). Knowledge, experiments and practical interests. In J. Brown & M. Gerken (Eds.), *New essays on knowledge ascription* (pp. 192–219). Oxford, England: Oxford University Press.

Schaffer, J., & Knobe, J. (2012). Contrastive knowledge surveyed. *Noûs, 46,* 675–708.

Causation

Alicke, M. D., Rose, D., & Bloom, D. (2011). Causation, norm violation, and culpable control. *Journal of Philosophy, 108*, 670–696.

Danks, D., Rose, D., & Machery, E. (forthcoming). Demoralizing causation. *Philosophy Studies*.

Dunaway, B., Edmonds, A., & Manley, D. (2013). The folk probably do think what you think they think. *Australasian Journal of Philosophical Studies*.

Hitchcock, C., & Knobe, J. (2009). Cause and norm. *Journal of Philosophy, 11*, 587–612.

Knobe, J., & B. Fraser. (2008). Causal judgment and moral judgment: Two experiments. In W. Sinnott-Armstrong (Ed.), *Moral psychology, volume 2* (pp. 441–448). Cambridge, MA: MIT Press.

Livengood, J., & Machery, E. (2007). The folk probably don't think what you think they think: Experiments on causation by absence. *Midwest Studies in Philosophy, 31*, 107–127.

Lombrozo, T. (2010). Causal–explanatory pluralism: How intentions, functions, and mechanisms influence causal ascriptions. *Cognitive Psychology, 61*, 303–332.

Rose, D., & Danks, D. (2012). Causation: Empirical trends and future directions. *Philosophy Compass, 7*, 643–653.

Sytsma, J., Livengood, J., & Rose, D. (2012). Two types of typicality: Rethinking the role of statistical typicality in ordinary causal attributions. *Studies in History and Philosophy of Science Part C, 43*, 814–820.

Intentionality

Adams, F., & Steadman, A. (2004). Intentional action in ordinary language: Core concept or pragmatic understanding? *Analysis, 64*, 173–181.

Guglielmo, S., & Malle, B. F. (2010). Can unintended side effects be intentional? Resolving a controversy over intentionality and morality. *Personality and Social Psychology Bulletin, 36*, 1635–1647.

Knobe, J. (2006). The concept of intentional action: A case study in the uses of folk psychology. *Philosophical Studies, 130*, 203–231.

Machery, E. (2008). The folk concept of intentional action: Philosophical and experimental issues. *Mind & Language, 23*, 165–189.

Mallon, R. (2008). Knobe versus Machery: Testing the Trade-Off Hypothesis. *Mind & Language, 23*, 247–255.

Nadelhoffer, T. (2006). Bad acts, blameworthy agents, and intentional actions: Some problems for juror impartiality. *Philosophical Explorations, 9*, 203–219.

Nichols, S., & Ulatowski, J. (2007). Intuitions and individual differences: The Knobe effect revisited. *Mind & Language, 22*, 346–365.

Pettit, D., & Knobe, J. (2009). The pervasive impact of moral judgment. *Mind & Language, 24*, 586–604.

Phelan, M. T., & Sarkissian, H. (2008). The folk strike back; or, why you didn't do it intentionally, though it was bad and you knew it. *Philosophical Studies, 138*, 291–298.

Phelan, M., & Sarkissian, H. (2009). Is the 'Trade-off Hypothesis' worth trading for? *Mind & Language, 24*, 164–180.

Pinillos, N. Á., Smith, N., Nair, G. S., Marchetto, P., & Mun, C. (2011). Philosophy's new challenge: Experiments and intentional action. *Mind & Language, 26*, 115–139.

Uttich, K., & Lombrozo, T. (2010). Norms inform mental state ascriptions: A rational explanation for the side-effect effect. *Cognition, 116*, 87–100.

Wright, J. C., & Bengson, J. (2009). Asymmetries in judgments of responsibility and intentional action. *Mind & Language, 24*, 24–50.

Young, L., Cushman, F., Adolphs, R., Tranel, D., & Hauser, M. D. (2006). Does emotion mediate the relationship between an action's moral status and its intentional status? Neuropsychological evidence. *Journal of Cognition and Culture, 6*, 265–278.

Contributors

Joshua Alexander is Assistant Professor of Philosophy at Siena College, where he also directs the Cognitive Science Program. His work focuses primarily on the nature of philosophical cognition and intellectual disagreement. He is the author of *Experimental Philosophy: An Introduction* (Polity, 2012).

Adam Arico is Visiting Professor at the University of Wyoming. Working at the intersection of philosophy, psychology, and cognitive science, his research focuses on issues surrounding folk psychology (especially everyday attributions of consciousness), moral psychology, and group minds.

Kenneth Boyd is currently completing a PhD in philosophy at the University of Toronto. His research interests lie primarily in epistemology, specifically concerning how the ways in which we make epistemic evaluations informs norms of action, as well as the relationship between epistemic and moral evaluations.

Brian Fiala is a postdoctoral fellow in the Philosophy-Neuroscience-Psychology Program at Washington University in Saint Louis. He has co-authored articles in *Behavioral and Brain Sciences* and *Mind and Language.*

Joshua Knobe is a professor at Yale University, appointed both in the Program in Cognitive Science and the Department of Philosophy. Much of his work is concerned with the ways in which people's moral judgments can impact their intuitions about questions that might at first seem entirely non-moral.

Edouard Machery is Professor in the Department of History and Philosophy of Science at the University of Pittsburgh, a fellow of the Center for Philosophy of Science at the University of Pittsburgh, and a member of the Center for the Neural Basis of Cognition (University of Pittsburgh-Carnegie Mellon University). He is the author of *Doing without Concepts* (Oxford University Press, 2009) as well as the editor of *The Oxford Handbook of Compositionality* (Oxford University Press, 2011), *La Philosophie Expérimentale* (Vuibert, 2012), and *Arguing about Human Nature* (Routledge, 2013).

Genoveva Martí is ICREA Research Professor at the Universitat de Barcelona and coordinator of the Logos research group. From July 2014, Professor of Philosophy at the University of Western Ontario in London, Canada. Her research focuses on the theory of reference, the semantics of general terms and modality.

Jennifer Nagel is Associate Professor of Philosophy at the University of Toronto. Her recent work focuses on the relationship between intuitive knowledge attribution and knowledge itself.

Eddy Nahmias is Associate Professor of Philosophy and Neuroscience at Georgia State University. His research focuses on philosophy of mind, moral psychology, especially free will and responsibility, and experimental philosophy. He is co-editor of *Moral Psychology: Historical and Contemporary Readings* (Wiley-Blackwell, 2010).

Shaun Nichols is Professor of Philosophy at the University of Arizona. He is the author of *Mindreading* (co-authored with Stephen Stich, Oxford University Press, 2003) and *Sentimental Rules: On the Natural Foundations of Moral Judgment* (Oxford University Press, 2004).

Elizabeth O'Neill is a graduate student in the Department of History and Philosophy of Science at the University of Pittsburgh. Her primary research interests currently lie in moral epistemology and moral psychology.

Justin Sytsma is a lecturer in the Philosophy Programme at Victoria University of Wellington. His research focuses on issues in philosophy of psychology and philosophy of mind. As a practitioner of experimental philosophy, his research into these areas often involves the use of empirical methods. He is co-author of a forthcoming volume on *The New Experimental Philosophy* from Broadview Press, in addition to authoring or co-authoring articles appearing in journals such as *Australasian Journal of Philosophy, Philosophical Studies, Philosophy of Science, Journal of Consciousness Studies,* and *Philosophy Compass,* among others.

Morgan Thompson is a graduate student in the Department of History and Philosophy of Science at the University of Pittsburgh. She has an MA in philosophy from Georgia State University. Her interests are in philosophy of cognitive science, philosophy of science, and moral psychology.

Jonathan M. Weinberg is an Associate Professor in the Department of Philosophy and the Cognitive Science Program at the University of Arizona. He received his PhD in Philosophy from Rutgers University in 2002. His research focuses on intersections between cognitive science, epistemology, philosophical methodology (including experimental philosophy), and aesthetics.

Index

abstract cases 74, 75, 83–4n2, 94, 96, 101n4
acceptability judgments 13, 14, 34
action 69, 70–83, 86–100, 102n14, 102n15;
    belief-desire explanation for
    71–2, 76–8, 83, 89, 93, 96, 99;
    causal explanation for 96, 97,
    99; controlled 64; intentional xx,
    xxiv; nonvoluntary 98; reasons
    explanation for 96, 97, 100
actor/observer bias 147
agency 32, 35, 43, 46n11, 46n14, 86, 89, 91,
    93, 99, 100
agency model 35–7, 40, 51, 62, 65
agent, categorizing entity as 35, 36, 37, 40,
    41, 43, 46n6, 48, 51, 55, 62
Alexander, Joshua xxv2, 118, 121, 142n3,
    142–3n7, 146
American subjects 6, 7, 73
analytic functionalism 45n3
anger 33, 36, 53
animacy 40
arbitrariness critique 115
Arico, Adam xxii, 35, 36, 48, 49, 51, 63–5
armchair xx, 120, 133, 134, 138, 139, 141
arousal 41

Bartneck, Christoph 40, 41, 43, 44, 46n12
baseline accuracy of intuitions 128–31,
    134–6, 138, 139, 141, 142n5
Bealer, George 131
Beebe, James 7
belief-desire explanation for action. See
    action
Boyd, Kenneth x, 128–30, 132–6, 138–41,
    142, 142n4–5, 143n9
brain 34, 37, 86, 87, 88, 90–9, 101n6,
    102n16, 114, 118, 135; computer
    metaphor for 34, 49, 69–70, 79,
    80, 88, 98; in a vat 114;
    lesions 135
brain states 87, 93, 95, 98, 99
brain in a vat 114
Buckwalter, Wesley xvi, xxvn3, 33, 34, 45n3,
    64, 115, 117, 118, 146
bypassing 92–8, 101n10

Cappelen, Herman xviii, xix, 142n3
Carey, Susan 35
Carnap, Rudolf x
causes: of judgments xxi; of actions 69–84,
    86–100

causal competition principle 86–8, 95,
    97–100
causal explanation for action. *See* action
causal modeling 82
causal-historical theories 3, 5, 7, 9, 10, 13,
    17, 19, 21, 24n2, 25n8, 27
China 49
Chinese subjects 6, 7
Choi, Incheol 21, 116, 136
Coates, Justin 98, 104
cognitive reflection test (CRT) 52
Colaço, David xvi, 146
compatibilist theory of free will.
    See free will
computer, metaphor for the brain.
    See brain
concrete cases 74, 75, 82–3n2, 94, 96, 97
consciousness vii, xx, xxii, 34, 35, 37, 48,
    49, 50, 51, 61–4, 65, 88, 91, 93,
    99, 100, 101n13, 102n16, 110;
    phenomenal 32–6, 39, 44, 48, 50,
    51, 62, 64, 65
contextualism about knowledge. *See*
    knowledge
contrast effects 110
counterfactual cases xiii, 5, 10, 11, 13, 20,
    22, 27
CRT. *See* Cognitive Reflection Task
culture. *See* intuitions
Cummins, Robert 131

Danks, David xxi, xxii, xxvn7
Davidson, Donald 77
Dedekind/Peano case 10, 13
deep self 88, 102n14; *see also* self
deliberation 35, 37, 51, 88, 93,
    101n13–102n13
demographic variation. *See* intuitions
Dennett, Daniel 45n4
DeRose, Keith 114, 123
descriptivism xiii, xxvn1, 3, 5–11, 13,
    17–25, 27
desire. *See* action

determinism 72, 73–8, 80, 81, 83n2–84n2,
    89, 94–9, 101, 101n13–102n13,
    104
deterministic universe 72–7, 78–81,
    83n2–84n2, 94, 97, 98, 101n4,
    101n6, 102n15
Deutsch, Max 3, 7–12, 15, 21, 23, 142n3
Devitt, Michael 13, 19, 22, 27
disagreement x, xi, xviii, 23, 109, 116, 117,
    121, 123, 132, 142n7, 143n8
Donnellan, Keith 19, 23
Doris, John 102n17, 105
dual-process 31, 35, 45n5, 51, 52
dualism, folk 90, 101n4

East Asians 6, 7, 21, 24n3, 27, 114–16
ELIZA effect 42
embodiment 82, 90
emotion xxi, xxiv, xxv, 37, 41, 42, 46n12,
    53, 79, 81, 83, 83n2–84n2, 90, 94,
    101n11, 104
error argument 19, 20, 22, 24n2, 25n6
error fragility 137, 138, 140, 143n19
error robustness 137, 143n17
error theory x, 94, 114
experiential states 31, 34
experts viii, ix, xx, xviii, 7, 8, 10, 11, 13, 23,
    24, 25n10, 109, 112, 120, 121,
    139, 140, 147, 148
expertise defense xxvn5, 25n10, 121,
    139, 140
explanatory gap 100
externalism about knowledge. *See*
    knowledge

face perception 37, 40–3, 46n13
fake-barn case xvi, xix, xxvi, 119, 122, 123,
    133, 146
fear 32, 42, 79
feeling ix, 33, 34, 43, 44, 48, 50, 51,
    53, 62, 90
Feltz, Adam xxii, 104
Fiala, Brian 49, 54

fictional cases 20, 22, 135
first-person experience 48–9, 51, 63–4
flatness 113
Fodor, Jerry 130
Foot, Philippa xiv
folk: concept of free will 69–83, 86–100; concepts vii, ix, x, xii; epistemology 130, 134–6, 138, 139, 143n13, 146–7; mind attributions 32, 33, 34, 44, 45n3; psychology 31–4, 63–4, 88, theory of consciousness 49–50, 63–4, 65; theory of mind 90, 99, 101n5
free will vii, viii, ix, xiii, xxi, 70, 71, 75, 76, 83, 86–96, 98–100, 101n4, 101n6, 101n10, 101n12, 101, 101n13–102n13, 104; compatibilist theory of 88, 89, 102n14, 104, 105; incompatibilist theory of 87, 93, 96, 101n4, 104; folk concept of. See folk
Frederick, Shane 52
Frege, Gottlob 18
Friedman, Ori 121, 122, 147
function: of epistemic intuitions 109, 111, 119, 124; of robots 33–5, 41, 44, 45n3, 61–2
functionalism 45n3, 64–5, 82, 90, 101n5

general reliability thesis (GRT) 130, 131, 134, 141, 142, 142n6, 143n8
general terms 17, 25n6, 25n9
Gödel case xiii, xvi, xix, xxvn1, 5–7, 9–13, 20–5
Gettier cases ix, xv, xviii, 114–16, 118, 121, 122, 129, 133–5, 143n9, 143n13, 147
Goldman, Alvin 119, 123, 130, 131, 142n7, 143n17, 146
grammaticality 13, 14
Gray, Kurt 31, 41
Griffiths, Paul ix, xxi, xxv
GRT. See general reliability thesis

Harris, Samuel 86, 87, 95, 99
hedonic value 32, 33, 35, 45n1, 50; see also valence
Henrich, Joseph 136
high-road process 35, 37, 40, 44, 45, 46n14, 51, 52, 53, 62
Hong Kong 6, 21, 73
Huebner, Bryce 34, 118
human-computer interaction 40–2
humdrum cases 20, 22
Hyde, Janet 118
hypothetical cases 11, 20, 22, 23, 121, 129, 131, 135

ignorance argument against descriptivism 19, 20, 24, 24n2, 25n6, 25n7
India 21, 73, 116
incompatibilist theory of free will. See free will
intentional stance 45n4
intentional states 32, 33, 35, 36, 39
internalism about knowledge. See knowledge
intuitions: age variation in xvi, 133; cultural variation in ix, xvi, 6, 21, 24n3, 73, 101n4, 111, 116, 117, 148; demographic variation in xiii, xvi, xvii, xviii, 3, 4, 6, 11, 12, 14, 15, 109, 110, 114, 115, 118, 132, 143n15; ethnic variation in 110, 114, 115, 116, 132; as evidence xxi, 9, 10, 12, 22, 23, 25n10, 27, 45n3, 50, 65, 110, 115, 128, 129, 132, 133, 134, 142n2, 148; gender variation in xvi, 110, 114, 115, 117, 118, 132; reliability of vii, xvii, xix, 8, 109–24, 128–42; sensitivity of 129, 132–4, 136–9, 142; trustworthiness of xx–xxii, 119, 128–31, 134–7, 139, 141

Jack, Anthony 65
Japanese subjects 6, 7

Johnson, Susan 35, 41
Jonah case 7

Kahneman, Daniel xxiii
Kanwisher, Nancy 41
Knobe, Joshua ix, xiii, xxiii, xxiv, 49, 50,
        51, 64, 65, 86–9, 93–100, 100n1,
        101n4, 102n15, 104
knowledge ix, x, 109–24, 129, 130, 133–5,
        137, 146–7; and moral consid-
        erations 82; attributions of xv,
        xvi, xviii, xxiv, 39, 40, 46n10,
        132–6, 143n13, 146; contextual-
        ism about 114; externalism about
        124; internalism about 124
Korean subjects 6
Kornblith, Hilary xx
Kripke, Saul xiii, xvi, xxvn1, 5, 6, 8–13,
        18–24, 25n8, 27

Lam, Barry 21, 24n4
Laudan, Larry xi
laypeople viii–x, xx, xxv, xxvn5, 14, 23,
        25n10, 50–3, 55, 58, 61, 62n2,
        63n3, 65, 88, 104, 109, 120–2,
        147; *see also* folk
Livengood, Jonathan xxii, 28
Lehrer, Keith 114, 118
Lloyd, Elisabeth xxv
Lombrozo, Tania 25n6, 25n9
low-road process 35–7, 40, 44, 45, 51–3, 62

Machery, Edouard xvi, xvii, xxi, xxii, 7, 11,
        14, 19–21, 24, 24n4, 27, 28, 32,
        33, 34, 38, 39, 45n1, 48–56, 62,
        63n2, 63n3, 64, 65–6, 146, 147
Machiavellian Intelligence Hypothesis 111
Mackie, John x, xi
Malle, Bertram 91
Mallon, Ron 6, 8, 9, 19, 21, 25n9, 27
manifest image 101n3
manipulation of brain states 95, 99
Martí, Genoveva 3, 11–15, 24n3, 24n5,
        27, 28

Mele, Alfred 91, 101n6
mental state ascription (attribution) ix, xv,
        32, 34, 45, 48, 51, 52, 53, 55, 61,
        62, 65, 114, 115, 146
Mercier, Hugo 136
method of cases viii–xxi, 4–8, 22–4
mind perception 31, 64
mind reading: by animals 111, 112; by
        humans 111, 112, 117; by tech-
        nology 94, 95
Mongolia 21
moral standing 65
Murray, Dylan 76, 77, 78, 80, 81, 96, 104

Nadelhoffer, Thomas xxi, 74, 90, 104
naturalism xix–xxv, 88–91, 95,
        101–102n14; metaphysical xix;
        methodological xx, xix, xxiv, xxv
naturalistic vision of the human mind
        86–91, 94, 100, 102n16
Nagel, Jennifer x, xvii, xix, 116, 124,
        128–30, 132–6, 138–42, 142n4,
        143n9, 147
Nahmias, Eddy ix, xxi, 74, 76–7, 78, 80,
        81, 90, 96, 98, 100–101n2, 101,
        101n13–102n13, 102n17, 104
Naming and Necessity 5, 12, 18, 20
Nichols, Shaun xiii, xv, xxii, xxiii, xxiv, xxv,
        6, 9, 19, 21, 25n9, 27, 48, 49, 59,
        63–4, 71, 74, 83n1, 83n2, 94, 96,
        97, 104, 142n7, 148
Nisbett, Richard 6, 21, 24n3, 116, 117, 136
Norenzayan, Ara 21, 116, 136
North American subjects 115

Olivola, Christopher 21
Oppenheimer, Daniel 52
order effects xvii, 55, 56, 60, 120, 132, 147

pain ix, 32, 34–7, 44, 46n7, 48, 50, 51, 53,
        62, 62n2, 63n2, 63n3, 66
Papineau, David vii, xx
Peng, Kaiping 21, 116, 136
person 90; *see also* soul, self

personal control 88, 89, 102n15, 111
personal stance 45n4
personality xvi, 104, 132, 147; of robots 43
personhood 35; *see also* agency
Peter of Mantua 109, 110
Phelan, Mark 33, 34, 45n3, 64, 65
phenomenal stance 65
physicalism, reductive and nonreductive 88, 89, 91, 93
phenomenal states 32, 33, 35, 39
Pinillos, N. Ángel 25n9, 147
Prinz, Jesse ix, xxi, xxii, xxv, 49, 50, 51, 64, 65
psychological states 70, 71, 76, 78, 79, 82, 88, 96, 98, 99, 102n15, 142n2
proper names xiii, xvi, xviii, xix, xxi, 3–15, 17–19, 21–4, 25n6, 27, 147

rationality wars 130
reasoning style 116, 117
reasons 80, 81, 83, 84n4, 86, 88, 89, 93–100, 101n12, 102n15, 102n16
reason explanation for action. *See* action
reasons-responsiveness 88, 97, 98
reference: case judgments as evidence about 5, 9–15, 22–4; causal-historical theory of 3–5, 7, 9, 10, 13, 17, 19, 21, 24n2, 25n8, 27; descriptivist theory of 3, 5–11, 17–24, 27; speaker's 7, 9, 20, 23; use as evidence about 4, 5, 11–14, 18–20, 22, 23, 24n3, 24–25n5, 25n11
reliability xvii, xiii, xv–xviii, xix, xxvn2, xxvn5, 8, 9, 72, 109–15, 118, 120, 122–4, 128–32, 134, 136–9, 141, 142, 142n4; baseline accuracy sense 128, 130, 131, 134–6, 138, 139, 141, 142n5; trustworthiness sense 128–31, 134–7, 139, 141
religion 90
responsibility, moral xiii, 73–6, 81, 83n2, 87, 92–6, 98–100, 101n10,

101n12, 102n14, 102n17, 104, 105, 147
restrictionist challenge 132–4, 138–42, 143n11, 143n15, 143n16
Robbins, Philip 65
robot 31–45, 48–62; robot "faces" 41, 42; *see also* function; personality
Rose, David xxi, xxvn7
Russell, Bertrand 18

Sarkissian, Hagop 73, 101n4
Saxe, Rebecca xxii
Schwitzgebel, Eric xxii
scientific vision of the human mind 69–73, 76, 78, 81, 82, 87, 88
Schupbach, Jonah x
seeing, attributions of 38, 48, 50, 53, 54, 61, 62, 63n2, 63n4, 63n5
seeing vs. detecting 38, 39, 46n9, 54–7, 58–61
self 70, 73, 76, 87–91, 93, 94, 102n14
semantics 14, 19, 24, 25n10, 27, 124
skepticism: about the method of cases xvi–xix; about the reliability of epistemic intuitions 113, 114, 131, 143n10; Pyrrhonian 113
singular terms 17
smelling 33, 34
Sosa, Ernest xv, 119, 133, 142n7, 147
soul, and free will 90, 91, 94, 99
Sperber, Daniel 112
Stanovich, Keith 45n5
Starmans, Christina 121, 122, 147
Sterelny, Kim 19
Stich, Stephen xvii, xxv, 6, 9, 19, 21, 27, 115, 117, 118, 131, 142n5, 146, 147, 148
Swain, Stacey 118–20
System 1, 65; *see also* low road process
System 2. *See* high road process
Sytsma, Justin xxii, 7, 21, 24n4, 28, 32–4, 38, 39, 45n1, 48–56, 62, 63n2, 63n3, 64, 65, 66, 146

Talbot, Brian 52, 65
teleology 33, 45n3
theory-laden folk views 90, 99
theory-lite folk views 86, 88–91, 93, 95, 100
thickness defense of philosophers' intuitions 140, 141
transcendence vision of the human mind 69, 70–3, 75, 76, 78–82, 84n2, 86–90, 94–6, 99
Thomson, Judith Jarvis xvi
Truetemp case 114, 118, 119, 120, 124, 143n9, 149
Tsu Ch'ung Chih case 6, 7
Turri, John 116, 147
Tversky, Amos xxiii

"uncanny valley" effect 46n13
Unger, Peter 113, 114
use: of epistemic concepts 110, 111, 129, 130; of names. *See* reference

valence 32, 35, 36, 38, 41, 44, 45n1, 50, 51, 53, 64, 65; moral xxi, 133
variation in judgments. *See* intuitions

Weatherson, Brian 27, 137, 143n18, 147
Wegner, Daniel 41
Weinberg, Jonathan xxvn2, 115, 116, 118, 121, 131, 132, 142n3, 143n9, 143n10, 143n17, 146, 147–8
Westerners 6, 8, 21, 24n3, 27, 116, 136
WEIRD (Western Educated Industrialized Rich Democratic) populations 136
Williamson, Timothy 122, 142n3
Woolfolk, Robert 105
Wright, Jennifer 120, 148

Young, Liane xxii

Zamzow, Jennifer 142n7